Deliberate Practice for Psychotherapists

This text explores how psychotherapists can use deliberate practice to improve their clinical effectiveness. By sourcing through decades of research on how experts in diverse fields achieve skill mastery, the author proposes it is possible for any therapist to dramatically improve their effectiveness. However, achieving expertise isn't easy. To improve, therapists must focus on clinical challenges and reconsider century-old methods of clinical training from the ground up. This volume presents a step-by-step program to engage readers in deliberate practice to improve clinical effectiveness across the therapists' entire career span, from beginning training for graduate students to continuing education for licensed and advanced clinicians.

Tony Rousmaniere is on the clinical faculty at the University of Washington, Seattle where he also maintains a private practice.

DELIBERATE PRACTICE FOR PSYCHOTHERAPISTS

A Guide to Improving Clinical Effectiveness

Tony Rousmaniere

Routledge
Taylor & Francis Group

NEW YORK AND LONDON

First published 2017
by Routledge
711 Third Avenue, New York, NY 10017

and by Routledge
2 Park Square, Milton Park, Abingdon, Oxon, OX14 4RN

Routledge is an imprint of the Taylor & Francis Group, an informa business

© 2017 Taylor & Francis

The right of Tony Rousmaniere to be identified as author of this work
has been asserted by him in accordance with sections 77 and 78 of the
Copyright, Designs and Patents Act 1988.

Library of Congress Cataloging in Publication Data
A catalog record for this book has been requested

ISBN: 978-1-138-20318-1 (hbk)
ISBN: 978-1-138-20320-4 (pbk)
ISBN: 978-1-315-47225-6 (ebk)

Typeset in ITC Legacy Serif and Bodoni
by Saxon Graphics Ltd, Derby

This book is dedicated to my supervisors,
from graduate school to the present,
who have taught me how to learn with courage,
patience, and self-compassion.
I stand on their shoulders.

CONTENTS

Prologue   ix
Acknowledgments   xvi

PART I: THE PATH TO DELIBERATE PRACTICE   **1**

1 The Path to Competence   3
2 The Path to Expertise   26
3 The Experiment, Phase 1: Deliberate Practice   32
4 The Experiment, Phase 2: Solitary Deliberate Practice   44

**PART II: THE SCIENCE OF EXPERTISE: LEARNING
FROM OTHER FIELDS**   **55**

5 Expertise in Medicine: Focus on Clinical Outcomes   57
6 Expertise in Performing Arts: Focus on Skills   73
7 Expertise in Difficult Situations: Experience Refined by
   Feedback   86
8 Expertise in Spiritual Practices: Addressing Experiential
   Avoidance   96

PART III: DEVELOPING YOUR OWN DELIBERATE PRACTICE ROUTINE   **111**

  9 The Principles of Practice   113
10 Deliberate Practice Exercises for Basic Skills   125
11 Deliberate Practice Exercises for Specific Models   143

PART IV: SUSTAINING DELIBERATE PRACTICE   **155**

12 The Inner Game: Self-Regulation, Grit, and Harmonious Passion   157
13 Advice for Supervisees: Finding Your Path to Expertise   165
14 Advice for Supervisors: Integrating Deliberate Practice into Supervision   173
15 Advice for Mid- and Later Career: Lifelong Learning   180
16 Challenges to Deliberate Practice   186
17 Looking Forward   190

Epilogue   193
Appendix: Videotaping Psychotherapy   195
References   198
Index   214

PROLOGUE

Me (as a psychologist trainee): I don't think therapy is helping Karen.

My supervisor: What's wrong?

Me: I don't know. We've got a great therapeutic relationship. But she's not getting better.

Supervisor: How so?

Me: Her drug use is getting worse. She's lost her job. Her boyfriend left. I'm worried about her four-year-old son. I've tried working dynamically in the relationship, cognitive reframing, and behavioral interventions. Nothing seems to work.

Supervisor: How about we talk with our social workers about getting financial and caretaking support for her son?

Me: Great, but how do I help *her* more?

Two weeks later my client[1] died from a drug overdose. Her son was shipped off to foster care.

This tragedy was the capstone of a long series of therapeutic disappointments. I, like all therapists (whether they admit it or not), was all too familiar with clients stalling, dropping out of therapy, and even deteriorating. However, my client's death and her son's abandonment brought painful clarity to the harsh consequences of clinical failure. I had become a therapist because I wanted to help my clients, not watch them die.

This event sparked a crisis within me—one that I believe is shared by therapists around the world, across all the treatment models: *How do I become a more effective therapist?*

Luckily I wasn't alone in my quest. Although I didn't know it at the time, prominent psychotherapy researchers were wrestling with the same dilemma: the urgent need for more effective methods of psychotherapy training. At the same time that I had my crisis, these researchers were on the cusp of discovering a promising path to clinical excellence: *deliberate practice.*

This book proposes that the science of expertise, backed by decades of research on how experts in a wide range of other professions—from sports to math, medicine, and the arts—may help psychotherapists achieve skill mastery. This mountain of research can be distilled into two major findings. First the good news: expert performance *is* achievable by most people, with effort and perseverance. Now the bad news: achieving expert performance isn't easy. In fact, it's hard.

What This Book Is About: Deliberate Practice

The idea of deliberate practice has its origins in a classic study by K. Anders Ericsson and colleagues (Ericsson, Krampe, & Tesch-Romer, 1993). They were curious about what methods top-performing professional musicians used to achieve expert performance. To examine this, they went to a famous music conservatory in Germany and asked the students to complete a survey regarding their training activities. Ericsson and colleagues hoped to discover which training activities were associated with the very best musicians.

When they compiled the data, only one variable reliably predicted the skill level of the musicians: the amount of time the students had spent practicing their instrument alone. Further investigation revealed that the students were not just simply practicing their instruments but were primarily working on goals to improve particular aspects of their performance identified during the weekly meeting with their master teachers. The students were engaging in a comprehensive series of activities designed to maximize skill acquisition. According to Ericsson (2006), these activities are:

1) Observing their own work.
2) Getting expert feedback.
3) Setting small incremental learning goals just beyond the performer's ability.

4) Engaging in repetitive behavioral rehearsal of specific skills.
5) Continuously assessing performance.

They termed this process deliberate practice. Notably, all of the top performers at the music conservatory had accumulated a minimum of thousands of hours of solitary deliberate practice. This finding led to the widely known "10,000 hour rule" popularized by Malcolm Gladwell in his 2008 book *Outliers*, although the actual number of hours required for expertise varies by field and by individual (Ericsson & Pool, 2016). The widespread misunderstanding that 10,000 hours of work performance leads to expertise is not accurate: 10,000 hours of *solitary deliberate practice* was found to be the minimum for expertise. As I discuss in Chapter 4, this misunderstanding holds considerable significance for the field of psychotherapy, where hours of work experience with clients has traditionally been used as a measure of proficiency.

Many professions rely on solitary deliberate practice to improve performance. When a basketball player is told by his coach that he needs to sharpen his 3-point shots and then arrives an hour early every day to practice his shots until he improves, that's solitary deliberate practice. When a chess player loses a tournament, identifies a specific opening sequence that would have helped him, and then spends hours repetitively trying out that sequence against a computer chess training program, that's solitary deliberate practice. When a surgeon learning a new laparoscopic procedure spends hours repetitively practicing on a simulator that provides continuous feedback on his accuracy, that's solitary deliberate practice.

What about psychotherapists? While professional dancers, musicians, athletes, orators, etc. would never expect to improve their performance without investing many, many hours in solitary deliberate practice, most psychotherapists will get through years of training, licensure, etc. without having spent even a full hour in solitary deliberate practice. I sure didn't, and I had never met a therapist who did.

It's not because we are lazy or don't care. The vast majority of us care deeply about helping our clients and are willing to invest substantial time and money in becoming better therapists. However, unlike most other professions, our field simply does not have a model for how to use solitary deliberate practice to improve our work.

Why don't we have a model for solitary deliberate practice for psychotherapy? Certainly our work is as challenging, complex, and high stakes as any of the fields listed above. We help our clients with an incredibly diverse range of challenges (anxiety, depression, relationships, work performance, etc.), often with high-stakes consequences (ending a marriage or helping a client not take their own life) and under constrained work conditions (managed care, limited financial resources, etc.). Furthermore, we have to do all this while maintaining eye-to-eye, empathic attunement with clients who are often in severe emotional distress or caught in cycles of self-destructive behaviors. Doesn't sound like an easy job to excel at, does it?

In my experience, psychotherapy is actually a very hard job to excel at. In fact, throughout my training, I found that while I was good at helping some clients, a large amount of my caseload was simply not improving. Despite doing everything I was supposed to do—including supervision, studying theory, attending workshops—I wasn't helping a full 50% of my clients. This caused me years of growing frustration.

Then one day I had a fateful interview with Scott Miller, the first psychologist to call for the use of deliberate practice in psychotherapy. This interview led me to Scott's other work (Miller, Hubble, Chow, & Seidel, 2013; Miller, Hubble & Duncan, 2007) and the work of other prominent psychologists (Tracey, Wampold, Lichtenberg, & Goodyear, 2014) who had been studying the potential use of deliberate practice for psychotherapy. Building on their research, I started experimenting with using deliberate practice for myself and my trainees.

From this experience, I have developed a routine for using deliberate practice for psychotherapy training. The main goal of this routine is to help me and my trainees improve our effectiveness by using deliberate practice to learn from our clinical nonimprovers and failures, the "other 50%" of our cases. This routine aims to help us break through a competency plateau by engaging in a never-ending gradual improvement process towards psychotherapy expertise.

My routine uses these five deliberate practice processes:

1) Observing our own work via videotape.
2) Getting expert feedback from a coach or consultant.
3) Setting small incremental learning goals just beyond our ability.
4) Repetitive behavioral rehearsal of specific skills.
5) Continuously assessing our performance via client-reported outcome.

These processes are repeated throughout a career, beginning with graduate school and continuing through licensure into middle and later career.

Additionally, my routine includes learning principles gleaned from how other fields (e.g., medicine, performing arts, and emergency management) use deliberate practice:

- We use the clinical outcomes of our individual clients as the most valid empirical basis for our work (see Chapter 5).
- We learn best by focusing on specific incremental skills just beyond our current ability and repetitively practicing those skills (see Chapter 6).
- We maximize learning from our clinical experience, particularly our clinical failures, by reviewing our own work via videotape (see Chapter 7).
- We address our own experiential avoidance by developing emotional self-awareness and nonreactivity (see Chapter 8).

How Is This Book Different?

In the decades since Ericsson and colleagues' first study of musicians, the body of research on deliberate practice has grown rapidly. Deliberate practice is now a well-researched field. The *Cambridge Handbook of Expertise and Expert Performance* has over 40 chapters and 900 pages exploring how a vast range of fields use deliberate practice (Ericsson, Charness, Feltovich, & Hoffman, 2006). I have recently had the good fortune to edit a volume with prominent colleagues on how to use deliberate practice specifically for psychotherapy (Rousmaniere, Goodyear, Miller, & Wampold, in press).

This book is different from the other literature on deliberate practice in one main way: it is personal. Although I cite research literature, I did not write this book from an academic perspective. Rather, it is a highly personal narrative of the arc of my training from beginner trainee to licensed clinician and beyond, throughout which I faced significant clinical challenges that ultimately led me to find deliberate practice. I am including my personal story because I know the path I took in my clinical training was not unique. Rather, the challenges, both professional and personal, that I experienced will sound familiar to many therapists. Facing these challenges together with open eyes and a compassionate heart will provide a strong foundation for the hard road ahead: the journey to expertise.

How This Book Is Organized

This book is divided into four parts.

Part I: The Path to Deliberate Practice tells the story of the arc of my professional development, starting with my initial experiences and including the clinical challenges and failures that led me to discover and use deliberate practice.

Part II: The Science of Expertise: Learning from Other Fields delves deeper into the science and research on deliberate practice, including exploring (a) the history and evolution of deliberate practice, (b) what we can learn from how other fields use deliberate practice, and (c) empirically based components of expertise.

Part III: Developing Your Own Deliberate Practice Routine aims to help you start experimenting with deliberate practice. To get you started, I describe the deliberate practice principles and exercises I have used for clinical training: *what* I practice and *how* I practice. Because the processes of deliberate practice are transtheoretical, these exercises can be used to enhance the effectiveness of clinical practice and supervision in any field of mental health (e.g., clinical psychology, counseling, marriage and family therapy, etc.) and to benefit any therapeutic modality (e.g., cognitive behavioral therapy, psychodynamic psychotherapy, etc.).

Part IV: Sustaining Deliberate Practice discusses key empirically based methods that therapists can use to strengthen and support their deliberate practice. Because solitary deliberate practice is difficult, Part IV focuses on strategies and techniques to make solitary deliberate practice more viable, such as developing grit, tips for trainees seeking a mentor, and strategies for integrating deliberate practice into supervision. This part provides guidance for clinicians at all career stages, from trainees to seasoned, licensed therapists in independent practice.

What This Book Is *Not* About

This book does not contain clinical instruction from a master psychotherapist. I cannot write that book since I have not achieved clinical mastery. I can say this with confidence because I have collected my outcome data for the past half-decade. My outcomes are good but not superb; my dropout rate is decent but not zero; my deterioration rate is about average for the field. I have had many clients who report substantial life-change improvements. But I have also had some who left disappointed after a few sessions or, even worse, left after many sessions with no positive change to show for their investment of time and money.

If this is disappointing to you—if you are looking for guidance or clinical wisdom from a master psychotherapist—there are many other books available for this purpose.[2] However, while I am not a master psychotherapist, I am passionate about becoming one, which has led me on a never-ending quest to find more effective clinical training methods. That is what this book is about: learning *how to become an expert psychotherapist*. This process starts by acknowledging our clinical failures (the "other 50%"), dropping our assumptions about what constitutes effective psychotherapy training, and reexamining the whole endeavor of psychotherapy skill acquisition from the ground up.

Let's begin.

NOTES

1 All psychotherapy cases presented in this book have been modified to preserve the confidentiality of the clients.

2 It is worth noting, however, that the claims of clinical expertise in these volumes are usually not based on actual outcome data, but instead on the authors' decades of experience as therapists, or the quality of their writing. These claims are dubious. Several large studies have recently suggested that years of clinical experience is not in itself a reliable indicator of clinical expertise (Goldberg et al., 2016; Tracey et al., 2014). I do not mean this as a criticism of these authors; not collecting or reporting outcome data is the norm in our field. As I suggest in Chapter 5, this is a problem that needs to be addressed if our field is to achieve substantial improvement in effectiveness.

ACKNOWLEDGMENTS

This book and my personal journey to deliberate practice have been possible only because of the generous guidance and encouragement I have been fortunate to receive from others. Scott Miller is at the top of this list. Scott is a true visionary and never content with the status quo. Always a decade ahead of the rest of the field, Scott was the first psychologist to see how the science of expertise could benefit psychotherapy. Scott's team at the International Center for Clinical Excellence is leading the effort to bring deliberate practice to mental health. His fearless pursuit of improvement and client-centered focus have been an inspiration to me throughout my career and have reached through me to benefit every one of my clients.

In addition to Scott, I have had the great fortune to work with Rodney Goodyear and Bruce Wampold on an edited volume on deliberate practice in psychotherapy. From them I have learned not only a lot about deliberate practice but also how to approach psychotherapy outcome and supervision research more scientifically. I am blessed to have the generous mentorship of such talented senior psychologists.

This book is based on ideas originally developed by K. Anders Ericsson in the early 1990s and on the large body of writing he produced over the following decades. Dr. Ericsson provided valuable advice for this book, and for that I am especially grateful. Among other topics, Dr. Ericsson pointed out new developments in the definition of different forms of practice that delineate between naïve practice, purposeful practice, and deliberate practice (see Chapter 16). A thorough discussion of these alternate definitions is beyond the scope of this book; readers are referred to Ericsson and Pool (2016) for an in-depth review of these topics.

William McGaghie also provided important assistance for this project. As we will review in Chapter 5, Dr. McGaghie is one of the leading proponents of using deliberate practice for the reform of medical training. His pioneering work in medicine is a model of what we can hopefully achieve in psychotherapy over the next few decades. I am also indebted to Daryl Chow for inspiration and advice on this topic. Daryl ran the first empirical study on deliberate practice and psychotherapy, which was instrumental in opening my eyes to the potential in this area. Additionally, I am thankful to Noa Kageyama for his generous assistance and encouragement.

Allan Abbass, Patricia Coughlin, and Jon Frederickson helped this project in many ways. First, they are case examples of psychotherapists who strive tirelessly to improve their clinical skills and openly discuss their outcomes. Additionally, all were willing to discuss their personal training methods with me. Allan and Jon provide invaluable clinical supervision that greatly benefits my clinical work. Just as important, Patricia provided my first experience of truly top-notch psychotherapy. Jon was the first psychotherapist to show me how to use the principles of deliberate practice for psychotherapy supervision. I am deeply indebted to all three.

This book is based on the intersection of two major domains of research: psychotherapy outcomes and clinical supervision. I am very fortunate to have benefited from encouragement and mentoring by psychotherapy researchers in both domains. Jason Whipple, a researcher in routine outcome monitoring, provided important advice on every section of this book. Michael Ellis and Ed Watkins, who produced some of the key clinical supervision literature that serve as the foundation for this book, generously provided valuable guidance throughout my career, as well as encouragement for this project.

I am also indebted to the therapists who experimented with the exercises in this book, including the trainees I have supervised and the licensed therapists who have attended my classes on deliberate practice. Their curiosity and courage have been an inspiration. Much of the information in Parts III and IV of this book was gleaned from their experiences experimenting with deliberate practice.

George Zimmar, my publisher at Routledge, saw the potential in an early draft of this book and provided valuable advice throughout the publishing process. Len Sperry, Nicholas Ladany, and an anonymous reviewer provided encouragement and helpful suggestions for improving the text. Joanne Freeman offered excellent editorial advice for every part of the book. Nat Kuhn identified key problems in earlier drafts of the book and helped me get back on track. Chip Cooper and Simon Goldberg raised questions about the text that helped me clarify important points. Jennifer Callahan and her two anonymous graduate students provided insightful advice and encouragement. Dawn Preston and Alaina Christensen contributed valuable editing and proofing of the book.

At the heart of this book is my family. My wife, Laura Prugh, is my inspiring model of a successful scientist and has taught me how to approach research and data in a level-headed way. More than anyone, my lively and wonderful four-year-old daughter, Evelyn, lights up my days and keeps me humble by generously providing moment-to-moment feedback on my fathering skills.

Most of all, this book is founded on the work of my clients. Their courage, effort, persistence, and feedback have taught me more about psychotherapy than anything else. To them I am endlessly grateful.

Part I

The Path to Deliberate Practice

CHAPTER 1

THE PATH TO COMPETENCE

My entry into the field of psychotherapy was typical. Like many therapists, I was drawn to the field because I was a "people person." I had a knack for talking with people about their inner life, I enjoyed introspective work, and I felt like I could be good at it. Furthermore, I was quite confident of the potential benefits of psychotherapy. Although I had never read any psychotherapy research, my gut told me that many individual and social life challenges were caused by psychological blocks, and psychotherapy offered the keys to healing, growth, and empowerment. (Turns out my gut was right: decades of research have shown psychotherapy to be, on average, very effective for helping people with a wide range of problems; Lambert, 2013.)

Like many aspiring therapists, no small part of my inspiration to enter the field came from my personal experiences in psychotherapy (Farber, Manevich, Metzger, & Saypol, 2005). In my late teens I had become deeply depressed; a psychologist's evaluation recommended that I be removed from school due to risk of suicide. A mentor at my school connected me with a kind and compassionate psychologist. Using a patient, non-confrontational Rogerian style, the psychologist melted my angry and rebellious persona. My first few years of therapy with him were instrumental in helping me pull myself together, graduate high school, and enter college. I became an evangelist for psychotherapy and the power of introspection to transform lives. Now an adult, I wanted to provide that life-saving help for others.

When I started graduate school, I found myself among peers who also were enthusiastic and optimistic about the opportunity to help people change their lives through psychotherapy. In fact, I can't recall a trainee from my graduate program—or any of the supervisees I've had since—who wasn't clearly driven by the inherent motivation to help others. The research in this area mirrors my personal experience: 90% of trainees in a recent study reported a desire "to help others" as a main motivation to become a therapist (Hill et al., 2013). We are truly fortunate to work in a field where so many choose this work for such positive reasons.

Like many trainees, I entered the field with strong feelings about psychotherapy models. Specifically, I was convinced that psychodynamic therapy was the best model. Even more specifically, I felt sure that long-term psychodynamic therapy was the best. I say that I *felt* this because I had not yet bothered to actually read any psychotherapy-outcome research. Unburdened by the facts, I found peers who agreed with me, and together we enjoyed the clarity of confidence that only comes from a lack of contact with real data, which is invariably messier.

One year into my training I started working with actual clients. One of my first practicums was at a high school near Palo Alto, where I helped students with a wide range of problems, from academic concerns to depression to eating disorders. Although the school was in a wealthy suburb, my client population was very diverse. About half of my clients were children of undocumented immigrants. Many were in gangs. I initially felt a strong, heady rush of exuberance as I sat down with this diverse group of young people to help them change their lives.

A Good Start

My first few months working as a therapist trainee were very positive. I connected quickly with my clients. I still had something of a rebellious streak left over from my teenage years, and this probably helped me bond with my teenage clients, many of whom were in trouble at school, with their parents, or law enforcement.

Quickly bonding with clients gave me great hope. The therapeutic relationship is the basis for psychodynamic work. Additionally, we were taught in graduate school that the therapeutic relationship is the variable most associated with successful psychotherapy, across all models of treatment (Norcross, 2011).

I was lucky to have a practicum where clients were not mandated to be in therapy: they came of their own free will and were largely very eager to get help. My clients were enthusiastic and resilient despite having a wide range of multisystemic stressors at home, including poverty, domestic violence, peer pressure, and prejudice because of their skin color, culture, nation of origin, and sexual orientation.

My clients' initial successes in therapy occurred very quickly. Roughly 25% of my clients were like rocket ships blasting off from a launch pad: all it took was a bit of empathy and advice to achieve ignition and send them tearing off into the sky. These clients worked hard in therapy and implemented our work in their daily lives. I didn't know it at the time, but psychotherapy research has identified that a large number of clients have a dramatic positive response to therapy, called "sudden gains" or "rapid response" (Lambert, 2013).

Another 25% of my clients took a bit longer to respond positively to therapy. Like a rocket ship struggling to gain altitude, they sputtered at first, showing no initial improvement. Sometimes their symptoms even worsened for the first few sessions. However, after three to six sessions they righted themselves, started to recover, and settled into a pattern of gradual improvement. This pattern of initial symptom deterioration followed by gradual improvement has been recently identified in large research studies (e.g., Owen et al., 2015). Like the fast responders, these clients worked hard in therapy and actively tried to implement what they learned in their daily lives.

A QUICK HONEYMOON

Then came the disappointment. After a few months at my practicum, I started to notice that a sizable percentage of my clients were not improving. By sizable percentage, I mean *half*. While the fast responders were rocket ships that blasted off towards the stars, 50% of the clients couldn't even find the ignition switch. They engaged in therapy; we talked about their challenges, their goals, their relationships, their history, their *everything*. But these clients simply didn't improve.

Like the 25% of my clients who were slow responders, some of these 50% experienced worsening of initial symptoms during their first few sessions. However, unlike the slow responders, they didn't then get better. Instead, about 10% of my clients continued to get worse. In clinical terms, this is called *deterioration*. Some deteriorated so much that they dropped out of school or ended up in a hospital psychiatric ward. Rather than taking off, these clients were like rocket ships that blow up on the launch pad.

I felt frustrated and guilty about my clients who showed no improvement. Curiously, these cases were not correlated with the clients' socio-economic status or other variables that could cause stress at home and thus impede progress. Caucasian clients from wealthy families were just as likely not to respond as children of undocumented immigrants living in poverty and surrounded by gangs.

Then came the dropouts.

I responded to my first few dropouts with outright denial. I assumed they couldn't come back to therapy because of some external reason: maybe their schedule had changed, or possibly their friends convinced them to stop. However, as more and more of my clients stopped coming back, I had to acknowledge that maybe it was because therapy wasn't actually helping them.

In summary, about 50% of my caseload was not benefiting from therapy. The psychotherapy research literature has a term for these cases— clients who don't show improvement, who deteriorate, or who drop out: "nonresponders" (a less gentle term is "treatment failures"). I know now that my therapy batting average was actually pretty typical. Research suggests somewhere between 40% and 60% or more of clients do not benefit from therapy (Lampropoulos, 2011).

CLINICAL SUPERVISION TO THE RESCUE?

I was quite embarrassed about my therapy nonresponder and dropout problem. But I knew the solution: clinical supervision. Called the "signature pedagogy of the mental health professions" (Bernard & Goodyear, 2014, p. 2), clinical supervision is the primary method of clinical instruction. In a field characterized by intense antagonism among treatment models, one constant point of agreement is clinical supervision. Every major model of psychotherapy relies on supervision for clinical training.

The primary goals of clinical supervision fall into two broad domains. The first is aiding supervisee professional development. For example, supervision serves a critical role in helping supervisees improve their sense of self-efficacy, develop a professional role identity, reduce performance anxiety, and increase professional autonomy (Bernard & Goodyear, 2014).

The second goal of supervision is to improve and protect client welfare. Unsurprisingly, there is wide consensus among scholars that this second goal is primary. Supervision scholars Carol Falender and Edward Shafranske (2004) succinctly summarized this point when they wrote, "The most important task of the supervisor is to monitor the supervisee's conduct to ensure ... the best possible clinical outcome for the client" (p. 4). Michael Ellis and Nicholas Ladany, two prominent supervision researchers, famously called client outcome the "acid test" of good supervision (Ellis & Ladany, 1997, p. 485).

Although I had not yet read the work of these supervision scholars, I shared their view. Specifically, what I wanted most from supervision was help with the "other 50%"—the clients who stalled, deteriorated, or dropped out. I had great confidence in supervision to help me navigate through my clinical impasses towards better clinical effectiveness. If it worked for Sigmund Freud, it would work for me.

My faith in clinical supervision was not unique. Data from a survey I conducted some years later with colleagues at the University of Alaska Fairbanks suggest widespread confidence in supervision's ability to improve clinical outcomes. From a national pool of 185 supervisees and 189 supervisors, almost all participants affirmed that supervision *should* have a positive impact on client outcome (92% of supervisees and 89% of supervisors), and large majorities reported that supervision *does* have a positive impact (70% of supervisees and 79% of supervisors). When given an opportunity to voice concerns, only six supervisors and seven supervisees (out of 374 participants) expressed hesitation or doubts about supervision's impact on client outcome (Rast, Herman, Rousmaniere, Swift, & Whipple, in review).

While supervisees and supervisors may be largely convinced that supervision improves client outcomes, the research literature in this area is, unfortunately, less clear. Some studies have suggested that supervision may improve clinical effectiveness (e.g., Bambling, King, Raue, Schweitzer, & Lambert, 2006; Callahan, Almstrom, Swift, Borja, & Heath, 2009; Reese et al., 2009). However, three large reviews of the literature in this area all raised concerns about the reliability of these findings. Likewise, supervision scholars voiced caution in assuming that supervision improves client outcomes. Ladany and Inman (2012) urged modest expectations for supervision's impact on client outcome: "Supervision may have an effect on client outcome; however, supervisors should recognize that the effect in many instances may be minimal" (p. 195). Beutler and Howard (2003) stated simply, "Supervision does not work" (p. 12). In his review of the literature in this area, noted supervision scholar Ed Watkins (2011) summarized this perspective more diplomatically, "We do not seem to be any more able now, as opposed to 30 years ago, to say that supervision leads to better outcomes for clients" (p. 252).

Fortunately, I had not read this literature, so my faith in supervision was undeterred.

My supervisor was smart, friendly, and approachable. He had over three decades of experience as a therapist and supervisor. We met for an hour each week to discuss my cases, and I also had two hours of group supervision with five of my peers. The group felt comfortable and supportive. We were all genuinely trying to learn how to be better therapists. There was very little competition among trainees.

I told my supervisor and the group about my concerns regarding my "other 50%"—the clients who stalled, deteriorated, or dropped out. My supervisor listened compassionately. He told me that my experience was common, which was simultaneously both relieving and disheartening. In retrospect, I now know that my supervisor's comment about my experience being common was correct: clinical research has shown that trainees (like all therapists) can have poor outcomes. In a striking example, my colleague Jennifer Callahan at the University of North Texas published a study that showed dropout rates of up to 77% at a training clinic (Callahan, Aubuchon-Endsley, Borja, & Swift, 2009).

As I talked about my dropouts and deteriorations, I saw a look of recognition in the eyes of my peers. I could tell I was not alone in my clinical failures. I felt support and camaraderie, which was helpful. Unfortunately, support and camaraderie do not themselves lead to improved effectiveness.

Biased Data

In supervision we discussed my challenging cases in detail. Unfortunately, the detail was highly biased. I say biased because my description of the session was based on my memory and notes; I did not have videotapes of the session. A large body of research has repeatedly shown that human memory has extensive biases in self-appraisal (Myers, 2015; Greenwald, 1980) and is generally as truthful as a politician giving a press conference (Chabris & Simons, 2014).

Our memory is a petri dish of biases, blind spots, ulterior motives, and projections—all totally unconscious—driven by our desires, fears, past experiences, self-image, vanity, shame, and God knows what else. Memory researcher Charles Fernyhough describes memories as "shaped by who we are now. They're shaped by what we feel, what we believe, what our biases are" (Martin, 2013). Importantly, memories reported in supervision are subject to distortion at two stages: once when the memory is encoded during the initial experience of the event (the therapy session) and then again during the memory retrieval in supervision (Buchanan, 2007).

I cannot stress this enough: our memory is biased up, down, and sideways. Repeat after me: I have biased memory, you have biased memory, we all have biased memory. This is one of the reasons why the American Psychological Association (APA, 2014) and Association for Counselor Education and Supervision (2011) recommend the use of audiotape or videotape for supervision.

As we discussed my cases, my supervisor gave me advice. His advice usually involved new ways of looking at a case, understanding my own internal emotional reactions to a case (countertransference), and suggestions for new approaches I could take in session that might be more helpful for the client. He often assigned reading in psychotherapy textbooks to help me conceptualize the case or learn new treatment approaches.

I was a dedicated supervisee. Every week I read the assignments carefully. I then went back to my office at the high school, saw my clients, and tried to apply my supervisor's guidance. His advice was often helpful for my clients who were already responding well. Unfortunately, very little changed for the clients in the "other 50%," those who were not responding or deteriorating. And my dropout rate remained uncomfortably high.

I had a nagging feeling that I was learning a lot about psychotherapy but not becoming a more effective therapist.

What was I doing wrong? Why all the dropouts, and why were so many of my clients not getting better? In retrospect it was impossible for me to know because I had no empirical perspective on my work. While my supervisor was very clinically astute, he was working with biased data (i.e., my notes and memory), and thus his ability to give corrective feedback was limited.

Although I was very open about my clinical failures in supervision, I was less forthcoming about how supervision didn't seem to be helping. My supervisor was very nice, and I could clearly see that he was trying his best to help me. In retrospect I know that the limited benefit of supervision wasn't his fault but rather a systemic problem across our field. I also now know that I was not alone in keeping silent about the limited benefit of supervision. A growing body of research shows that supervisees routinely withhold important information (e.g., Ladany, Hill, Corbett, & Nutt, 1996). Supervision is a very hierarchical relationship; supervisors have tremendous personal power over their supervisees and little accountability. Supervisees have little to gain but much to risk if their supervisor doesn't appreciate their feedback. In one recent study, 84% of trainees reported withholding information, with a "negative perception of supervision" being the most common topic withheld (Mehr, Ladany, & Caskie, 2010).

That said, I want to emphasize here that I think my supervisor was very good by the current standards in the field. His knowledge of psychotherapy was excellent, his engagement with me was open and collaborative, and his advice was solid. He was a very competent supervisor doing everything a supervisor is supposed to do (with the exception of videotaping, which wasn't recommended by the APA at the time). While that was sufficient to help me become a *competent* therapist based on the prevailing clinical training standards, it was unfortunately not sufficient to help me significantly improve my effectiveness with the "other 50%" of my caseload that was stalling, deteriorating, or dropping out.

A GOOD AVERAGE

I also want to emphasize that my overall effectiveness at that time was not bad. Roughly half of my clients were getting better—some very dramatically and quickly. If a researcher were to have used my personal caseload as data for a clinical study, she would have determined that my average client was doing better (especially since clinical studies routinely exclude dropouts from data analysis, which gooses up the results). The overall mean would likely mask the number of significant failures in my caseload.

I was baffled by the split between the clients who had quick, dramatic improvement and the clients who deteriorated or dropped out. How could this be? I now know why this split makes sense and is, in fact, entirely predictable: the vast majority of variance in client change is accounted for by the *client* (Bohart & Wade, 2013). As Tallman and Bohart (1999) wrote in *The Heart and Soul of Change*, "the client's abilities to use whatever is offered [in therapy] surpass any differences that might exist in techniques or approaches" (p. 95).

One of the great challenges of clinical supervision and training is that we have very poor leverage. In one hour a week we're trying to right problems caused by years, or decades, of the client's history, genetic/biological makeup, circumstances in the client's life, state of the economy, physical health, financial situation, etc. And we're trying to fix these problems by simply talking (in contrast to providing financial support, education, housing, etc.). This is why therapy can sometimes feel like trying to help someone get free from a strait jacket with both of your hands tied behind your back. On the face of it, it's amazing that psychotherapy ever succeeds.

As hard as it can be for therapists to affect clients' well-being, it is exponentially harder for supervisors. To affect client outcome, supervisors' interventions, in effect, have to travel through three layers of mediating variables: client variables, therapist variables, and supervisor variables. For example, for a supervisor to impact client outcome, the following conditions must be met: (a) the supervisee or supervisor must be able to identify an opportunity to improve client outcome, which may require enough supervisee trust to disclose uncomfortable information; (b) the supervisor must have the psychotherapy skills necessary to understand and address the opportunity; (c) the supervisor must have the supervision skills necessary to provide developmentally appropriate interventions in supervision (e.g., explain therapeutic goals and tasks, or address the supervisee's countertransference); (d) the supervisee must have the capacity to understand the supervisor; (e) the supervisee must trust the supervisor enough to truly accept the supervision rather than just pretend to comply; (f) the supervisee needs to have sufficient skill or talent to be able to remember and implement the supervision; (g) the client needs to have the capacity and openness to receive the effects of the supervision; (h) other factors in the client's life must not block their efforts to implement the change; (i) the effects need to have an impact that is within the sensitivity of an outcome measure; and (j) the client needs to be able to accurately report that difference on the outcome measure.

Describing the weakness of the link between supervision and client outcome, Wampold and Holloway (1997) anticipated, "Detection of a relation between supervision process and the patient's rating of patient change (the most distal outcome) would be expected to be extremely small" (p. 23). Their concerns were prescient. Later in my career, I was part of a research team that examined the amount of variance supervisors had in client outcomes, using a large five-year data set from a large counseling center in Canada (6,521 clients seen by 175 trainee therapists supervised by 23 supervisors; Rousmaniere, Swift, Babins-Wagner, Whipple, & Berzins, 2014). The findings were nothing less than shocking: supervisors accounted for *less than .01%* of the variance in psychotherapy outcome, a finding that a colleague called "horrifying." (When we presented the data at a conference, we rounded the results to "less than 1%" in the abstract because we were concerned that readers would think that "less than .01%" was a typo.)

Effectiveness of Psychotherapy Training

I now know that my experience with clinical supervision and training was not unique but rather the norm. Many studies have shown that clinical training can be effective for teaching basic psychotherapy skills such as the ability to create and maintain therapeutic relationships, the component of psychotherapy most associated with positive outcomes (e.g., Crits-Christoph et al., 2006; Hilsenroth, Kivlighan, & Slavin-Mulford, 2015; Wampold & Imel, 2015). However, very few studies have shown that psychotherapy training actually results in improved clinical outcomes, and multiple studies have shown that beginning trainees or even paraprofessionals can have better outcomes than fully trained and licensed therapists (Goldberg et al., 2016; Tallman & Bohart, 1999).

This disconnect between clinical training and client outcomes is scandalous, and has been known for decades. Questions have been raised as far back as the 1950s (Watkins, 2011). If this is not a sign that our training methods need a major overhaul, then I don't know what would be. Yet our field plows ahead with business as usual. Current clinical supervision and training models are largely the same now for trainees as they were 50 years ago. This would be inconceivable in other fields. Can you imagine if trained surgeons had outcome equivalent to or worse than paraprofessionals? If professional basketball players had the same

3-point shot percentage as amateurs? If musicians in the National Symphony had the same level of musical skill as high-school musicians?

CRISIS OF FAITH

Back to my first year of clinical training. As my awareness of being stuck in my work with the "other 50%" was growing, I was simultaneously having less than stellar experiences in my own therapy. The depression from my teenage years had begun to return, and psychotherapy wasn't seeming to help as much as it had when I was younger. I was seeing the same psychologist who had helped me in high school. He had the same style of psychodynamic therapy: patient, compassionate, accepting, and congruent. Unfortunately, this time around it wasn't working. We had a great therapeutic relationship, and I gained valuable insights into my own self-destructive habits. But I didn't feel better. My friends frequently observed that my ever increasing proficiency with introspection rarely resulted in my making actual important changes in my life. I was, in the words of psychotherapy researchers Werbart and colleagues (2014), "spinning my wheels."

The gap between expectations and results in my clinical work and my own personal therapy sparked a crisis of faith in dynamic therapy. (I use the term "faith" because my belief in the superiority of dynamic therapy was not based on evidence from research or outcome data.) My faith stood in stark contrast to my actual experience of dropouts, nonimprovement, and deteriorations in my own caseload.

Like many therapists, I had found a handful of research studies that supported my psychotherapy model. These had been passed around in email lists and academic courses. Every psychotherapy model has a handful of studies that show outstanding results and thus imply superiority to other models. So we have evidence that all major psychotherapy models are similar in that they can produce amazing results. Unfortunately, they all share another similarity: therapists using all psychotherapy models have unacceptably high rates of nonresponders, dropouts, and clinical deterioration (Imel, Laska, Jakupcak, & Simpson, 2013; Swift & Greenberg, 2014; Wampold & Imel, 2015).

Over time, after conversations with many therapists, I've come to see that the process I experienced—starting with faith-based idealism of a treatment model followed by disillusionment—is common for therapists.

This makes sense, given that the process by which we adopt our psychotherapy models usually bears more resemblance to how one chooses a religion than to a scientific process based on empirical data.

Most therapists choose a model based on two factors. First, their community: people they respect such as professors, mentors, and their own therapists. Second, their feeling of congruence with the model: how well the theory makes sense to them, how well the level of therapist activity and directedness matches their own interpersonal style, etc. Put simply, we pick a psychotherapy model because it feels right for us.

These community-and-feeling methods for picking a psychotherapy model lead therapists to grandiose expectations for effectiveness that aren't tethered to reality. However, after a period of time, most clinicians who take an honest look at their own practice will see dropout and deterioration rates that weren't advertised in the literature.

Science or Faith?

We have put ourselves in a double bind. In an attempt to achieve scientific credibility, leaders in our field have asserted that therapists should pick a psychotherapy model based on scientific evidence. However, unlike physics, chemistry, biology, and medicine, psychotherapy is a field with *no basic science*. Although decades of outcome data show that therapy works, we still don't know why or how at the level of basic science. Eminent psychotherapy researcher and past president of the APA Alan Kazdin (2009), a fierce advocate of empirically based treatments, expressed this well when he wrote, "There is no evidence based explanation of how or why even the most well-studied interventions produce change, that is, the mechanisms through which treatments operate" (p. 418).

We might cite a select few empirical studies on our websites to give the impression that we have gone through a logical process of elimination in picking a treatment model. This can give our work a veneer of scientific credibility. However, most of us haven't read the studies we cite, and our confidence in the superiority of our model is maintained primarily by avoiding similar evidence from other models.

Our field suffers from a vacuum of performance data from actual clinicians in the field. While every model has clinical research data to support it, few individual clinicians track their own outcome data or make that data available to the public. Proof of this can be found by looking at the websites of prominent clinical trainers and supervisors in your preferred treatment model. Can you find even one who reports their treatment outcome data with clients? Websites like goodtherapy.com and psychologytoday.com have therapist profiles that report almost everything one could want to know about a therapist—education, license, training, treatment model—everything *except* the most important thing: data about how effective that therapist actually is.

THERAPIST VARIABILITY: THE GOOD, THE BAD, AND THE UGLY

Why is it important for therapists to track their own outcome data? Recall that decades of research have shown that psychotherapy *on average* produces good results: about 80% of clients in treatment do better than those who don't attend psychotherapy (Lambert, 2013). With results this good, why bother with outcome data? Because the average treatment outcome across an entire caseload masks the variability in individual clients (as in my own caseload). And it turns out that therapists have great variability in their effectiveness.

A classic study on this topic was conducted by Okiishi, Lambert, Nielsen, and Ogles (2003). They examined the outcome data from 1,841 clients seen by 91 therapists over two and a half years and found a substantial difference in the client outcomes among therapists. The authors summarized their findings:

> There was a significant amount of variation among therapists' clients' rates of improvement. The therapists whose clients showed the fastest rate of improvement had an *average rate of change 10 times greater* than the mean for the sample. The therapists whose clients showed the slowest rate of improvement actually showed an *average increase in symptoms* among their clients.
>
> (p. 361, emphasis added)

This finding has been replicated in many large studies since (e.g., Baldwin & Imel, 2013; Wampold & Brown, 2005; Minami, Brown, McCulloch, & Bolstrom, 2012; for a review of this topic, see Wampold & Imel, 2015).

A notable recent study expanded on this research by not just looking at variability among therapists but also by examining variability in outcomes within individual therapist caseloads, depending upon the clinical focus

(Kraus, Castonguay, Boswell, Nordberg, & Hayes, 2011). In other words, the study aimed to explore whether therapists were more or less effective working on different diagnostic categories (depression versus anxiety versus substance abuse, etc.). The authors examined outcome data from 6,960 patients seen by 696 therapists. They found that many therapists had good results with some diagnoses but bad results with others, sometimes with dangerous implications: "we found large numbers of therapists whose average patient ends treatment worse off than when they started (38%) depending on the [clinical focus], with 20% of therapists' average patients left more suicidal and 36% more violent" (Kraus et al., 2011, p. 273).

THE DATA BECOMES PERSONAL

Let's return to my story. It was now nearing the end of my first year of training. My clinical outcomes by the end of the year were largely unchanged from the beginning: about half of my clients were getting better, some very quickly. However, the rest, my "other 50%," were not improving, dropping out, or even deteriorating.

I was also feeling the variability in therapist effectiveness personally. My work as an adult with the same therapist who had helped me when I was a teenager was going nowhere. Over time I finally had to acknowledge that the many hundreds of hours and thousands of dollars I was investing in my own therapy wasn't actually helping me improve my life in any real terms. My relationships consisted of a long series of short, rocky alliances with abrupt endings. I was bitter about my upbringing and avoided meaningful contact with my family. My social life increasingly centered around partying late into the night with alcohol and drugs. I was becoming a deterioration statistic in my own therapy.

Unfortunately, my therapist seemed to be as helpless and trapped as I felt. Although the content of our sessions (anger at my parents, mistrust of society, fantasies of a better life) might have sounded meaningful, I never actually made any important changes in my life. We spent countless hours dancing in passive tense. As we cycled yet again through the same topics, he would assure me that we were making progress because our therapeutic relationship was becoming stronger, which somehow would produce unconscious change that would liberate me. However, as I was about to find out, waiting for the unconscious to fix a growing substance-abuse problem is like waiting for gravity to tame a horse: it only works when the horse is dead.

Like many psychology graduate students, the tipping point of my awareness of the severity of my personal problems occurred in psychopathology class. As we reviewed the DSM-IV section on addictive disorders, and discussed the minimizing and denial prevalent in those disorders, I realized that I met many of the criteria for clinical substance abuse. I had two immediate reactions: my first thought was "But this is just how I relax and have fun with my friends," followed very closely by, "Oh crap."

I needed to find good therapy, fast.

REALLY GOOD PSYCHOTHERAPY

The first time I saw really good therapy was in narrative therapy class. I had wanted to focus my clinical training on dynamic therapy, but luckily my graduate program required exposure to multiple treatment models. My professor, Mary Herget, showed us a demonstration video of her using narrative therapy with a real client. I was awestruck.

First, I had never seen a video of a real psychotherapy session before. The idea that we could watch what actually happens in therapy was revelatory. The clinical video let my professor guide us step by step through her clinical decision-making process and let us examine the client's reaction to each of her interventions. We were able to discuss her successes and mistakes based on the client's actual reactions, rather than notes compiled from biased memory. Furthermore, the video enabled us to participate in the emotional experience of the therapy from both the therapist's and client's perspective.

In contrast, all of my psychodynamic clinical training was from textbooks. This might be fine for math, physics, or chemistry but is inadequate (in my experience) when learning a deeply emotional interpersonal skill. Learning therapy without watching clinical videos is like learning to play sports without watching competitions, or to play music or dance without watching performances. Learning therapy from master clinicians' case reports is like learning how to paint by hearing a master painter describe their paintings without being able to actually see the paintings directly.

Second, the actual content of the session was shockingly good. Using her own style of narrative techniques, my professor helped her client proceed through a process of emotional self-discovery that was clearly quite powerful. Seemingly paradoxically, she was both fully engaged and transparent with the client while simultaneously being neither directive or intrusive. The client was clearly working at the cusp of his emotional capacity, simultaneously challenged and supported by my professor's close emotional attention. This was quite different from the therapy I was providing (and attending) myself, which all too often consisted of the client (or me) engaging in endless, detached, ruminative complaining, dressed up as sophisticated self-reflection.

As a class we learned more from watching the interpersonal dance between my professor and her client than we ever could from reading a psychotherapy textbook or case transcript. Most important, I had seen proof of what my gut had told me all along, and which research has confirmed: really good psychotherapy is possible. Unfortunately, clinical videos are the only way to see if a therapist is really good, because few in the field keeps personal outcome data or makes it available to the public.

The other important lesson I learned from my professor's video was that psychodynamic therapy does not hold the exclusive license to good therapy. I didn't know it at the time but I had personally discovered what psychotherapy research had discovered a few decades previously: there is far more variance in outcome between individual *therapists* than between psychotherapy *models* (Wampold & Imel, 2015).

DOES EXPERIENCE LEAD TO BETTER EFFECTIVENESS?

I had always assumed that my personal therapist was good, despite my recent poor personal experience with him, because he had over four decades of experience. In fact, there is striking evidence to the contrary.

That evidence comes courtesy of my colleague and mentor Jason Whipple. I met Jason some years later, after I had become a supervisor myself at the University of Alaska Fairbanks. Jason is first and foremost an athlete. He was a competitive wrestler for 15 years, and even now at age 40 he spends many hours a week at mixed martial arts, getting thrown onto the mat by men half his age. When Jason's not beating people up, he's supervising psychology trainees. Jason runs the student-training clinic for the University of Alaska psychology training program in

Fairbanks. In addition to being a supervisor and researcher, he also works as a therapist and devotes considerable energy to continually improving his own clinical skills.

Jason and I spent many hours in his underground windowless office (called "the cave" by his students) discussing the challenges in clinical development, which we knew both from our personal experience and from watching our trainees struggle. One day we were discussing a classic study on therapist development by David Orlinsky and Michael Ronnestad (2005). In the largest study completed on this subject to date, Orlinsky and Ronnestad surveyed nearly 5,000 therapists about their self-perceptions of professional development over decades of work experience. The majority of therapists reported thinking that they had experienced significant clinical skill development from their years of work. Jason, who is something of a skeptic, like any good researcher, raised his eyebrows at this finding. "Sure, they think they're developing. But are they *really* getting better?"

I knew the basis for his doubt. A decade previously, Jason's graduate-school advisor noted that psychotherapy-outcome researcher Michael Lambert and colleagues (Walfish, McAlister, O'Donnell, & Lambert, 2012) had done a study examining the accuracy of therapists' self-perceptions about their personal effectiveness. In a survey of 129 mental health professionals, the average therapist rated his or her own work performance in the 80th percentile, no participants rated themselves below average, and 25% of participants rated themselves in the 90th percentile.

In another study, 48 therapists were asked to predict which of their personal cases were at risk of deterioration. The therapists were informed that the average deterioration rate in psychotherapy is 5–10%. Despite this information, only one of the 48 therapists accurately identified their clients who were at risk for deterioration (Hannan et al., 2005). Notably, the only therapist who correctly predicted their client's deterioration was a trainee; the licensed therapists all predicted that *none* of their clients were at risk of deterioration. These concerns about therapist self-appraisal have been supported by a large body of research (e.g., Ægisdóttir et al., 2006; Spengler et al., 2009).

Jason summarized his concerns, "We know that therapists *think* they are getting better with experience, but we also know that their self-perception can be faulty. How about we examine this empirically?" From this idea was born the first large-scale longitudinal study of therapist clinical-skill development based on client outcomes. Simon Goldberg, a talented graduate student at the University of Wisconsin, led the project. He got help from his advisor Bill Hoyt, an expert in psychotherapy-outcome research, and his mentor Bruce Wampold, who is co-author of the classic text *The Great Psychotherapy Debate* (Wampold & Imel, 2015) and an expert in comparing large-scale psychotherapy-outcome studies. We examined outcome data from 6,591 psychotherapy patients seen by 170 therapists at a large university counseling center over a period of many years. Some therapists in the dataset had up to 18 years of data; the average was almost 5 years of data.

When Simon finished the data analysis, Jason's doubts were confirmed. While some therapists' effectiveness did improve with time, many didn't show improvement, and the average therapist actually had a small but statistically significant decrease in effectiveness over time (Goldberg et al., 2016).

We're on the Road to Nowhere …

Back to my story. If my first year of clinical training was any indication, I was on track to be no more effective after 18 years myself. I was now at my second clinical-training placement at a community mental-health center in San Francisco. I was again working with a very diverse group of clients who presented with a wide range of problems. Like those in the previous practicum, these clients were voluntarily in therapy. They really wanted help. Also like the previous practicum, I had a very experienced and talented supervisor who did everything a supervisor was supposed to do. She even let me videotape my sessions, which was no small feat in a city mental-health system run by a bureaucracy terrified of litigation. Unfortunately, similar to my previous practicum, I was only able to help about half of my clients, while the other half languished, dropped out, or even deteriorated.

Please note: I wasn't a bad therapist. In fact, I was quite competent. I knew this because I was regularly assessed by both my supervisor and my university according to a long laundry list of 18 different criteria for competency, including my professionalism, record keeping, collegiality with staff and peers, openness to supervision, knowledge about psychotherapy theory, etc. Notably, the only thing *not* included in my competency assessments was outcome data with my actual clients. Are you sensing a pattern here?

The problem was that I didn't want to just be competent. I wanted to be *better*.

At about the same time, a friend turned me on to a psychotherapy textbook that had provoked a lot of discussion at our university: *The Heart and Soul of Change*, by Mark Hubble, Barry Duncan, and Scott Miller (1999). *The Heart and Soul of Change* is possibly the most important book for therapists of my generation. The central thesis of the book, based on four decades of clinical research, was exactly what I had been discovering in my own clinical work: all major psychotherapy models show roughly equivalent results. This finding was humorously termed the "dodo bird verdict" by Rosenzweig (1936) after the scene in Alice in Wonderland where the queen says "everyone has won and all must have prizes." In the book the authors propose that the key to improved psychotherapy effectiveness is to stop the fruitless fighting between models and instead focus on helping each individual therapist improve his or her outcome with each individual client through the use of clinical feedback tools.

The Heart and Soul of Change, now in its second edition, was well received by clinicians. The mountain of evidence pointing to the general equivalency of all major therapy models kept growing with each following study (for a review, see Wampold & Imel, 2015). Over a decade later it finally broke through to general acceptance: 13 years after *The Heart and Soul of Change* was published, the APA approved the Resolution on the Recognition of Psychotherapy Effectiveness, which states:

> Comparisons of different forms of psychotherapy most often result in relatively nonsignificant difference, and contextual and relationship factors often mediate or moderate outcomes. These findings suggest that (1) *most valid and structured psychotherapies are roughly equivalent in effectiveness* and (2) patient and therapist characteristics, which are not usually captured by a patient's diagnosis or by the therapist's use of a specific psychotherapy, affect the results.
>
> (APA, 2012, emphasis added)

Breaking Ranks

I had heard about the Dodo Bird Verdict previously but had dismissed it due to my strong faith in my treatment model of choice, psychodynamic therapy. However, after my limited experiences of effectiveness as a therapist using psychodynamic therapy and my poor experience with it as a client, followed by the videotape of excellent narrative therapy, my faith was fragile. Reading *The Heart and Soul of Change* broke the last cords of loyalty I had.

I simply wanted more than anything to be a better therapist, and dynamic therapy (at least the way I was learning it) was clearly not the path to improved effectiveness. I gave myself permission to break ranks from the dynamic therapy fold and sought out experts from other psychotherapy models. Much to her credit, my supervisor wasn't threatened by my trying new psychotherapy models, but instead gave me her 100% support. "Videotape your work. We'll review it here in supervision and learn together what works and what doesn't," she said.

I quickly discovered that our field is rich in clinical-training opportunities, and I tried many: training videos, conferences, clinical workshops, weekend immersions, webinars, and more. I became a psychotherapy-training groupie. Witnessing the masterful skill of expert psychotherapists was truly inspiring. I was like a psychotherapy sponge, trying to absorb as much of their methods as possible. I filled a stack of lined pads with careful notes and accumulated a large library of books on psychotherapy models, techniques, and theory. When I attended conferences or workshops, I asked the instructors for their advice about my challenging cases. My plan was simple: I would learn techniques from a wide range of psychotherapy models. Like a mechanic with a toolbox full of shiny new tools, I would then be able to reach the 50% of my clients that I had previously failed to help.

Unfortunately, my plan fell flat. After a year of immersing myself in every training opportunity I could find, I still had the same problem. The new techniques and methods seemed to help the clients that were already responding well to therapy but didn't help the significant portion of my cases that simply did not respond to treatment, the "other 50%." Although I had some dramatic successes, my dropouts continued at an alarming pace, some clients clearly deteriorated, and many didn't get better.[1]

I started to notice a pattern: I'd come back from a clinical workshop or conference with lots of new techniques and enthusiasm to try them with my clients. The clients who were already responding well to therapy would continue to do well. Sometimes a few of the other 50% would initially respond as well, almost like they were absorbing my enthusiasm. Within a few weeks, however, we'd end up stuck in the same clinical ruts we had been in previously.

Because I didn't have any follow-up training in the new models I was learning, I didn't know how to respond beyond what I had originally learned at the workshop or conference. I could follow the script, but without continued feedback I couldn't learn how to make the techniques fit within my personal therapy style, so they often felt odd and disjointed. I was like a psychotherapy mockingbird: I could copy the notes but the music was wrong.

My psychotherapy toolbox was growing larger by the day, but I wasn't getting any better at using the tools. How could I get that damn good? What was I missing?

Now in my third year of clinical training, I had learned three key lessons:

1) It is possible to become a really good therapist (regardless of the model).
2) I really wanted that.
3) I had no idea how to achieve it.

PATTERNS IN THE MESS

Over time, I also noticed that continually learning new treatment models wasn't helping. Bouncing among disparate models—psychodynamic to cognitive behavioral therapy to eye movement desensitization and reprocessing to solution focused—confused clients and resulted in muddled work. While no psychotherapy model is superior to another, I paradoxically discovered that I needed to pick a specific approach and stick with it.

At this point I had graduated from my doctoral program. I was in my postdoctoral internship and was starting my own part-time private practice on the side when I saw a psychotherapy-demonstration tape by Patricia Coughlin, who teaches intensive short-term dynamic psychotherapy (ISTDP; Coughlin, 2006; Davanloo, 1990). Her tape was, simply put, amazing. Through an artful balance of challenge and encouragement, Patricia guided her client through a careful process of self-discovery about her unconscious habitual behavioral and cognitive patterns as they appeared moment to moment in the therapy session. As the client saw and then relinquished her own defenses in the session, old emotions of rage, guilt, sadness, and love that had been buried since childhood burst forth in waves of intense cathartic expression. Patricia helped her client link the previously unconscious feelings with her current self-destructive behavioral patterns and encouraged her to make healthier choices for herself.

I was excited to see this video example of very high-quality dynamic therapy, and went on a search for more. I saw a video by Jon Frederickson, another ISTDP expert, in which he artfully helps a man with sociopathic traits face his own intense guilt. In another video Allan Abbass (2015), a psychiatrist who specializes in using ISTDP to treat somatization and medically unexplained disorders, helps a client see how avoiding his feelings leads to medical symptoms. The session, perhaps the most astounding psychotherapy video I've ever seen, begins with the client hobbling in on a cane, barely able to walk, dejected and hopeless, reciting a long list of medical complaints. By the end of the session the client is so energized that he simply stands up and leaves, carrying his cane!

The work of these experts felt simultaneously very hard and effortless. On one hand, they courageously facilitated feelings more intense than I had seen in any previous therapy video. On the other, their interventions seemed perfectly natural. There were no elaborate interpretations or therapeutic jargon, leaving the impression that this model of therapy was quite easy to use. (Later I would discover that their effortless application of the model was only possible because of the years of hard, deliberate practice all three master therapists had invested.)

ISTDP seemed perfect for me: it is a dynamic therapy where the therapist takes a very active and engaged stance that also integrates cognitive and behavioral components. The model is based on the healing power of unconscious affect but emphasizes conscious personal responsibility to relinquish self-destructive behaviors and move towards healing. Like most major models, ISTDP has been proven empirically effective in multiple clinical trials (Abbass et al., 2014).

I was convinced that I had found the key to unlock a new level of therapeutic effectiveness. Learning ISTDP would be my path to therapeutic mastery. I read all the ISTDP books I could get my hands on. I attended ISTDP conferences, weekend trainings, and week-long immersions. My dive into ISTDP was an N of 1 case study of intensive immersion in psychotherapy training. What were the results of all this effort (and money)? On a personal level, it was very beneficial. I built camaraderie with motivated and bright clinicians. I expanded my referral network, which is crucially important in the first few years of private practice.

However, the impact on my clients was more of the same. It benefited the clients who were previously getting better but largely didn't help the other 50% who were stalled or deteriorating. Additionally, my dropout rate actually increased for a little while. Like my previous clinical supervision and training, this split experience (good for me, not impactful for my clients) matched the body of research on the impact of clinical supervision that shows significant benefits for the development of the trainee but questionable impact on client outcome (Watkins, 2011). I was still stuck with the same dilemma: How do I get better?

Then one of my clients at my postdoctoral internship died from her addiction to methamphetamines, leaving her four-year-old son alone. She died on my watch. She had been deteriorating for a while, and I had tried everything I knew to help her. This event crystallized my emerging clinical crisis. Out of desperation, I had an idea: I knew therapists who had achieved clinical mastery. Why not ask them how they did it?

NOTE

1 Assessing reasons for dropouts is actually quite tricky, in part because the client isn't there to tell you (this will be discussed more in Chapter 7). Research on this topic shows that, as expected, a majority of clients drop out of therapy due to dissatisfaction with treatment. However, a minority of clients actually drop out due to clinical improvement (Swift & Greenberg, 2014). Our own research from a large mental-health clinic showed that over 20% of dropouts showed improvement in their clinical-assessment scores prior to their last session (Swift, Rousmaniere, Babins-Wagner, Berzins, & Whipple, in review).

CHAPTER 2

THE PATH TO EXPERTISE

My goal was to get to the root of clinical expertise by interviewing master psychotherapists about their training methods. I approached three of the master therapists I had previously seen in videos: Allan Abbass, Patricia Coughlin, and Jon Frederickson. Fortunately, they were all very open to talking about their paths to clinical mastery. From our discussions, four common themes emerged.

Theme 1: They watched videos of their own work. They watched *a lot* of videos of their own clinical work. Allan Abbass reported that in his first three to four years of post-graduate training and studying ISTDP, he watched every hour of every therapy session at least once on video (Abbass, personal communication, 2014; see also Kenny, 2014, pp. 216–17).

Theme 2: They got frequent feedback from experts. The second common theme reported by these experts was getting frequent feedback on their tapes from other experts, particularly during the first three to five years of training in a new model. They deliberately focused on tapes of cases with which they needed help and used the feedback to identify clinical problems and areas for growth in their work. It is noteworthy that this kind of personalized feedback is not available at most clinical workshops and continuing education because the usual format is a lecture by a presenter, perhaps with a demonstration video, while the audience passively observes.

This wasn't just a few weekend workshops, but years of frequent feedback.

Importantly, the experts reported seeking to identify and address their own limits interpersonally (the interaction between them and their clients) and intrapsychically (their own internal emotional reactions during therapy sessions and in their daily lives). All three emphasized that both were vital for improving their own performance—the lowest limit of either their interpersonal or intrapsychic functioning served as a glass ceiling for their progress with clients.

Theme 3: They practiced specific psychotherapy skills. The third theme is that the experts practiced specific skills aimed at improving the areas identified from expert feedback. Some practiced alone using their own clinical videos, while others practiced in consultation with experts through clinical role play.

Theme 4: They assessed their own effectiveness. The fourth and final theme reported by the experts I contacted was an intense focus on assessing their clinical outcomes. This went far beyond the norms of clinical practice. For example, Patricia Coughlin published a book about her outcomes with clinical follow-up data (Coughlin, 2007). Allan Abbass published a summary of outcome data from his first six years in clinical practice (Abbass, 2002). All of these experts developed their own intense training regimens that exceeded what was required by their graduate training and licensing boards.

At about this time, I did an interview with Scott Miller for psychotherapy.net, a psychotherapy video website run by my friend and mentor Victor Yalom, an excellent therapist in his own right. The interview was on "why most therapists are just average" (I told Scott I was interested in this topic "for a friend"). Scott Miller is one of the authors of *The Heart and Soul of Change* (Hubble et al., 1999), which had influenced my work in two important ways: by introducing me to the "common factors" literature that showed general equivalency among psychotherapy models (e.g., Lambert, 2013; Wampold & Imel, 2015), and by teaching me how to use outcome and alliance feedback in my clinical practice. To my surprise, in the interview Scott described how he and his team at the International Center for Clinical Excellence had been working on exactly my problem: finding a more effective method for clinical training. Their answer was a term I had never heard before: deliberate practice.

DELIBERATE PRACTICE

Deliberate practice is a term introduced by K. Anders Ericsson and colleagues in the field of expert performance (Ericsson, 2015; Ericsson et al., 1993). Defined as "the individualized training activities specially designed by a coach or teacher to improve specific aspects of an individual's performance through repetition and successive refinement" (Ericsson & Lehmann, 1996, pp. 278-9), deliberate practice involves an intensive training process with repetitive skill-building exercises informed by expert feedback and performed throughout a professional career.[1]

Professionals across many fields, from music to sports to chess to medicine, rely on deliberate practice to achieve expert performance (Ericsson, 2006). However, as Scott noted, deliberate practice is conspicuously lacking from psychotherapy training (Miller, Hubble, & Chow, in press). If most other professionals use deliberate practice for training, then why don't we?

Scott's words sparked my curiosity, so I dug into the literature on expertise. Ericsson (2003, p. 67) described his team's discovery of deliberate practice:

> Analyzing a review of laboratory studies of learning and skill acquisition during the last century, we found that improvement of performance was uniformly observed when people were given tasks with well-defined goals, were provided with feedback, and had ample opportunities for repetition. These deliberate efforts to increase one's performance beyond its current level involve problem solving and finding better methods to perform the tasks. When a person engages in a practice activity (typically designed by teachers) with the primary goal of improving some aspect of performance, we called that activity deliberate practice.

Focused deliberate practice is a psychologically challenging, iterative process of intentional continuous strain and repair that intentionally aims to cause disequilibrium in the professional and thus break old habits that impair performance:

> Elite performers search continuously for optimal training activities, with the most effective duration and intensity, that will appropriately strain the targeted physiological system to induce further adaptation without causing overuse and injury.
>
> (Ericsson, 2006, p. 11)

> Lengthy engagement in some training activity has minimal effect unless it overloads the physiological system sufficiently to lead to associated gene expression and subsequent changes (improvements) of mediating systems.
>
> (Ericsson, 2003, p. 73)

Achieving expert performance requires continually repeating this process day after day, year after year: "When adults expose themselves to demanding and physiologically straining activities ... they are eventually able to transcend the stable structure of abilities and capacities that mediate activities in everyday life" (Ericsson, 2003, pp. 55–6).

A large body of research over the past few decades has made clear that deliberate practice is not just important but is in fact *necessary* for achieving expert performance across a wide range of fields, including competitive sports, music, and chess (Ericsson, 2006). Over the past two decades, researchers have explored using deliberate practice to improve performance in a range of other fields. For example, deliberate practice has been used to improve performance in surgery and nursing (Ericsson, 2015; see Chapter 5).

Neurobiological research has shown that focused deliberate practice can change brain-activation levels and produce structural changes in the nervous system. For example, one study showed that an hour of focused practice can reduce brain activation by 85%, primarily in the anterior regions of the brain that involve task control and working memory as well as posterior regions that involve attention control. Behaviorally this is represented by reduced errors, faster response time, and less effort. Regions of the brain that are involved in detecting stimuli (perception) and making responses (decisions) remain fully active, presumably because these tasks cannot be consolidated and are thus required for both novice and expert performance (Hill & Schneider, 2006).

To summarize the findings of this large body of research, deliberate practice is based on five main processes for the practitioner (Ericsson, 2006): observing your own work, getting expert feedback, setting incremental learning goals just beyond your ability, repetitive behavioral rehearsal of specific skills, and continuously assessing performance.

Can deliberate practice benefit psychotherapy as well? This question was first raised by Scott Miller and colleagues (Miller et al., 2013, 2007). More recently, other prominent researchers have joined the call to explore the use of deliberate practice for psychotherapy training (e.g., Tracey et al., 2014).

Daryl Chow and colleagues (2015) examined this question by asking a group of 17 therapists about their professional activities and comparing that information with their outcome data from 1,632 clients. They found that the "amount of time spent targeted at improving therapeutic skills was a significant predictor of client outcomes" (p. 337), while therapist experience level and psychotherapy model were not.

As I read the deliberate practice literature, I thought back to the conversations I had with my informal panels of master therapists—Allan, Patricia, and Jon—about their training regimens. Although none of them had mentioned the concept of deliberate practice, all had attributed their clinical expertise to (a) engaging in an intensive repetitive process of observing their own work, (b) getting feedback from experts, (c) practicing specific skills, and (d) assessing their outcomes—core elements of deliberate practice. Could deliberate practice be the way that these therapists had achieved expertise? Intrigued, I decided to try it for myself. I called Patricia Coughlin and signed up for my own therapy.

No-Nonsense Therapy

Psychotherapy with Patricia was completely different from what I had experienced before.

It was efficient. Instead of meandering around many topics, we kept our focus on a few specific productive goals. It was simultaneously tighter and more flexible. Patricia was clearly guided by her psychotherapy model but also was highly flexible. There was a feeling that we were moving in a clear direction, but it never felt artificial or forced.

It was very responsive. Patricia asked for my feedback at the end of every session, not just in the pro-forma manner that many therapists use: "Was the session okay?" Instead, Patricia was clearly very open, curious, and doggedly tenacious in getting my honest opinions about anything in the session that could have been better, including any mistakes she may have made. We had a strong working alliance built on shared hard work, not just on liking each other.

It was harder. Although we were working as collaborative partners, Patricia kept a firm stance that the responsibility for change was mine, and it wasn't going to happen just by rehashing the same old stories about myself or sitting back and passively waiting for a breakthrough. It was clear from the first few minutes that I was only going to achieve my goals if I were willing to confront my own self-destructive patterns. I expended considerably more energy in one hour of therapy with her than I had in ten hours of previous therapy.

Most important, it worked. Almost every session helped me achieve not just insight but real behavioral change in my life. The results of our therapy kept building and emerging over months and years after we ended our work together. I say *almost* every session because one of our sessions stood out as an exception. I ended the session feeling unclear and unsure. Patricia's response to this session is representative of her approach to psychotherapy. First, she was able to determine that something wasn't right by earnestly asking for my feedback at the end of the session. Second, she had a videotape of the session available to review so she could assess her errors (she taped all of our sessions). Third, she actually did the hard (and unpaid) work of reviewing the videotape before our next session. I know she reviewed the tape because she started the next session by openly acknowledging that she had missed something important in the previous session, described what it was, and asked if I were open to discussing how we could improve our work together.

Could deliberate practice be the reason that Patricia was an excellent therapist? Could deliberate practice make *me* a better therapist? I decided to find out.

NOTE

1 Ericsson and Pool (2016) have recently clarified the definition of deliberate practice to only apply to fields that are reasonably well developed with teachers who are widely recognized as experts and know effective methods for training students, and use the term *purposeful practice* to describe practice activities where these two factors are not present. This is an important distinction, but beyond the scope of this book. Interested readers can find a thorough discussion of this topic in Ericsson and Pool (2016).

CHAPTER 3

THE EXPERIMENT, PHASE 1

Deliberate Practice

My plan was to attempt to integrate all five deliberate practice processes into my personal training. I would observe my own work, get expert feedback, set small, incremental learning goals just beyond my ability, repeatedly rehearse specific skills, and continuously assess my performance.

The first step was to find a mentor. Deliberate practice requires expert direction to provide feedback and guide training: "More accomplished individuals in the domain, ideally professional coaches and teachers, will play an essential role in guiding the future experts to acquire superior performance in a safe and effective manner" (Ericsson, 2004, p. S74). Who could be my mentor?

In the previous few years I had attended clinical trainings run by many different supervisors. Of them all, one supervisor caught my attention as having a notably different approach to clinical training. This was Jon Frederickson (2013), one of the master therapists I had interviewed earlier. Jon is a prolific teacher and writer who conducts clinical trainings around the world, including Australia, Europe, India, the Middle East, and throughout the United States. Although he is not a techie, he has embraced technology as a medium for clinical training, including his clinical-training website (istdpinstitute.com) and his Facebook page, through which he answers questions from an international community of students.

BRINGING JUILLIARD TO TAVISTOCK

Before becoming a therapist and supervisor, Jon was a professional musician. (His wife, Kathy, plays the oboe for the Kennedy Center Opera House in Washington, DC.) To become a professional musician, one goes through a rigorous training program that includes many years of intense deliberate practice. Ericsson and colleagues' original 1993 study on deliberate practice found that the top-performing professional violinists had logged over 10,000 hours of solitary deliberate practice by age 20. This is a highly effective method of training that reliably produces excellent performers. Modern professional musicians routinely achieve or exceed technical skill that previously was only attainable by geniuses like Mozart (Lehmann & Ericsson, 1998).

When Jon became a therapist, he was struck by how differently psychotherapy training was conducted, and how it doesn't contain the key elements of deliberate practice. After Jon completed graduate school, he developed his own training regime that included an intensive process of watching videotapes of his work, getting feedback from experts, and practicing key skills, as Allan Abbass and Patricia Coughlin also did.

Jon's unique approach to psychotherapy training is based on the same principles he learned in music training. When I asked him recently to describe his approach to psychotherapy training, he replied:

> Unlike the field psychotherapy instruction, the field of music teaching has evolved over thousands of years. But only in the eighteenth century did instructional books emerge, putting together exercises which would develop the specific skills needed to perform a musical instrument. In the nineteenth and twentieth centuries, these books of etudes or "studies" evolved so that all students have access to exercises which will develop the skills musicians need and in the order in which they can be acquired systematically. Although the teacher is teaching an art, the student must have technical command of the instrument to create great art. Thus, in music there is a clear understanding of the relationship between technical competence and artistry.
>
> The field of psychotherapy has been strong on the teaching of theory but weak on the teaching of craft. As a result, students often know theory but not how to put it in practice. In fact, the learning of skills has traditionally been devalued in our field as mere "technique," something of a lower order than empathy, or the emotional bond.

Jon's unique approach to psychotherapy training sounded like a great fit for my deliberate practice project. Importantly, I had also heard from Jon's supervisees that he is a warm, patient, and compassionate teacher. Deliberate practice is "challenging, effortful, requires repetition and feedback, and may not be inherently enjoyable or immediately rewarding" (Coughlan, Williams, McRobert, & Ford, 2014). No one enjoys having their weaknesses pointed out to them repeatedly. Thus, it is essential to have a supervisor who is attentive to the emotional responses of the student and can create a positive and supportive training relationship. Unfortunately, positive and emotionally attuned relationships are not always present in clinical training. I knew this from both research and personal experience.

Harmful and Inadequate Supervision

My dissertation had been on collaboration in supervision. This was inspired by horror stories I had heard from my peers in graduate school regarding their supervision. In contrast, my personal experiences with supervision in graduate school were positive. This made me curious if the nightmare supervisors my peers described were one-off anecdotes or if there really was a widespread problem with supervision.

My dissertation advisor was Mary Herget, the narrative therapist whose clinical video I described earlier. With her assistance, I created a survey that asked a nationwide pool of supervisees to assess their supervisors efforts at collaboration in supervision. For the data analysis, I partnered with Michael Ellis, a prominent supervision researcher who specializes in bringing solid scientific methodology and advanced statistical methods to clinical supervision research (e.g., Ellis & Ladany, 1997). Michael has also done groundbreaking research on "harmful and inadequate" supervision, so he was a good fit for this project (Ellis et al., 2014).

A nationwide sample of 252 supervisees took the survey. When the results came back, we were shocked: fewer than 5% of supervisees reported that their supervisors were regularly engaging in explicit collaborative supervision, defined as "mutually agreeing, understanding, and working together on the relationship, process, and endeavors of supervision" (Rousmaniere and Ellis, 2013, p. 3). One third of supervisees reported that their supervisors were minimally collaborative, and over 10% reported that their supervisors were explicitly noncollaborative.

Little did I know we were just scratching the surface. Further research by Michael Ellis and his team at the University of New York at Albany found that 93% of the supervisees are in "inadequate supervision" and "over half of the supervisees had received harmful clinical supervision" (Ellis et al., 2014, p. 461). The authors note that these findings should not be surprising, given that most supervisors "are either not formally trained or have received minimal training in clinical supervision" (p. 462).

I also knew about the negative effects of harsh supervision personally, since I had recently experienced them first hand. Although I had been fortunate in graduate school to have warm, open, and patient supervisors, some of the post-graduate clinical training programs I had attended were led by supervisors who were degrading or even outright contemptuous of their students. While these individuals were excellent therapists, they displayed no knowledge of effective pedagogy and group process, essential components of clinical training. Rather, they simply provided supervision the way it had been provided to them years earlier, in a hierarchical, top-down, "you do as I say" manner. This can create an almost cult-like environment in which the teacher takes on the aura of an infallible guru to be obeyed, and the students often feel anxious, embarrassed, or ashamed of their mistakes.

Needless to say, this kind of training relationship was not conducive to the emotional vulnerability required for deliberate practice, where one repeatedly shows videotapes of his or her clinical weaknesses and mistakes. From these experiences I learned that being an effective supervisor is a double duty: one must be both an expert therapist *and* an expert supervisor.

Given his unique approach to clinical training and his personal characteristics as a supervisor, it was clear that Jon could make a promising supervisor for my experiments with deliberate practice. I approached him about starting supervision, and he agreed.

VIDEOTAPE SUPERVISION

We started with videotape in our supervision sessions. I selected videotapes of my cases from the "other 50%," clients who were not responding, deteriorating, or at high risk of dropout. I used routine outcome measurement data to help identify these clients (see Chapter 9 for more information on using multiple sources of data to identify clients at risk for deterioration). Video is a natural tool for deliberate practice, as it allows precise performance review (in contrast to biased memory). Ericsson (2015) described the use of videotape for deliberate practice by surgeons:

> Perhaps one of the most exciting developments in the measurement of behavior during surgery is the systematic video recording of surgeries followed by detailed analyses of the videotapes ... The methodology of using video recordings and their independent assessment seems to offer a potential feedback loop through which weaknesses and potential problems can be identified. These areas requiring improvement could then be addressed through targeted training focused on the relevant technical skills, the perceptual skills necessary to sense and understand the critical anatomical structures, the ability to plan the surgery, and/or the capacity to detect and deal with unexpected deviations or events (pp. 8–9).

Jon's perception and psychodiagnostic skills are incredible. It often takes him less than a minute of watching a video to see a host of clinical errors on my part. Like spotting a snowball that grows and grows until it causes an avalanche, he could quickly predict how these errors would cause problems later in the therapy session. Notably, most of the problems Jon identified included visual cues that require videotape to spot; case transcripts or audiotapes would not have been sufficient.

Jon's advice over our first few months of supervision focused on helping me find the right intensity of work for each client. He noted that,

> A common reason that clients become stalled, deteriorate, or drop out is that the therapist is working above or below their specific threshold of tolerance for anxiety and feelings. If you work above this level, then the client will be flooded, and won't be able to learn or heal. If you work below this level, then the client won't be challenged sufficiently to make progress. The key is to find each client's exact threshold of tolerance and work right there.

This concept of a threshold is similar to Russian psychologist Lev Vygotsky's (1978) theory of the "zone of proximal development," which focuses training on skills just beyond the learner's abilities but still within their reach.

Sure enough, as we reviewed the tapes of my "other 50%" cases, Jon identified multiple instances where I was working above or below the client's threshold. I'll describe an example of both.

Example 1: Working above the Zone of Optimal Learning

At the beginning of one video, Jon noticed that the client came into the session holding his stomach. I asked the client how he was feeling, and he replied, "Oh, fine, maybe a bit sick, but I'm always like this. Probably something I ate. Let's move on, I'll get over it." Jon suggested that

> the client's nausea might be a sign that he actually started the therapy session beyond his anxiety threshold before he even sat down in the chair. He might be minimizing his anxiety with you due to obedient relational patterns he had learned from his past attachment figures. But let's watch some more tape and see what happens.

As predicted, the client's nausea increased as the session progressed.

> Nausea is a common sign that the client's anxiety has gotten so high that it has passed over the threshold into the parasympathetic nervous system. This can cause a client to deteriorate in therapy. Although the client may try to comply and follow you in session, proceeding while his anxiety is this high only reinforces the client's habit of self-neglect. This is a relationship based on following you rather than attending to himself. The client really wants to make progress but is simply overwhelmed with cortisol [a stress hormone] from his anxiety. What I recommend here is to pause and try to help the client downregulate his anxiety.

Example 2: Working below the Zone of Optimal Learning

In another video I was helping a client who was struggling with depression. At the beginning of the session, I asked the client what she wanted to focus on. Jon noticed that the client didn't answer but instead sat quietly and waited for me to talk. He commented, "This might be a problem of passivity. Let's watch more video and see." I asked her again what she wanted to focus on, and she again sat quietly, with an air of polite deference. I asked yet again, to which she replied, "Oh, I don't know ... maybe ... ummm ... tools to be more confident?" Jon paused the video and said, "Notice how the client's answer suggests that she wants to work with you, but her body language is passive, compliant, and detached? Do you think she *really* wants to work with you? Is her will driving the therapy or yours?"

As the tape progressed, the same pattern continued: I did most of the talking, while the client was hesitant and ambivalent. Jon paused the tape and pointed to the client's eyebrows. He said, "Watch her eyebrows. She's unconsciously making nonverbal facial microexpressions that are provoking you to talk more." He played another few seconds of tape. "Right here, notice how her eyebrows arch slightly when she is quiet? That is an unconscious cue for you to talk. Each time she does that, you speak up. Let's replay the tape and watch this pattern." We replayed the tape and, lo and behold, there was a clear pattern of the client going quiet, arching her eyebrows, and then I would speak. "The client is unconsciously using nonverbal signaling to provoke you to be more active. This colludes with her passivity and will block progress."

Jon continued,

> Here, the client is working below the zone of optimal learning. Although the client's words might sound like she wants to work with you—and a transcript would read as such—her body language clearly conveys the lack of internal motivation. The words are correct but the music is wrong. Instead of an *internal* struggle within her, she's engaged in an external conflict with you. You are trying to convince the client to feel better rather than addressing the passivity and compliance that is keeping her depressed. You're trying to relate to the client you want to have—motivated and engaged—rather than relating to the client who showed up, who is passive and ambivalent. This client could spend years in therapy without any real progress.

Jon continued,

> We're often taught in graduate school that clients will tell us what's wrong with them. However, that's crazy. While many clients can tell us their symptoms, they can't tell us what's actually wrong inside them, what's producing the symptoms. Instead, these clients *show* us what's wrong; they enact it. This patient is a good example. She is unable to tell you her problem with her words, so instead you have to learn about her from her behavior in relationship with you.

DEEP DOMAIN EXPERIENCE

Jon's speed and accuracy in psychodiagnosis was at first quite disconcerting, as if he had x-ray vision for psychotherapy. But over time I came to see that his skill comes from the very deep well of experience and knowledge that he has built through thousands of hours of deliberate practice himself. For example, he had over ten years of videotape supervision, in addition to countless hours of intensive study of his own tapes. This deep well of clinical experience was referred to by Scott Miller in our interview as "deep domain-specific expertise" and as "mental representations" by Ericsson and Pool (2016). Ericsson (2004) noted:

> The rapid reactions of expert athletes are not due to greater speed of their nerve signals, but depend rather on their ability to better anticipate future situations and events by reactions to advanced cues. For instance, expert tennis players are able to anticipate where a tennis player's serves and shots will land even before the player's racquet has contacted the ball.
>
> (p. S74)

Master performers have attained domain-specific expertise. Weisberg (2006) studied the development of creative genius, including artists Mozart, Picasso, Calder, and engineers and scientists such as Thomas Edison and the Wright brothers. Common among all was years (more than a decade) of laborious effort building deep domain-specific expertise.

SKILL-FOCUSED CLINICAL EXERCISES

After we identified a problem in a tape, Jon led me through skill-building role-play exercises to help me learn the solution. Jon played the client, and I played the therapist. We repeated each exercise not once or twice but five times, ten times, or more, until it was clear that I had internalized each skill.

For the client who was above threshold and minimizing his anxiety, Jon directed me to rewatch the video with the sound off. "The client's words can mislead you, so try to do psychodiagnosis using only your eyes. Let's see what visual cues you can use to identify when the client's anxiety spikes above threshold." We replayed the tape. Each time I correctly pointed to nonverbal signals of high anxiety, Jon would pause the tape and say "Now practice saying to the video what you will say to the client next time you see him." When I missed nonverbal anxiety signals, Jon would rewind the tape, identify my error, and we'd then try it again. We repeated this process until it was clear that I was comfortable with the skills.

For the client who was below the threshold and passive, the exercise was quite different. Jon said, "Let's do a role play with you as the therapist and me as the client. When I am passive and quiet, resist the urge to jump in and talk more. Instead, let there be silence, and notice your own internal experience." We started the role play. As Jon played the quiet client, I noticed a spike of anxiety within me, and a corresponding urge to speak up. I resisted the urge. As we looked at each other, Jon then moved his eyebrows like the client did in the video, and I felt another spike of pressure to speak. After some time, Jon finally spoke, breaking the tension.

> Feel that rise of anxiety? That is the client's anxiety that you are sympathetically attuning to. When you speak, it discharges the anxiety, so neither of you have to feel it. While that provides you both with temporary relief, it also blocks clinical progress because the client never learns to notice and deal with her own feelings, and she stays stuck. If this client had lower capacity, such as psychotic or with borderline personality disorder, then we would need to speak up more and lead the session, as you have been doing. However, for this client we shouldn't compensate for her passivity. Let's try it again.

We repeated the role play many times, until I felt more comfortable not rescuing the client from the silence.

Simulation-Based Mastery Learning

Repetitive clinical role play is a form of "simulation-based mastery learning" (McGaghie, Issenberg, Barsuk, & Wayne, 2014). Defined as "contrived social situations that mimic problems, events, or conditions that arise in professional encounters," simulation-based mastery learning has been used in medical education since at least the eighteenth century (McGaghie et al., 2014, p. 375). Ericsson (2004) described the benefits of simulation-based training:

> Unlike surgery with actual patients, practice in the simulator can be stopped at any time, allowing trainees an immediate chance to correct mistakes and

even repeatedly perform challenging parts of procedures ... simulators offer the possibility of presenting rare problems and emergencies that would better prepare performers to deal with such situations. A recent study of military pilots showed that those pilots who had trained for a specific emergency situation in a simulator were more effective at responding to the same situation when it occurred during an actual flight mission. Similarly, surgeons who can experience rare emergency procedures when they are mentally ready in the simulator will be able to make necessary adjustments through additional training. These learning experiences are likely to better prepare surgeons for rare and challenging situations that occur unexpectedly.

(Ericsson, 2004, p. S78)

What about the risk of these exercises producing a mechanical approach to therapy? I asked Jon about this. He said:

Some students initially object to these exercises, thinking that they are "mechanical" or impeding their creativity. After doing them, however, they find that doing interventions that lie outside their habitual relational responses results in personal growth. In addition, they realize, once they have mastered a technique, that they now know the principle of intervention "in their bones" and, as a result, can now improvise based on their understanding of the principle of intervention. As I point out to them, improvisation in jazz is not random noise making, but a specific elaboration of a melody based upon a precise understanding of the scales, modes, and underlying chord structure. Just as in music, the student must know these underlying patterns very well so that he knows what he is improvising upon and why.

At the conclusion of supervision Jon assigned homework. The homework usually included reading on topics we had discussed. Assigning reading is a fairly common practice for clinical supervision (Bernard & Goodyear, 2014). Like most psychotherapy training, reading is aimed at building knowledge about psychotherapy theory.

Unfortunately, while reading about psychotherapy is interesting and even enjoyable, in my experience it has very limited impact on improving actual *skills*. I wouldn't expect reading about golfing to much improve a player's swing or reading about music to much improve a violinist's performance. That requires repetitive simulated performance—deliberate practice—exactly what our field lacks.

A UNIQUE APPROACH TO PSYCHOTHERAPY HOMEWORK

To address this gap, Jon has added a new (and in my experience, unique) component to his clinical homework assignments: solitary video study with behavioral rehearsal. Based on the errors identified in each supervision session, Jon identified a few skills (and only a few; two or three at most) for me to practice while watching my own videos.

Jon's homework assignments are based on his experience in professional musician training, in which students are assigned challenging parts of music to play again and again. Recall that the first major study on deliberate practice by Ericsson involved classical violinists. "Musicians can spend hundreds of hours mastering challenging pieces in their practice room by working on selected difficult passages" (Ericsson, 2004, p. S78). Solitary repetition allows the student to get a very deep understanding of the work at a bodily level. The skills move into procedural memory, so they become automatic and effortless, an experience described as "being in the zone" or *flow*[1] (Csikszentmihályi, 1990). This is crucial for professionals who have to perform in high-arousal states, such as musicians and athletes who perform in public or surgeons whose work is a matter of life and death. Whether one is performing in Carnegie Hall, the World Series, or the hospital emergency room, the skills need to be 100% automatic.

Is psychotherapy different? Some may think so because we don't perform in public (unlike musicians), our work is not competitive (unlike athletes), and our work is not a matter of life and death (although we do often help clients who are at high risk of self-harm or suicide). Despite these differences, I actually feel the opposite: that therapists work in *higher* arousal states than possibly any other profession. My reasoning is based on two factors. First, we help clients who very often present with symptoms of psychological trauma. Second, our job is to be open to that trauma, listen carefully, empathize, and attune to extremely painful feelings despite a very natural urge to avoid our client's painful experience.

Unlike other professions, we need to hold our clients' intense emotional suffering eye to eye while still making complex decisions quickly and accurately. To do this effectively, we have to address our own experiential avoidance (Hayes, Follette, & Linehan, 2004). This challenge is unique to our field and constitutes one of the major impediments to expertise (discussed further in Chapter 8).

I spent about an hour a week total, 15 minutes at the beginning of each day, doing Jon's homework assignments, focusing on videos of cases that were stuck or at risk of deterioration.

Jon's videotape supervision and homework helped. Cases that were previously stuck opened up. In session I felt more prepared, and my clients could tell. My dropout rate slowed, and more of my clients achieved clinical breakthroughs.

My experiment with deliberate practice was an initial success. However, I quickly saw that there was a major constraint in my plan: insufficient time for supervision. Jon's availability is very limited and individual supervision is expensive. At any given time, at least 30% of my clients were either stalled or at risk of dropout, and around 5-10% of my cases were deteriorating. In total, about half of my cases could benefit from supervision, meaning 15 out of my average caseload of 30. In one hour of supervision we could only cover one or two cases. Covering all of the cases that needed help would take 10-15 hours of supervision, which would cost more than the total income from my practice.

I needed something more.

Note

1 Note, however, that although experts are in flow while performing, they strive to stay out of flow while practicing. Deliberate practice achieves automaticity by aiming for the exact opposite of flow: a continuous process of disequilibrium that allows for continual improvement, discussed further in Chapter 9.

Chapter 4

THE EXPERIMENT, PHASE 2

Solitary Deliberate Practice

Searching for a solution, I returned to the literature on expertise. Among other papers, I reviewed the original study in which Ericsson and colleagues (1993) proposed the concept of deliberate practice. In this study they examined the differences in study habits among three different groups of violinists: best performers, middle performers, and lowest performers.

Rereading this study, something stood out to me that I had not noticed before. The skill of the violinists was predicted by the amount of time they spent in *solitary* deliberate practice: "There is complete correspondence between the skill level of the groups and their average accumulation of practice time alone with the violin" (Ericsson et al., 1993, p. 379). When the authors asked the violinists which activities were most important for their skill acquisition, all three groups of violinists (27 out of 30 participants) agreed on the answer: solitary deliberate practice. "Violinists rated *practice alone* as the most important activity related to improvement of violin performance" (p. 375, emphasis added).

Could solitary deliberate practice be the next step towards clinical expertise? I decided to find out.

SOLITARY DELIBERATE PRACTICE PLAN

I made a plan. Based on the deliberate practice research, my practice would follow this format:

1) I would watch my own clinical videos, focusing on cases that were stuck or those where I felt confused.

2) I would run through the homework exercises Jon had assigned (at this point I had a small library of homework exercises from previous supervisions).

3) Throughout the practice sessions I would pay close attention to my internal emotional state, following the process described by Allan Abbass (Kenny, 2014, pp. 216–17).

I then considered how much time I should spend in deliberate practice. I knew from the literature that professionals routinely spend many hours a day practicing. For example, the best chess players spend up to four hours per day in solitary study (Ericsson et al., 1993). In their research on expertise, Ericsson and colleagues (2006, 2016) estimated that it takes many thousands of hours of deliberate practice to become an expert in most fields. This is referred to as the 10,000-hour or 10-year rule by Malcolm Gladwell in the book *Outliers* (Gladwell, 2008), although the actual number of hours required for expertise varies by field and by individual (Ericsson & Pool, 2016). A common misconception about this idea is that it takes thousands of hours of routine work experience to achieve expert performance. In actuality, researchers have found something much more challenging: thousands of hours of solitary deliberate practice, on top of hours spent in routine work performance, is often required for expert performance.

I didn't have four hours per day available for solitary practice. In fact, it was going to be a struggle to do even one hour a day. My job duties at the time included clinical work (psychotherapy), providing supervision, paperwork, consultation with other treatment providers, networking, teaching graduate students, and more. So I decided to aim for a more modest goal: two hours a day, five days a week.

Solitary Deliberate Practice Plan 1.0

My plan was set. Enthusiastic and optimistic, I blocked off time in my schedule and was ready to go.

The first thing I noticed in my experiment with solitary deliberate practice was nothing. Specifically, I didn't do it. Although I had blocked off time in my schedule, I somehow always ended up doing something else. I answered emails, wrote research papers, went to the gym, cleaned my office—everything but the deliberate practice. This went on for two full weeks. I gradually became aware of an internal struggle. My mind had a strong intention to try solitary deliberate practice, but my heart had an equally powerful avoidance reaction. Why was this so difficult? What was I avoiding?

Solitary Deliberate Practice Plan 2.0

I made two changes to my plan. First, I aimed for a more modest goal. Although I might need more hours in the future, I would start with just one hour of practice for now. Second, I made a forced march plan. I would brew a pot of coffee, turn off all distractions, make myself sit down at my computer, and then just see what happened. I remembered that part of my plan was to tune into my internal emotional reactions to deliberate practice. If nothing else, I would simply do that.

Feeling invigorated and optimistic by my new plan, I tried again. This time it worked. Through no small amount of willpower and caffeine, I managed to sit at my desk and engage in deliberate practice almost every weekday for a month, watching my videos and alternating focusing my attention on the therapy process and my internal reactions. Success! Or at least a half-success, because I only averaged 30 minutes per day, while my plan called for a full hour. But it was a step in the right direction, so I gave myself full credit.

At the conclusion of the month, I took some time to reflect on the experience and assess what I learned. Reviewing my notes, four broad categories of benefits had emerged:

1) Deeper attunement to my clients.
2) Clearer awareness of my own work.
3) Sharper understanding of where my therapy model was and was not working.
4) More emotional self-awareness.

Each of these is described in more detail below.

DEEPER ATTUNEMENT

First, I noticed that I was developing a much deeper and more nuanced awareness of my clients. Watching the videos let me carefully study their body language, including their posture, eye contact, and vocal patterns. I noticed nonverbal microexpressions (Ekman, 2003) that often communicate feeling more honestly than words. These are all critical elements of communication that I would miss in the heat of the moment in therapy but could catch later in a video that I could pause, rewind, and replay.

For example, I noticed that one client always broke eye contact and looked away from me whenever she talked about her feelings. Another client unconsciously made tight fists with her hands while telling me that she never felt anger towards her father, who had abused her. Another client absentmindedly scratched her arm, right where she had scars from cutting herself, when saying she felt guilty for avoiding her family.

In the now-classic volume, *Psychotherapy Relationships that Work*, John Norcross (2011) listed variables that have substantial impact on therapy outcomes. The top three are considered "common-factor" variables because they apply across all therapy models: the working alliance, empathy, and goal consensus/collaboration. These variables require deep and accurate awareness of the client's experience, including nonverbal and unconscious communication. Notably, each of the above variables accounts for more variance in psychotherapy outcome by a factor *ten times* greater than the psychotherapy model, therapist adherence to the model, and competence in a model (Norcross, 2011; see also Wampold & Imel, 2015, p. 257).

Surgeons rely on precision, athletes rely on stamina, musicians rely on their hearing. Therapists rely on attunement.

A MIRROR INTO MY WORK

The second thing I noticed was improved awareness of patterns in my own work with clients. I knew that my memory is unreliable (Loftus & Loftus, 1976) and biased (Myers, 2015). However, I hadn't realized how much of my own words and actions I was unaware of and remembered incorrectly. For example, in one video I noticed that I talked over the client for most of the session. In another video I changed the subject when the client started crying. In another session I was simply trying too hard to make the client change and was ignoring her ambivalence.

Watching my own videos day after day, week after week allowed me over time to recognize patterns of similar clinical missteps across many cases. I wrote these problematic patterns down and made a list of areas in which to improve my work.

For example, I noticed in many videos that my clients were in a passive or compliant stance, following me rather than being motivated by their own will to change. Studying these tapes, I also noticed that I was frequently interrupting or talking over these clients, which could encourage their passivity or compliance. To address this, I wrote "DON'T INTERRUPT" on a post-it and put it on the desk next to my chair. Over time, I stopped interrupting clients. (I knew this was really working when, some weeks later, my wife commented, "I've noticed you're quieter than usual. You haven't interrupted me all evening. Is anything wrong?")

Where the Model Meets the Road

The third benefit from watching my own videos was learning a lot about my psychotherapy model. In the videos I could clearly see how well the model's theory fit each client. Did the model help me understand the client and help the client understand herself? Did the model's interventions make sense to the client and help the client grow or heal? What aspects of the client aren't explained by the model, or don't even fit the model?

Examining the fit of the model for each client is critical because my psychotherapy model, like all models, isn't actually real: it's a myth. My psychotherapy model, ISTDP, is based on a medical model of treatment (Laing, 1971) in that it proposes reasons for the cause of a client's problems (etiology), the solution (method of treatment), and predicted patterns of change (prognosis). However, unlike modern medicine, psychotherapy models are not empirically based on basic science research (in contrast to, for example, treatment for lung disease or broken bones). This is because we simply don't have sufficient basic science research into the brain, personality, and emotions.

Instead, psychotherapy theories are just that: theories, elaborate metaphors based on each particular model founder's insight and clinical experience. Frank and Frank (1993) described models as "A rationale, conceptual scheme, or myth that provides a plausible explanation for the patient's symptoms and prescribes a ritual or procedure for resolving them" (p. 42). While most theories make rather confident and sweeping assertions about the causes and solutions of clients' problems, all practicing therapists will tell you that the actual practice of implementing therapy is often quite messy. As television commercials sometimes say in rapid speech at the end of their sales pitch, "results may vary." Human beings are incredibly complex. Psychotherapy models may predict and explain some aspects of human behavior but invariably miss others. This is probably one reason why specific psychotherapy techniques within models account for less than 1% of the variance in psychotherapy outcome (Wampold & Imel, 2015).

As Field Marshall Helmuth Moltke, chief of staff of the Prussian Army, famously said, "No battle plan ever survives contact with the enemy" (Detzer, 2005). While half of my clients were winning their war, the other half were in rout.

Psychotherapy-session videos bring empirical science back to psychotherapy at the N of 1 case level. Watching my videos helps me identify the client's response to the model: where the model is helping, where it isn't helping, and where it might even be misguiding me.

EMOTIONAL SELF-AWARENESS

The fourth insight I gained from deliberate practice was the most surprising: awareness of my own very strong emotional reactions when watching the videos. As I watched, I tuned in to my own reactions. Most often the first experiences I noticed were anxiety: tension in my chest, rapid breathing, legs crossed tightly, arms tense, hands fidgeting. These were frequently accompanied by negative thoughts: embarrassment ("my sessions are no good"), pessimism ("this isn't going to work"), helplessness ("I can't do this; I should give up"), among others.

What was causing all this anxiety and self-attack?

I sat with these experiences and focused on just taking deep breaths while I watched the tapes. After 10–15 minutes, or more at first, I gradually noticed that my negative thoughts subsided and were replaced by a rising, chaotic tide of feelings. I felt sadness when watching my client, a survivor of horrific childhood abuse, shut down and withdraw into emotional isolation as I inquired about her feelings; hope when watching another client struggle to be honest with himself about his addictions; fear when facing the reality that another client might kill herself and not asking her to pretend otherwise with a suicide contract; anger at another client's boiling rage without trying to talk him out of it; guilt when hearing another client talk about the loved ones she had hurt and remembering my own list of relationship casualties.

In my videos I saw my clients and me struggling with our raw and frail humanity. As I watched these videos, I cried.

The cycle repeated itself with each video: tension, followed by negative thoughts, followed by deep feelings, ending with me in tears. Watching psychotherapy videos is hard because we face ourselves in our clients. Our clients' feelings evoke and reveal our own feelings. Their hope evokes our hope, their grief evokes our grief, their guilt evokes our guilt. As the Roman playwright Terence wrote, "Nothing which is human is alien to me."

I realized that psychotherapy is hard work because psychological suffering has interpersonal impact. Psychotherapy requires facing extreme pain eye to eye. Every day we confront human existential crises without flinching; minimizing, avoiding, or papering them over.

These reactions were occurring within me, in my emotional "background," during every therapy session of every day. However, I had previously not been aware of this because my attention had been wholly focused on helping the client. Solitary deliberate practice with my session videos let me gradually build self-awareness of the internal emotional process that occurs in my work. As I grew more aware and accepting of my own feelings, I became less tense and defended in session, and more open to clients' experiences. (The challenge of experiential avoidance is discussed further in Chapter 8, and solitary deliberate practice exercises to help are provided in Chapters 9 and 10.)

Deliberate Practice Is Hard

Solitary deliberate practice felt very different from videotape supervision with my expert supervisor. Specifically, it was much harder. In supervision I follow my supervisor's guidance. In solitary deliberate practice I am in the captain's chair, responsible for my own learning and training my own perception. This requires considerably more effort. Focusing on staying attuned to the video and my internal reactions and keeping my mind from wandering over to check email or Twitter is exhausting.

My experience of difficulty matches that described in the literature, first noted by Ericsson and colleagues (1993) and later confirmed by additional research (Ericsson, 2015). Coughlan et al. (2014) report that deliberate practice is "challenging, effortful, requires repetition and feedback, and may not be inherently enjoyable or immediately rewarding" (p. 449). Ericsson (2003) stated that:

> The core challenge of deliberate practice then is for performers to maintain effort at improvement for as long as they wish to improve performance beyond their current level ... With such an approach, as each individual's level of performance increases, the demand for further effort is not reduced— if anything, *the demand for effort is actually increased.*
>
> (p. 80, emphasis added)

For example, solitary deliberate practice is harder than providing psychotherapy. In therapy I can get into a state of flow. Deliberate practice works by intentionally staying out of flow.

> In sum, the key challenge for aspiring expert performers is to avoid the arrested development associated with automaticity and the completed adaptation to the physiological demands of the current levels of activity ... The expert performer actively counteracts such tendencies toward automaticity by deliberately constructing and seeking out training situations in which the set goal exceeds their current level of performance.
>
> (Ericsson, 2003, p. 69)

In my life I've trained for many activities: rock climbing, scuba diving, piloting, and more. Solitary deliberate practice for psychotherapy is harder than all of these because it requires feeling vulnerable. All of the other training I've done required focusing my energy outwards. When rock climbing I look for the holds. When piloting I watch my altitude and the instruments. When scuba diving I monitor the gauges and my depth. In contrast, in psychotherapy solitary deliberate practice I focus some of my energy inwards as I observe myself—my thoughts, my feelings, my anxiety.

EMOTIONAL ENDURANCE

Solitary deliberate practice is also hard because it involves building emotional endurance. Psychotherapy requires maintaining an emotionally attuned focus on the client for a whole session, which typically is 50 minutes. After a few years of training I could sit with clients and talk for many hours on end. However, I didn't have the endurance to be accurately attuned and emotionally available during all of that time. I sure wouldn't want to be the client I saw at the end of a long work day or a busy week.

Solitary deliberate practice helps us build endurance by overloading us just enough to break homeostasis and causes adaptation: growth of new capacity.

> The human body is constantly trying to protect its homeostasis ... improvements of strength and endurance require that people continue overloading (i.e., increase intensity, frequency, or duration on a weekly basis) and that they keep pushing the associated physiological systems outside the comfort zone to stimulate physiological growth and adaption.
>
> (Ericsson, 2003, p.72)

From athletics or fitness training, many of us are familiar with this process of overload followed by adaptation. However, the same process applies to our mental and emotional abilities.

> The general rule (or perhaps even the law) of least effort theorizes that the human body and brain have been designed to find means to carry out activities at the minimum cost to the metabolism. Consequently, when physiological systems, including the nervous system, are significantly strained by new or altered activities, these systems produce biochemical signals that initiate processes that lead to physiological adaptation and mediation of simpler cognitive processes that reduce the metabolic cost. This phenomenon is evident in most types of habitual everyday activities, such as driving a car, typing, or strenuous physical work, in which people tend to automate their behavior to minimize the effort required for execution of the desired performance. After participants have engaged in the same activities on a regular schedule for a sufficiently long time that the physiological and cognitive adaptations have been completed, then further maintained engagement in this activity will not lead to any additional improvements and the performance will remain at the same level. The central claim of the expert-performance framework is that further improvement of performance requires increased challenges and the engagement in selected activities specifically designed to improve one's current performance—or in other words, deliberate practice.
>
> (Ericsson, 2003, p. 79)

From this realization I developed a deliberate practice exercise deliberately aimed at building psychotherapy endurance (see Chapter 10). Building endurance for psychotherapy is an arduous, gradual, and long-term process that simply requires many hours of focused practice. There are no shortcuts. Doing deliberate practice with my own videotapes is invariably the hardest thing I do every day. As my rock climbing partner says, "Climbing is hard because it isn't easy."

A Deliberate Practice Journal

From Daryl Chow and colleagues' 2015 study, I got the idea to keep a deliberate practice journal. The use of journals for tracking deliberate practice was originally adopted by Ericsson and colleagues in their 1993

Table 4.1 Solitary deliberate practice journal

Date/Time	Duration	Focus	Notes
8/28/2015 9am	30 mins	Assessment and intervention skills assigned by coach	Limited benefit; too tired after gym to focus
8/30/2015 9am	30 mins	Exercise 1 (emotional self-awareness while watching videos of my work)	Tense and avoidant; emotionally distracted by argument with daughter; wife traveling
8/31/2015 Noon	60 mins	30 mins Exercise 1 (emotional self-awareness), 30 mins practicing model-specific intervention skills assigned by coach	When doing Exercise 1 felt tense with considerable experiential avoidance for first 15 minutes, then crying
9/1/2015	Didn't practice		Got distracted by phone call from colleague
9/2/2015 1pm	60 mins	Endurance exercise	Started tense and avoidant; calm and focused in middle; ended tired and drained
9/3/2015 8am	50 mins	25 mins Exercise 2 (attunement: see) and 25 mins Exercise 3 (attunement: hear)	Distracted at first by earlier argument with friend; later felt invigorated and focused
9/4/2015 9am	55 mins	25 mins Exercise 4 (attunement: feel) and 20 mins Exercise 5 (activity/model assessment)	Tense and avoidant then strong emotional reactions to client in video
9/8/2015 8am	20 mins	Warm-ups before seeing clients	Felt optimistic and enthusiastic for upcoming sessions

study of expert violinists. In the journal I include a row for each day: the time I spent in solitary deliberate practice, my particular focus for that day, and notes from the practice. I also note any significant internal reactions I experienced (e.g., anxiety, sadness) and circumstances in my personal life that may have affected the practice (e.g., conflict at home, visits from family, etc.).

Next Steps

My initial experiments with solitary deliberate practice were a success, and I was eager to try more. Furthermore, I wanted to teach my trainees how to use solitary deliberate practice themselves.

It is said that you never really see how well you understand a subject until you try to teach it. As I reviewed my notes and prepared to teach my trainees how to use solitary deliberate practice, I became acutely aware that I still had a number of important unanswered questions. Namely, *what* should we practice and *how* should we practice it? I didn't have a clear or coherent model for using deliberate practice for psychotherapy. I was essentially winging it. This was working well enough for me personally, but would not be sufficient for supervising trainees.

Returning to the deliberate practice literature, it occurred to me that a wide range of other fields already had proven models for how to practice. Maybe it isn't necessary for psychotherapy to reinvent the wheel. Can we learn from how other fields achieve expertise? With this in mind, I reviewed the deliberate practice literature. The following is what I found.

Part II

The Science of Expertise

Learning from Other Fields

In Part II of this book I will explore what we can learn from the science of expertise in other fields. Every field that uses deliberate practice has its own model of what to practice and how to practice. Psychotherapy is unique, so we are not able to simply duplicate the deliberate practice model from another field. However, some other fields specialize in areas of work that are relevant to psychotherapy. Studying how these fields use deliberate practice can help us develop a model of expertise specifically for psychotherapy.

In my review of the deliberate practice literature, four fields stood out as having particular relevance for psychotherapy. These fields were medicine, music, emergency management, and spiritual practices. Each of these fields will be explored in the following chapters.

CHAPTER 5

EXPERTISE IN MEDICINE

Focus on Clinical Outcomes

Deliberate practice works through isolation, repetition, and focus. We isolate specific skills to be improved, repeat exercises to improve those skills, and maintain a focus until there is demonstrable evidence that learning has occurred. We then repeat the whole process, day after day, year after year, throughout the decades of a career. The story of peak achievement is often the story of sustained isolation, repetition, and focus.

It is not easy to successfully sustain isolation, repetition, and focus. Practitioners must have the right mix of personal traits and environmental circumstances to engage in solitary deliberate practice, as we will discuss further in Part IV of this book. One trait, however, stands out as a fundamental requirement, the *sine qua non* of deliberate practice: willpower.

Unfortunately, willpower is not one of my strengths. When I started supervision with Jon Frederickson, I was living in the San Francisco Bay area. I had a good group of friends, the weather was nice, and there was always something to do, 24 hours a day, seven days a week. While having a rich social life may have been fun, it was not very conducive to focusing on solitary deliberate practice. I often simply did not have sufficient willpower to overcome the distractions of my social life.

My motivation to engage in solitary deliberate practice was mostly fueled by my curiosity to learn and my ambition to be more effective. Curiosity and ambition are traits sufficient to experiment with solitary deliberate practice for a few months but inadequate to sustain prolonged practice. Fortunately for my professional development, fate was about to give my career a gift: the gift of isolation.

Moving to the Moon

In 2012 my family moved to Fairbanks, Alaska. Fairbanks is a one-hour drive south of the Arctic Circle. It is north of the town North Pole, which is the proud host of two military bases and a 40-foot-tall Santa Claus statue. We moved to Alaska because of my wife's career. She had been hired as assistant professor at the University of Alaska in Fairbanks.

The difference between Berkeley, California, and central Alaska was shocking. It was −40 degrees when we arrived on January 1, with about three and a half hours of "daylight." Actually it was more like twilight because it consisted of the sun rising to barely reach the horizon and then setting again 30 minutes later. Moving to Fairbanks felt like moving to the Moon.

I didn't fit in at Fairbanks. I'm urban, liberal, and technology focused. Most Alaskan men spent their youth hunting moose in the wilderness. I spent mine in my parents' basement playing Dungeons and Dragons and programming early computers. To say that I was a fish out of water would be an understatement. I was more like a goldfish taken from a warm tank and put into a box of ice in the freezer, surrounded by chunks of frozen game meat. (However, the people of Fairbanks are extremely friendly. I didn't have one negative social experience in three years there, while it's easy to meet unpleasantness on the streets of Berkeley or San Francisco in mere minutes.)

While moving to central Alaska freeze-dried my social life, it also provided a silver lining: ample distraction-free opportunities to focus on solitary deliberate practice. Fortunately I found a great job as the associate director of counseling at the University of Alaska Fairbanks Student Health and Counseling Center. Although life in Alaska was hard, one of the bright spots was my new boss, B. J. Aldrich, MD. B. J. encouraged me to experiment with expanding our counseling services at the center. One of the projects we experimented with was starting a practicum for Ph.D. psychology graduate trainees. I served as the trainees' supervisor.

Mindful of the limits of traditional clinical supervision, I assigned my trainees deliberate practice homework to help bolster their clinical skills. While the trainees reported that the homework was helpful, my process for assigning the homework was very ad hoc. I was just winging it each supervision session. It felt scattered and incomplete.

I realized that I needed a more cohesive plan or model for deliberate practice of psychotherapy. I searched the psychotherapy literature. While prominent researchers were advocating for the use of deliberate practice in psychotherapy (e.g., Miller et al., 2007), no one had yet developed a specific plan or model for how to do it. Specifically, I sought to answer these basic questions: (a) what should we practice, and (b) how should we practice it?

DEVELOPING A DELIBERATE PRACTICE MODEL FOR PSYCHOTHERAPY

Other fields took centuries to develop a model for deliberate practice. For example, classical music didn't develop études—short compositions designed to practice specific skills—until the nineteenth century.

Psychotherapy is a relatively young field. Freud just started talking to patients on his couch at the turn of the twentieth century. We've got a few thousand years less development than music, athletics, and medicine, so it makes sense that we're just getting started developing a model for deliberate practice.

I started by reviewing the basics. As discussed in Part I, deliberate practice is based on five core components:

1) Observing your own work.
2) Getting expert feedback.
3) Setting small incremental learning goals just beyond your ability.
4) Repetitive behavioral rehearsal of specific skills.
5) Continuously assessing your performance.

While deliberate practice in every field includes these five basic components, the *implementation* of deliberate practice is unique for each field. The way one practices chess is different from how one practices basketball, classical music, or dance.

To develop a model for deliberate practice for psychotherapy, what could we learn from how other fields do it? To explore this topic further, I turned to *The Cambridge Handbook of Expertise and Expert Performance* (Ericsson et al., 2006). This 901-page volume is the de facto encyclopedia of deliberate practice, with over 40 chapters that explore how professionals achieve expertise in a wide range of fields, including computer programming, writing, sports, music, acting, dance, chess, memory, math, history, and more. Mental health is notably absent from this volume. My question was this: If *The Cambridge Handbook of Expertise and Expert Performance* had a chapter on psychotherapy, what would be in it?

THE NATURAL METHOD OF MEDICATION EDUCATION

Fortunately, we are not the only field in health care to be experiencing a crisis in training. Similar to what has occurred recently in mental health, weaknesses in the field of medical training have also been exposed by a series of studies since the 1990s (McGaghie & Kristopaitis, 2015). These studies have prompted leading figures in medical education to reexamine the previously established methods of clinical training and experiment with new approaches gleaned from the science of expertise (e.g., Hashimoto et al., 2014).

Traditional medical education is based on the theory of a natural method of teaching brought from Europe in the nineteenth century (McGaghie, in press). Before then, medical education took place largely in lecture halls. In reaction to the limits of book learning for clinical training, the natural method of teaching emphasized actual clinical experience as the primary and most effective method for medical training. Medical reformer Oliver Wendell Holmes, Sr., the first doctor to propose the then controversial idea that doctors could spread fevers from patient to patient, summarized the main theory of the natural method of teaching:

> The most essential part of a student's instructions is obtained, as I believe, not in the lecture room, but at the bedside ... Before the student is aware of what he has acquired he has learned the aspects and causes and probable issue of the diseases he has seen with his teacher.
>
> (Oliver Wendell Holmes, Sr., 1867, cited in Osler, 1932)

In the natural method, prolonged clinical experience is viewed as both necessary and sufficient for the acquisition of medical expertise: "Student exposure to patients and experience over time is sufficient to ensure that physicians in training will become competent doctors ... [the natural method] made no place for structured, graded, educational requirements; skills practice; objective evaluation with feedback" (McGaghie & Kristopaitis, 2015, p. 220). Sir William Osler, a prominent physician from Oxford and Johns Hopkins, summarized this approach in an address to the Academy of Medicine in 1903 titled "The hospital as a college": "Teach him how to observe, give him plenty of facts to observe, *and the lessons will come out of the facts themselves*" (Osler, 1932, p. 315, emphasis added).

Since that time, the framework of the modern medical education system has been based on the natural method. Medical education, like psychotherapy training, is organized around a series of clinical training sites at which the student's primary learning activity is supervised clinical experience. Internships, residencies, and fellowships for medicine; practicums, externships, and internships for psychotherapy.

Moving physicians in training from lecture halls to patients' bedsides undoubtedly improved clinical training, and few modern medical professionals would discount the importance of clinical experience in training. However, a series of studies on medical education in the late twentieth century raised questions about the limitations of supervised clinical experience for aiding the acquisition of specific clinical skills. For example, three studies in the 1990s that examined specific clinical skills found that licensed physicians were no more skilled than medical students at performing a range of medical interventions such as cardiac auscultation and evaluating heart sounds (McGaghie & Kristopaitis, 2015).

Concerns raised from these studies have led to a growing push for reform of medical training. One of the leading figures in this movement is William McGaghie, a psychologist who has spent the past few decades working to improve modern medical education, largely from lessons learned from the science of expertise. McGaghie's efforts at medical education reform have been focused on moving away from "a passive clinical medical curriculum based solely on longitudinal patient experience" (McGaghie & Kristopaitis, 2015, p. 220) and instead toward skill-focused, outcome-informed deliberate practice. While McGaghie recognizes the value of real-world clinical experience in training, he laments the natural method's view that experience itself is sufficient to provide expertise:

> Structural and operational expressions of Osler's *natural method of teaching* are seen every day at medical schools, residency and fellowship programs where traditional, "time-honored" educational practices, such as morning report and professor rounds, are preserved and sustained. Key learning outcomes among medical students or residents (e.g., clinical skill acquisition, medical record documentation and health-care team communication) are rarely evaluated with rigor, or based on reliable data that permit valid decisions about medical learners and their progress.
>
> (McGaghie & Kristopaitis, 2015, p. 220)

In contrast to the natural method, McGaghie proposes that deliberate practice be used as a core component of medical education: "Deliberate practice in medical education settings means that learners are engaged in difficult, goal-oriented work, supervised by teachers, who provide feedback and correction, under conditions of high achievement expectations, with revision and improvement" (McGaghie & Kristopaitis, 2015, p. 223).

In 2011 McGaghie and colleagues published a paper in which they examined 14 studies that compared traditional medical education with skill-focused exercises using deliberate practice and clinical simulations. The result was, in his words, "unequivocal": deliberate practice and simulation-based training greatly outperformed traditional medical education. "The traditional Oslerian approach to medical education featuring clinical experience alone is obsolete" (McGaghie & Kristopaitis, 2015, p. 224).

You may be familiar with the classic medical training adage of "see one, do one, teach one." In contrast, McGaghie's approach to training can be summarized as, "see one, do many more, and keep doing it until you get it right."

As I read through McGaghie's papers on medical education, I felt like I was catching a glimpse of where I hoped psychotherapy training could head over the next few decades. I emailed him for an interview and he responded right away.

THE NAVY SEALS OF PHYSICIANS

I asked Dr. McGaghie how his trainees have responded to deliberate practice. Do they consider the extra work and effort worth it? He responded affirmatively.

> Once trainees get in lab and understand what they are up to, there is no trouble with motivation. The data convinces them. Trainees have an inherent motivation to be not just good but great. I tell them, "We're going to turn you into the Navy Seals of physicians," then they get it right away. They understand that expertise comes from hard work and sweat. It's not supposed to be easy.

He also noted, "It's important to show them early on that you're using evaluation as a tool and not a weapon."

I then asked him what he thought of the potential for deliberate practice to improve psychotherapy training. His response was encouraging,

"Deliberate practice works well for other fields, so there's no reason to believe that it won't work for psychotherapy." However, he also sounded a few notes of caution.

TRANSLATIONAL SCIENCE

First, he emphasized that "it's important to measure downstream outcome to make sure it's really helping." The academic term for this concept is *translational science*. We shouldn't just assume that practice is making us better therapists, but rather we should continuously evaluate whether training methods actually translate into improved outcomes. Translational science proposes four levels of training effects (McGaghie et al., 2014):

T1: Improved performance in the classroom or simulation (i.e., competency).

T2: Improved delivery of service to patients (i.e., adherence).

T3: Improved patient outcomes.

T4: Collateral effects (e.g., cost savings, skill retention, etc.).

Unfortunately, psychotherapy research to date has scant research to show the impact of training beyond T2 (see Figure 5.1). In other words, we can train trainees to follow a psychotherapy model, but we have limited

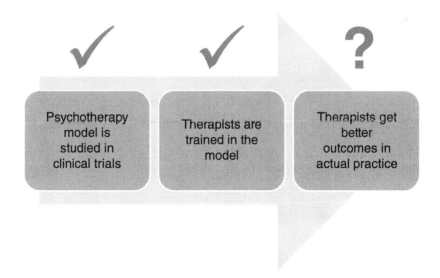

Figure 5.1 Implementation of psychotherapy research

evidence showing that the training actually improves client outcomes. For example, a recent meta-analysis of 36 different studies found evidence that "therapist adherence and competence play little role in determining symptom change" (Webb, DeRubeis, & Barber, 2010, p. 200).

An example of this recently appeared in the headlines in Sweden. Over the past decade the Swedish national health service, under the banner of empirically based treatments, spent 7 billion krona (approximately $1 billion) training and cajoling psychotherapists to use CBT. The result of this massive investment on actual patient outcomes? Zilch (Bohman, Blessed, & Ögren, 2015). A review of the program by the Swedish National Audit Office summarized their findings: "Steering patients towards specific treatment methods [CBT] has been ineffective in achieving the objective" (Riksrevisionen, 2015). This is a striking failure of training to translate into actual clinical improvements.

Another example of Dr. McGaghie's concern can be found in a recent study that examined the results of a similar large-scale training in CBT in England (Branson, Shafran, & Myles, 2015). The study found that training in CBT increased therapist CBT competency and adherence (T1 and T2). However, the study notably found that therapists' level of competency in CBT was not associated with better clinical outcomes (T3). As expected, data from the study indicated variability in therapist effectiveness. Some therapists had significantly better outcomes than others, but competency in CBT was not correlated with better client outcome.

I want to emphasize here that I am in no way criticizing CBT. In fact, I'd be surprised if similar efforts to promote adherence to other psychotherapy models performed any better. The challenge we are facing is not picking the right model of therapy but instead figuring out how to help therapists become more effective regardless of the model they are working from (Miller et al., 2007).

In contrast, skill-focused training using deliberate practice and clinical simulations in medicine has demonstrated strong effects all the way "downstream" to T3 (patient outcomes) and T4 (collateral improvement of public welfare). For example, research by McGaghie and others has shown deliberate practice to result in "reduced ICU infection rates, lower childbirth complications, faster surgical recovery, reduced hospital length of stay and fewer blood transfusions and ICU admissions" (McGaghie & Kristopaitis, 2015, p. 226).

I found myself wondering: if we could find better methods of training, what would our list of T3 and T4 effects be?

At the end of our talk, I asked Dr. McGaghie for his guidance, "We'd like to bring deliberate practice to psychotherapy. What is your advice, given your experiences bringing it to medicine over the past few decades?"

He replied with two points. First, he cautioned about the difficulty of change, and inevitable resistance to change. "The most powerful force in medical training is inertia," he warned.

Second, he emphasized the importance of serious research in this area.

> Translational education outcomes are difficult to reach and cannot be achieved from isolated, one-shot studies. Instead, translational results in medical education research come from integrated education and health services research programs that are thematic, sustained and cumulative ... usually involve interdisciplinary teams, composed of a diverse group of scientists and scholars, and must be carefully designed and managed to yield strong results.
>
> (McGaghie & Kristopaitis, 2015, p. 226)

McGaghie outlined three necessary steps for a field to integrate deliberate practice: "The three stages represent: (i) the capture of expert performance in the laboratory or field settings; (ii) the identification of underlying mechanisms that account for expert performance, and (iii) the examination of how expertise developed" (McGaghie & Fisichella, 2014, p.106).

Implementing McGaghie's three-step plan to integrate deliberate practice into medicine is a formidable task. Unfortunately, for psychotherapy it's even harder. McGaghie's plan starts at step one, but in psychotherapy we're actually still at step zero: agreeing on what expert performance entails.

Implicit in McGaghie's steps is an unstated but foundational assumption for integrating deliberate practice in psychotherapy: a consensus about "objective criteria for superior performance" (Ericsson & Pool, 2016, p. 98). This demonstrates a considerable advantage the medical field has over psychotherapy. In medicine, doctors can easily agree on the effectiveness of most medical procedures. In contrast, in psychotherapy we still have very little agreement about the simplest of questions: What is good therapy?

MODEL AND STYLE TRUMP OUTCOME

Model and style of therapy: sounds more like a portfolio for an art school than a clinical science, doesn't it? That's because our clinical-training pedagogy has lost track of the variable that is actually most important for clinical training: the client's clinical outcome. Namely, did the client benefit from therapy? (For a recent review of this topic, see Goodyear, 2015.)

My graduate program, like most, concluded with a final exam. Each student had to present one of their clinical cases, called a clinical portfolio, from their training site to a faculty panel. The presentation consists of a case conceptualization and a transcript of a sample session.

At my university it was well known among students that one's odds of passing the clinical portfolio were largely dependent upon what faculty members were randomly assigned to your portfolio (the clinical portfolio lottery, as we called it). Each faculty member had a preferred model and style of therapy. If one or two of the faculty draws in the lottery didn't line up with your model and style of therapy, then you had a much higher chance of failing your clinical portfolio. For example, my girlfriend at the time failed her first clinical portfolio because of faculty misalignment despite her clinical and case conceptualization skills being much stronger than mine.

This is not a hit against my graduate program. Their clinical-portfolio process follows the best practice standards for the field. Furthermore, my graduate program is not alone in having challenges identifying good therapy. Accurate skill evaluation is a problem across our field. For example, in 1999 the California Board of Psychology ended its previous use of oral examinations after it found that the evaluation committees, comprised of licensed psychologists, could not consistently agree on their evaluations of case reports by applicants (termed poor inter-rater reliability; California Board of Psychology, 2001).

Some years ago I had a personal experience that is illustrative of this problem. Three months before we were married, my wife was offered a faculty job at a university in a western state. The university has a large and prestigious department in her field (wildlife biology). The job offer was a great opportunity for my wife, and we were excited to move. There was only one problem: the university is located in a very small town, and I was concerned about whether I could find work. Luckily the academic profession has a solution for this "two body problem": spousal hires, in which the university offers employment to the spouse of the job candidate. The dean of the department that was trying to hire my wife secured funding for me to work half time at the university counseling center, which also served as a training clinic for the psychology training program.

The director of the counseling center was very friendly when I contacted him. He explained that I would have to go through the standard employee interview process that included showing videos of my clinical work. I told him that would not be a problem, as I had been using video for clinical supervision and consultations for a few years.

The interview format was fairly typical. I presented a sample clinical case from my practice, with a video of a sample session and a case conceptualization. Additionally, I brought a report of my clinical outcome data to present to them. I had been collecting outcome data at my private practice for some time and had been growing increasingly interested in the potential uses of outcome data to better measure, use, and report our clinical effectiveness. I assumed that other psychologists would be eager to nerd out about psychotherapy-outcome data. Little did I know that my idealistic naïveté was about to shatter against the hard rocks of our clinical culture.

At the interview I met with the senior staff of the clinic and a handful of their trainees. The interview started innocuously enough. They asked me about my training, private practice, and so forth. This part of the interview went well. I then presented a video of one of my psychotherapy sessions. The client was a young adult woman with dysthymia and anxiety. She had a history of physical and emotional abuse from her childhood. She was very bright and articulate but unemployed and directionless. She had friends and romantic partners who treated her poorly. When painful feelings arose she would have sharp spikes of anxiety and turn to self-destructive coping behaviors, including drugs, cutting, or engaging in risky sexual activity.

This client had previously been in unsuccessful therapies with multiple therapists. From these experiences she was "well trained" for her role as a client. She could talk about herself and her problems like a pro. However, when she talked she was detached or even contemptuous of herself. Despite years of therapy, she never learned how to tolerate her own painful feelings in a healthy, self-compassionate manner, so she hadn't improved.

Our work focused on three main steps: 1) helping the client identify her emotional triggers, usually relationships, 2) helping her shift away from self-destructive coping behaviors, and 3) building her capacity to experience her painful feelings with more self-compassion and patience. We had met for about a year and a half, and the client had responded very positively to our work together. She hadn't cut herself or used drugs in over a year, had found friends and a relationship that was healthier for her, had part-time employment, and was enrolled in a community college. Her outcome data showed a positive trend towards recovery.

The video I showed was a ten-minute compilation of clips from one session with the client. The session had occurred about a year into her course of therapy. This session was particularly powerful for the client and had been a turning point in our work together. In the session she let herself experience and express strong feelings of rage towards her mother for not protecting her from abuse. Unlike previous sessions, she was then able to restrain the usual internal backlash of shame for expressing her feelings. Instead, she discovered very strong feelings of love and longing for her mother that she had previously warded off, guilt for the intensity of her rage towards her mother, and grief about the loss of an innocent childhood she wished that she could have experienced. The session concluded with the client feeling a heightened sense of confidence and a calm determination to improve her future.

I chose to present this video for two reasons. First, the client had responded positively to our work. Second, the session was a good example of my model and style of therapy, which incorporates a blend of affect-focused relational, cognitive, behavioral, and experiential techniques within a psychodynamic frame. This session in particular highlighted my use of techniques to interrupt the client's habitual and automatic self-attack behaviors (i.e., shame) that emerged whenever she had strong feelings towards her mother. Interrupting these unconscious behaviors in the moment let the client see them experientially as they happened and thus helped her differentiate herself from her shame. She moved from "I am ashamed" to "I learned to use shame against myself." This created some emotional space within the client, which in turn facilitated self-compassion regarding her very complex feelings toward her original attachment figures, particularly her mother.

As we watched the video compilation, I sensed anxiety rising in the room. Just a few moments after the video ended, questions started popping up from around the table: "Why did you interrupt your client when she was talking about her shame?" "How are you showing your client that you understand her?" "Aren't you showing disrespect or a lack of empathy for the client?"

These questions stood in stark contrast to the client's reactions in the video. At the end of the session she was sitting taller in her seat, talking with more strength and confidence, and clearly expressing optimism for her future. I tried to respond as politely as possible, "Do you want to watch the video again? The client expressed quite a positive response to the session."

I knew I was in trouble when someone asked "Doesn't what you are doing make your client feel attacked?"

My client in the video was clearly not feeling attacked. So who was feeling attacked? I suddenly understood that these questions weren't really about what my client was feeling but rather what the interview committee was feeling: attacked by my model and style of therapy because it was different from theirs. I didn't realize it until some days later, but the hiring committee and I were watching the video with two very different lenses. I was primarily watching the reaction of the client, while the interview committee was primarily watching me, the therapist. They weren't actually very interested in the client's reaction to the session. They just wanted to see my model and style of therapy.

I asked the committee if they would like to discuss my outcome data from this client or my overall caseload. There was a long moment of silence, followed by more questions about my model and style of therapy. In that moment I realized that my actual clinical outcomes were the aspect of my work that they were least interested in, almost as though my clients' outcomes were somehow irrelevant.

Someone asked, "How do you know the client isn't just complying with you and pretending to get better?" This is, of course, a very valid concern for psychotherapy with survivors of abuse. Many survive childhood abuse by becoming masters of compliance. Furthermore, I knew from previous cases that compliance was a clinical weakness in my work.

I had addressed the potential for compliance with this client by asking for her feedback at the end of every session, using the Session Rating Scale (SRS), a brief measure of the therapeutic working alliance (Miller, Duncan, Brown, Sparks, & Claud, 2003). I had discovered the SRS a few years previously from a talk given by Scott Miller and had been using it with all of my clients ever since. I gave extra emphasis to the SRS with clients who were prone to compliance.

I replied to their question,

> When we started therapy the client related to me through a superficial
> wall of compliance. However, over time she's grown increasingly willing
> to voice her negative feelings toward me and tell me when we are working
> in a way that she doesn't like. This change has been reflected on the SRS.
> Her scores have moved from originally being all 10s (perfect scores that
> indicate compliance) to more variable, including poor scores for sessions
> when I misattune with her. We use her feedback as an opportunity to help
> her experientially learn to be more clear and assertive with me, which has
> generalized to her other relationships.

I again followed up with a hopeful, "Would you like to see her outcome
data?"

Their response: blank stares. It was as though the interview committee
didn't even hear my answer. Someone asked, "Do you really think this
model of therapy is appropriate for her?"

A PRIEST APPLIES FOR A JOB AT A MOSQUE

The next day I had lunch at the university cafeteria with the assistant
director and a senior intern before my flight back home to San Francisco.
They were very friendly and approachable. The intern had taken me rock
climbing the day before the interview, and we had enjoyed a good time
together. They genuinely seemed to like me, despite my heretical approach
to psychotherapy.

I immediately knew from the look on their faces that I wasn't going to
be offered the job. The assistant director said, "This is a tough call for us.
Personally, you seem nice. However, your model of therapy might not be
a good fit for our center." A week later I got a call from the director saying
that they were going to pass on me. He repeated the assistant director's
sentiments, "You're just not a good fit for us."

My wife was flabbergasted. "But your salary would be paid for by my
department. You would be a free staff member! How bad a therapist do
they think you are?" she asked, incredulously.

It didn't matter that my salary was paid for, that I had agreed to
videotape all my work and review it with their staff in weekly supervision,
that I had presented outcome data from my practice showing good

outcomes, that I had gotten along personally with the staff. None of it mattered. The only thing that really mattered was whether my model and style of therapy was a good "fit" for them—meaning the other therapists, not the clients. They didn't care that my salary was paid for any more than a mosque would want a priest whose salary was paid for. They weren't interested in my outcome data any more than a church would want to see how many meals a Buddhist monk had provided to the poor.

The work I had shown at the interview was a short-term dynamic model of therapy. Given their adverse reaction to my work, one might assume that the clinic staff were primarily cognitive or behavioral in their approach. Wrong. They were working from a long-term dynamic model. The difference between long-term and short-term dynamic therapy is so small that a therapist who was trained in a cognitive or behavioral approach might not even be able to see any distinction.

Why am I telling this story here? Not out of bitterness: although the interview was an unpleasant process, my wife found another excellent job opportunity, and we have both done well since. Furthermore, I don't think this university clinic is different from most. The interview I had is emblematic of a pervasive problem throughout our field. We have lost our focus on clinical outcomes—on the clients. Instead, we've become obsessed with models, our field's version of professional identity politics. We are defining ourselves by our models rather than by our actual clinical outcomes. And while we engage in endless debates about our models, 50% of our clients don't improve from treatment.

Can you think of even one interview for a psychotherapy job that you have been involved in as an applicant or an employer that included a discussion of the applicant's clinical outcome data?[1] If so, please email me!

A PROBLEM WITH OUR PROFESSIONAL CULTURE

This book is ostensibly about new methods of training. However, it is also about a crisis in our professional culture. We have a void of clinical-outcome data for individual clinicians, and we've filled that void with professional-identity politics. For example, consider what might happen if professional athletes were never permitted to see their own performance statistics. Without actual evidence of their success or failure, they might over time gravitate towards increasingly abstract arguments about their form, or model, of play. The same can be expected of professionals in any field. Take away proof of their success or failure, and you'll end up with abstract arguments about models and identity politics. As Jon Frederickson said to me one day, "Our field has come to prize ritualism rather than results."

Why does our professional culture matter? And what does it have to do with deliberate practice?

Recall that deliberate practice relies *on accurate performance feedback* (Ericsson, 2006). In our field, performance feedback is clinical-outcome data, whether quantitative or qualitative. Unless our professional culture refocuses on clinical-outcome data as the primary method of work evaluation, we cannot successfully incorporate deliberate practice, or any other method of improving our work, into clinical training.

Recall the three steps William McGaghie outlined as necessary for a field to adopt deliberate practice: "capturing expert performance in laboratory or field settings, identifying the mechanisms that account for expert performance, and examining how expertise developed" (McGaghie & Fisichella, 2014, p.106). Unless expert performance is anchored in clinical-outcome data of individual clinicians, rather than the identity politics of clinical models, we will not be able to improve our success rates and our clients will continue to suffer unnecessarily.

NOTE

1 I want to emphasize that I am not advocating for outcome data to be the sole criteria for evaluating the effectiveness of psychotherapy. Psychotherapy outcome measures are still at a stage of early scientific development and have too many limitations for this purpose (McLeod, in press). For example, they are not reliable with some clinical presentations, they are easily influenced by therapists, and blind to many of the more subtle but important effects of psychotherapy. Outcome data must be used appropriately in conjunction with other sources of data (see Chapter 9). However, despite these limits, I strongly feel that we will not progress as a field unless we start using outcome data more comprehensively in our work, especially in the age of medical reform.

CHAPTER 6

EXPERTISE IN
PERFORMING ARTS

Focus on Skills

I saw my first psychotherapy client at the beginning of my second year of graduate school. I was very nervous and hadn't slept well the night before. I don't remember the exact dialogue from our first meeting, but it went essentially like this:

Me: Hi, nice to meet you. How are you feeling today?

Client: Oh, nice to meet you too. You seem nice.

Me: Um, thanks.

Client: I bet you're going to be a great therapist after some training. I can tell. I've had dozens of therapists over the years.

Me: Ummm … okay. How are you feeling today?

Client: Suicidal.

Me: Do you have a plan to hurt yourself?

Client: Not sure yet.

Me: What?

Client: Well, I called my two favorite hospitals and their beds are taken for tonight. I really don't want to go to the county hospital. So I'm going to wait and call them back in an hour or two and find out if anything has opened up.

Me: Ummm …

Client: So what do you think would help me?

I honestly had no idea how to help this client. However, I had read that being authentic could help build the therapeutic working alliance and knew that was important. So at least I could do that. I said, "Honestly, I'm not sure how to help you. What do you think?"

Unfortunately, my authenticity didn't help the client. Neither did it hurt. In retrospect, my ability to impact this client in any significant positive or negative way was probably similar to the odds of a fish changing the course of a battleship. My client had a diagnosis of schizoaffective disorder. I found this out before I met her by reviewing her case notes and talking with her previous therapist. When I saw the diagnosis, I looked it up in the Diagnostic and Statistical Manual. After reading an explanation of the diagnosis, I felt more confused than I had been previously.

Schizoaffective disorder is essentially a mashup of psychosis and a mood disorder, two diagnoses that are themselves broad collections of vague symptoms without clear empirical etiology or prognoses. It is the empirical equivalent of psychiatrists throwing up their hands and saying, "Hell if we know what's going on here." A recent review of the literature on the schizoaffective disorder highlights this mess:

> Despite a clear recognition of the existence of patients with co-morbid psychotic and mood symptoms, many studies conclude that schizoaffective disorder as a distinct diagnosis does not exist ... even if schizoaffective disorder exists as a separate diagnosis, it may not be useful clinically due to considerable variation in the general use of the term ... based on the limited extant evidence, it is not yet possible to make definitive treatment recommendations for schizoaffective disorder.
>
> (Kantrowitz & Citrome, 2011, p. 317)

A few weeks later I presented this client in my practicum class:

> My client is chronically mentally ill and has been on psychiatric disability for over five decades. She alternates between flat affect and labile mood. She experiences frequent visual hallucinations and is on over a dozen psychiatric medications. For the past two decades she has lived with her elderly mother who abused her when she was a child.

I spent at least 20 minutes describing the client's broad range of complex symptoms. When I was done, the professor said, "Well at least she doesn't have an addiction." I replied, "Oh, I forgot that part. She's addicted to pain medication." The professor smiled and said, "Perfect. Sounds like a great training case."

My professor wasn't being sarcastic. By "great training case" my professor did not mean that this was a good case to learn and refine specific psychotherapy skills. Rather, she meant that helping this client would provide me with an opportunity to have a very rich and complex range of psychological and interpersonal experiences. (This is the *natural method of learning* described in Chapter 5.)

This model of training, an intense immersion experience, has a number of benefits. First, it is excellent at maximizing the extent of face-to-face contact trainees have with a diverse range of real clients. Second, this model meets the needs of most psychological training sites, which often serve clients with complex histories and multiple presenting problems. (For example, at the university counseling center where I ran a practicum, I'd estimate that fewer than 10% of our clients had simple or discrete presenting problems.) Third, the immersive experience can serve to screen out trainees who are not suited for this kind of work.

Unfortunately, the immersion-experience model also has a significant limit. It is simply not effective at helping trainees learn and refine specific skills. Where the natural method of learning provides a wide breadth of experience, it is limited in the depth of learning.

This client had so many deeply entrenched psychological challenges that I simply didn't know where to begin. Additionally, she was in a complex relationship with the mental health-care system. Her symptoms provided her with specific benefits, also termed secondary gain. For example, her suicidality would get her access to free care at emergency rooms, and her medical problems got her access to pain medication. Her problems were so complex that my weekly supervision time could be quickly consumed just describing her symptoms du jour.

From the deliberate practice perspective, starting clinical training with this very complex client was the equivalent of learning to become a firefighter by being dropped off in the middle of a five-alarm fire ("There was fire everywhere and then the house fell down"). It is the athletic training equivalent of being thrown into the middle of a National Basketball Association game and getting an hour of coaching once a week ("Well coach, I got passed the ball, then a whole lot happened very quickly, then we lost"). Of course, exposure to real fires is important for training firefighters, and playing in real games is important for training basketball players. But these activities are balanced by many more hours of deliberate practice on specific skills in controlled settings, with immediate performance feedback.

I want to be clear: I am not arguing against the importance of face-to-face contact with real clients or against the value of learning from complex cases. Both are essential components of preparing trainees to be competent practitioners. However, the natural method of learning does not lead to expertise because it does not provide the opportunity to repetitively practice and refine specific skills.

TRAINING IN PERFORMING ARTS: FOCUS ON SKILLS

In contrast to the natural method of learning that emphasizes diverse experiences, the expertise model of learning uses deliberate practice to learn a sequential series of specific, discrete skills that are just beyond the learner's ability. A great example is training in the performing arts.

Recall that Ericsson's groundbreaking 1993 study focused on classical violinists. Musical training involves a sequential process of learning basic skills. For example, very early in their learning process most musicians have ear training, which teaches trainees to identify the basic elements of music (rhythm, pitches, chords, intervals, melody, etc.). Early trainees also learn other basic skills, like sight reading, composition, harmony, etc. Similarly, dance training focuses on a sequential mastery of specific skills. For example, in ballet:

> Sequential progression means teaching certain basic steps that are required before more difficult and technical steps can be given ... Before any turns such as a *pirouette* or *piqué/chaîné* can be learned, the student must be taught how to spot ... Along with spotting, *relevé* and *retiré* must be taught before a pirouette is given and *posé* before a *piqué* turn.
>
> (Foster, 2010, p. 25)

Recalling that Jon Frederickson developed his psychotherapy-training methods from the principles of music pedagogy, I became increasingly curious if there were any other areas of overlap between the performing arts and mental health. Could psychotherapy training learn from the pedagogy of music or dance? With this question in mind, I searched through the literature. This is how I found Noa Kageyama.

The Bulletproof Musician

Noa Kageyama is a psychologist and classical violinist. He runs the website bulletproofmusician.com, where musicians learn to improve their performance by improving their solitary deliberate practice routines. Noa summarizes the goal of his website as helping students "practice like a boss."

Since his very early years, Noa has practiced the violin 365 days a year. While still a child, Noa studied under the legendary violin teacher Dr. Shinichi Suzuki, founder of the Suzuki Method of classical music training that is used around the world. Later Noa attended the Juilliard School, one of the most prestigious and competitive music schools in the world. There he noticed discrepancies in his work. "Despite my successes, I struggled with inconsistency and felt that my playing often fell short of what I knew I was capable of. It was frustrating to play so well in rehearsals and then sound like a different person in performances and auditions" (Kageyama, 2016). This frustration drove Noa to seek out new methods to improve his work.

Noa's frustration resonated with me, as my own quest was born from an acute awareness that the quality of the psychotherapy I was providing was inconsistent and well short of my capability.

The Key to Effective Deliberate Practice: Practice Smarter, Not Harder

Noa initially attempted to improve his work by doubling down on his practice routine. "Like many musicians, I just assumed that I needed to practice more. I figured the nerves would fade away at some point. Neither was true; sometimes I'd sound great, sometimes just mediocre. I couldn't figure out how to control it" (Kageyama, 2016).

Noa's breakthrough occurred in his second year at Juilliard when he took a course on performance enhancement for musicians. This course taught techniques from sport psychology to help students develop better practice habits. Inspired by the psychology of expert performance, Noa then got a doctorate degree in counseling psychology at Indiana University. After graduating, Noa circled back to classical music and created bulletproofmusician.com to help teach musicians how to improve their deliberate practice routines.

Recall that classical musicians regularly spend five or more hours per day in solitary deliberate practice from an early age. Noa's focus is on how to make that time more efficient. He notes that simple, mindless repetition of basic skills is itself not very helpful.

I emailed Noa, describing my goal to try to develop a model for solitary deliberate practice for psychotherapy. We set up a time to talk by phone.

Noa suggested that psychotherapy is different from classical music, his specialty, because it is more "free form." The goal in classical music is to tightly follow a score, which comprises a very specific series of notes written by the composer. Every performance of a score will follow the same notes. In contrast, the goal of psychotherapy is to align with the unique presentation of each client at each session. Thus, no two psychotherapy sessions will be identical, even with the same therapist and client.

Rather than classical music, Noa suggested that psychotherapy is more like jazz. Jazz works through improvisation: a complex mixture of group collaboration, creativity, and interaction among band members. Like psychotherapy, no two jazz performances are identical. However, although jazz is improvisational, it is still grounded in strict rules that jazz students must master in order to improvise. For example, prominent jazz instructor Jerry Coker lists 18 different skill areas that students must master, each of which has multiple discrete skills including tone quality, intervals, chord arpeggios, scales, patterns and licks, etc. (Coker, 1990).

David Sudnow, another well-known jazz instructor, describes the importance of mastering "rule-governed paths" for improvisation:

> Jazz students spend a good deal of time practicing movements along rule-governed paths on the piano, like various scales, to have ways to keep on going with the music. Such pathways can be vital when you're first trying to improvise and not follow a musical score. You've got to know just where you're headed in order to get there correctly, not tripping up along the way, not hitting two keys together out of uncertainty, for instance. In most playing situations you must keep the action moving, can't stop and think about good next places to go.
>
> (Sudnow, 2001, p. 1)

(Interestingly, jazz has other parallels to modern psychology. Both are relatively young fields. Jazz is based on ragtime music, which started in the late nineteenth century with African American composers experimenting with syncopated rhythm, at the same time Freud was experimenting with the concept of unconscious conflict as the explanation for symptomatic presentation.)

Noa suggested that deliberate practice could potentially benefit psychotherapy as much as it does jazz. However, he noted that research and his personal experience have shown that deliberate practice does not automatically produce benefits. Certain conditions must be met for the benefits to appear. From our conversation, three elements of effective deliberate practice stood out as particularly promising (and challenging) for psychotherapy:

1) Persistent focus on specific skills.
2) Observing your own work.
3) Using failure productively.

ESSENTIAL ELEMENT OF DELIBERATE PRACTICE 1: PERSISTENT FOCUS ON SPECIFIC PSYCHOTHERAPY SKILLS

Noa noted that deliberate practice works by persistently focusing on a specific skill until the trainee gets it right. William McGaghie calls this "mastery learning" (McGaghie et al., 2014). This stands in sharp contrast to traditional psychotherapy supervision, which typically involves theoretical discussions about cases (e.g., case conceptualizations, diagnoses, treatment approaches, etc.) rather than focusing on performance of skills.

What does persistent focus on a specific skill look like for psychotherapy? I have an example from my supervision with Jon Frederickson. My supervision with Jon originally consisted of showing him videotapes of my sessions where therapy was stuck or the clients were not improving. This was overall very helpful for teaching me how to get those cases unstuck. However, over time I noticed that a few of my cases were "supervision resistant." Our work was staying stuck, even after we discussed them multiple times in supervision. I reviewed my supervision notes for these cases and noticed something peculiar. My notes were almost identical for each of the supervision sessions. Jon was observing the same problems in my videos week after week. He was teaching me the same points and giving me the same homework, yet my behavior in sessions with these clients wasn't changing. In other words, I wasn't learning. It wasn't the cases that were "supervision resistant"; it was me!

One of these cases involved a middle-aged woman with a history of trauma. While watching videos of my sessions with this client in our previous supervisions, Jon had noticed that I wasn't in rhythm with the client. I was talking over her at moments when she was having deep feelings and letting there be silence at times when she was detached or uninvolved. My lack of harmony with the client was limiting her benefit from our work together. Put simply, my timing was off.

In our supervisions Jon had tried all the usual methods of addressing this skill deficit. He pointed out specific examples of bad timing in my videos, we role played better timing, and he assigned homework for me to work on this specific skill. Unfortunately, none of this had been sufficient to help me improve my timing in session with this particular client.

I discussed this problem with my friend and mentor Philip Colgan at lunch one day. Philip is a psychologist in San Francisco with 30-plus years of experience who kindly took me under his wing and provided much-needed supervision and office space during my first years of private practice. Like me, Philip is keenly interested in constantly improving his therapeutic effectiveness. He is a great example of the intrinsic motivation most therapists have to become more effective. Despite being a fully established late-career psychologist with a full private practice, he spends substantial time, energy, and money on continuous psychotherapy training.

At lunch I told Philip about my frustration.

> I've got this case where the client has been stuck for months. I've shown videos of the case to Jon for a few weeks. He keeps telling me the same points in supervision. I understand the theory and know he's right. But I just can't seem to change how I'm working in session with this one client. I go into the session with a plan but then do something else. And it's clearly not helping the client.

Philip concurred sympathetically. "Training is hard, huh?"

I said, "I think part of the problem is that supervision is so far from the actual session, a few days or more later. I wish I could have Jon's guidance in the session."

Philip said, "Like the live one-way-mirror supervision we did in graduate school?"

"Yes," I said, "except Jon lives in Washington, DC, and we're in San Francisco."

At that moment a light bulb turned on in my head. "Wait a minute. What about videoconferencing? Maybe I can have Jon in the session!"

From this conversation was born the inspiration for remote live supervision (Rousmaniere & Frederickson, 2013, 2015). I emailed Jon and asked him if he would be willing to experiment with providing live supervision of an actual session in real time via a videoconference. Jon agreed. I then asked the client if she would be willing to experiment with having Jon observe one of our sessions and provide live feedback. The client agreed, so we set up the session.

Psychotherapy Skill Example: Therapeutic Timing

As Jon watched the live session in Washington, DC via videoconference, he typed suggestions into a chat window. These suggestions appeared on a computer monitor sitting next to the client, like a teleprompter for me. To help foster an environment of open collaboration in therapy, I invited the client to view all of Jon's suggestions after the session.

With the client's permission, I kept a copy of the transcript of Jon's comments to me. It is copied in Figure 6.1. Each line shows one comment Jon wrote for me, with the exact time he gave it. For example, when he wrote "wait," it was an instruction for me to wait in that moment with the client. Note the very short interval of time, some as short as two seconds, between his interventions.

The session went very well. At its conclusion, the client reported feeling that I understood her better than previously and that she had learned more about herself. When I asked the client for her impression of the session she replied, "You finally heard something I've been trying to tell you for months!"

After the session I emailed Jon to ask his impressions of the session. In his reply he explained that he had noticed my own hurry at the beginning of the session, possibly stemming from anxiety that was being aroused by this client. My anxiety was causing me to not hear the client and at times jump in and talk over the client. Jon specifically noted that the client's silence or passivity caused particular spikes in my activity. He wondered whether my reactive anxiety to the client's passivity was interfering with my ability to be in sync with the client and also learn from our supervisions.

[9:33:56 AM] jon.frederickson: wait
[9:33:59 AM] jon.frederickson: wait   3 seconds between
[9:34:23 AM] jon.frederickson: wait   Jon's interventions
[9:34:36 AM] jon.frederickson: [note her feeling deepening]
[9:34:49 AM] jon.frederickson: wait
[9:35:00 AM] jon.frederickson: wait
[9:35:05 AM] jon.frederickson: reflect what she said
[9:35:46 AM] jon.frederickson: wait
[9:35:51 AM] jon.frederickson: wait
[9:35:57 AM] jon.frederickson: wait
[9:36:01 AM] jon.frederickson: reflect what she said
[9:36:07 AM] jon.frederickson: "notice that"
[9:36:34 AM] jon.frederickson: wait
[9:36:42 AM] jon.frederickson: [note her feeling deepening]
[9:36:44 AM] jon.frederickson: wait
[9:36:46 AM] jon.frederickson: wait   2 seconds between
[9:36:50 AM] jon.frederickson: wait   Jon's interventions
[9:36:55 AM] jon.frederickson: wait
[9:37:28 AM] jon.frederickson: "notice that urge"
[9:38:01 AM] jon.frederickson: wait
[9:38:08 AM] jon.frederickson: wait
[9:38:19 AM] jon.frederickson: good
[9:39:06 AM] jon.frederickson: good

Figure 6.1 Excerpt of transcript from live one-way-mirror supervision

In other words, I had been learning the appropriate theory about what to do in our supervisions, but I had too much anxiety in the actual sessions with the clients to change my behavior. (This problem of *experiential avoidance* is discussed further in Chapter 8.)

Jon explained that he used very fast interventions throughout the supervision to address this problem. By commenting "wait" every few seconds, he could in effect hold me and help me experientially learn to sit with my own reactive anxiety rather than discharge it by talking over the client. And this is exactly what happened. During the next session I was calmer and more in sync with the client, who ended up having a positive outcome from our work together.

I present this transcript in Figure 6.1 because I think it is a great example of how much repetitive specific focus can be required for therapists to learn some skills. Traditional weekly supervision was simply not sufficient. Jon is tenacious. He kept the focus on one specific skill and simply wouldn't give up until I got it.

ESSENTIAL ELEMENT OF DELIBERATE PRACTICE 2: OBSERVING YOUR OWN WORK

As stated above, practicing doesn't help unless it targets specific skill deficits. Identifying these skill deficits requires observing one's own work with an eye out for mistakes or areas that could be improved. Unfortunately, this is a problem for psychotherapy because we largely work in isolation and in secret. Many therapists have never seen one minute of their own work on video. Some therapists are lucky enough to see videos of their work in graduate school but then typically none thereafter.

Psychotherapy has the most bizarre method of training: the trainee (a) works alone with the client; (b) some days later the trainee reports what happened to the instructor via memory or notes, which are unconsciously biased and incomplete; (c) the instructor gives feedback to the trainee based on that biased and incomplete report; and (d) the trainee returns to work alone and tries to implement that advice.

Is it any surprise that clinical training doesn't reliably improve trainees' skills (Owen, Wampold, Rousmaniere, Kopta, & Miller, 2016)? It would be inconceivable to get training in music, dance, or any other performing art without direct observation of your actual work live or via video and feedback about how it could be improved. In fact, I can't think of any field where instructors and students don't regularly review actual work performance.

Why don't therapists videotape their work? In my experience, the most common reason is worries about clients' reactions to video. A recent study examined this concern. It involved 390 clients at a university training clinic who completed a survey regarding videotaping their sessions. Clients overall were open to the idea of videotaping: more than half the clients reported no or slight concerns about audio or video recording, and 71% said they were willing to consider it. Comfort with session recording was not significantly related to "treatment refusal, duration, and outcome" (Briggie, Hilsenroth, Conway, Muran, & Jackson, 2016, p. 66). It is worth noting that two of the researchers in this study, Hilsenroth and Muran, work from psychodynamic models and have a strong focus on the working alliance, since the psychodynamic community can sometimes voice the loudest objection to videotaping.

One finding from this study stands out and is worth highlighting: therapists who were biased for or against videotape seemed to influence their clients in the same direction (Briggie et al., 2016). This finding leads us to another, and perhaps more important, reason that therapists avoid videotape: aversion to seeing our own mistakes. Watching our own work means tolerating not being perfect and enduring all the fears and painful feelings associated with imperfection. However, hiding from our own mistakes by not viewing our work isn't a solution because then we also don't see our own successes or opportunities for improvement. Without viewing our work we cannot ensure we are positively impacting the welfare of our clients. This can leave us in a state of perpetual insecurity, because we don't know what we are actually doing, good or bad. This can in turn lead to self-aggrandizing ("I know I'm really good") or self-devaluation ("I am probably no good")—neither of which is based on actual data.

I discussed this one day with Jon Frederickson and he remarked,

> There is much less bragging in professional music than in psychotherapy because everyone knows exactly how good everyone else is: they can simply hear it. In psychotherapy we never really know how good anyone else is, unless we see their videos. Instead, we only know how well they can talk or write about their work.

Instead, if we view our own work, then we have the opportunity for true self-compassion: identifying areas of strength and areas where we can improve with practice for the benefit of our clients. It is crucial for us to ground our self-perceptions in real data. No field can expect to improve its effectiveness while working in isolation. Let's join the rest of the world and view our own work.

ESSENTIAL ELEMENT OF DELIBERATE PRACTICE 3: USING FAILURE PRODUCTIVELY

You might have noticed a common thread in this chapter: deliberate practice requires searching out our own mistakes and using them productively. Simply put, we need to change our relationship with the other 50% of our cases that aren't improving. Instead of avoiding or denying failure, we need to focus tightly on it as our best guide to improvement.

In my experience with running deliberate practice groups for psychotherapists, often the hardest point for trainees is learning how to use their own failures—their other 50%—self-compassionately and productively. In their article titled "How being bad can make you better," Barry Duncan, Scott Miller, and Mark Hubble (2007) call this stance "failing successfully." Ideally, we would learn this approach to our mistakes in graduate school.

A struggle with facing one's own mistakes is, of course, not limited to psychotherapists. Noa reports that a turning point occurred for him when he shifted his approach from self-judgment ("I did it wrong") to curiosity about opportunities for improvement:

> I used to hate, hate, hate listening to recordings of myself, but I think that's because I was approaching it all wrong. I was focused on evaluating the performance and whether or not I sounded any good. Instead, I probably should have been focusing on evaluating my *preparation* and *approach* to the performance. To figure out what I could do to prepare myself most effectively for the next performance and keep me on the path of continued growth and mastery. Which at the end of the day is really what we're all striving for, no?
>
> (Kageyama, 2016)

On his website, Noa quotes Thomas Watson, the former chairman and CEO of IBM:

> Would you like me to give you a formula for success? It's quite simple, really. Double your rate of failure. You are thinking of failure as the enemy of success. But it isn't at all. You can be discouraged by failure or you can learn from it. So go ahead and make mistakes. Make all you can. Because remember that's where you will find success.

CHAPTER 7

EXPERTISE IN DIFFICULT SITUATIONS

Experience Refined by Feedback

I talk with a lot of psychotherapists and researchers about deliberate practice, and they are generally very receptive to the idea. In classes, conferences, and workshops around the world, the concept of deliberate practice resonates with therapists. It's not controversial that skill-focused training, focusing on clinical outcomes, and observing your own work, can improve your effectiveness. The basic principles of deliberate practice resonate with therapists as just good common sense.

With one exception. In my experience presenting deliberate practice to psychotherapists, I've found one component of expertise theory that is controversial: the theory that clinical experience does not itself lead to expertise. This idea is viewed with skepticism, or even outright scorn, by many (if not most) clinicians.

However, the limited benefit of experience is not just a theory. It is one of the most robust findings from decades of expertise research across a wide range of fields (Ericsson et al., 2006). Ericsson (2004, p. S70) summarized these findings:

> Nobody becomes an outstanding professional without experience, but extensive experience does not invariably lead people to become experts. When individuals are first introduced to a professional domain after completing their education, they are often overwhelmed and rely on help from others to accomplish their responsibilities. After months or years of experience, they attain an acceptable level of proficiency and are able to work independently. Although everyone in a given domain tends to improve

with experience initially, some develop faster than others and continue to improve during ensuing years. These individuals are eventually recognized as experts and masters. In contrast, most professionals reach a stable, average level of performance within a relatively short time frame and maintain this mediocre status for the rest of their careers.

Evidence from psychotherapy research suggests that our field is no different. Despite many attempts over more than three decades, a large body of research has found scant evidence that therapists with more experience have better outcomes (e.g., Beutler et al., 2004; Budge, Owen, Kopta, Minami, Hanson, & Hirsch, 2013; Hattie, Sharpley, & Rogers, 1984; Laska, Smith, Wisclocki, & Wampold, 2013; Minami, Wampold, Serlin, Hamilton, Brown, & Kircher, 2008; Okiishi et al., 2003; Okiishi, Lambert, Eggett, Nielsen, Dayton, & Vermeersch, 2006; Stein & Lambert, 1984, 1995; Strupp & Hadley, 1979; Tracey, Wampold, Goodyear, & Lichtenberg, 2015; Wampold & Brown, 2005).

A particularly striking recent example is Simon Goldberg's study, which showed that the effectiveness of 170 therapists using a wide range of therapy models did not reliably improve over an average of five years, while some did not improve with up to 18 years of experience (Goldberg et al., 2016).

Another example is from Paul Clement, a psychodynamic psychologist in private practice in California. A pioneer in using practice-based evidence, Dr. Clement tracked his clinical outcomes for 26 years. When he compiled his data, he found good news: the majority of his clients had improved (Clement, 1994). However, he also found that his outcomes had not improved over the two-and-a-half decades of work. Fourteen years later he repeated the process, now with 40 years of his own clinical-outcome data, and again found his outcomes had not significantly improved over the years (Clement, 2008).

However, despite this robust evidence from the expertise and psychotherapy literature, most therapists are simply incredulous when I suggest that they might not improve with experience.

This reaction was eloquently stated by Steven Hendlin, a psychologist with over 35 years of experience (and fellow of three APA divisions), who spoke for the majority of therapists when he wrote:

For those of us who have dedicated our careers to the practice of psychotherapy, it is counter-intuitive, incredible, and even insulting to accept research that tells us we are no more skilled after decades of practice than a student or early career psychotherapist, nor do we get any more proficient in our skills over time, let alone become experts. While it is certainly possible that this is true for some who never grow, it *flies in the face of common sense* when applied to the whole profession of those psychologists who spend their lives practicing psychotherapy.

(Hendlin, 2014, p. 9, emphasis added)

Echoing the common view of many, Hendlin emphasized the importance of clinical wisdom, which "comes only with the ripeness of time and experience" (p. 11).

Despite all the research, I must admit that I am sympathetic to Hendlin's focus on the value of clinical experience. This is primarily because psychotherapy is complicated, with poorly defined variables and goals.

Psychotherapy Is a Mess

In classical music, performers have a very clear goal: to closely follow a score. Even in jazz, where improvisation is the goal, there is close agreement about what each note represents. Everyone knows the difference between an A, A-flat, B, etc. Likewise, medicine also has clearly defined goals. When medical providers meet a patient, they usually know what kind of procedure they will be doing, whether it's a surgeon removing a kidney or an obstetrician delivering a baby. In fact, medical patients who keep presenting with poorly defined goals usually get referred to psychotherapy! Even when a medical case is complicated by multiple diagnoses, there is still a very high level of agreement in the field about the fundamental treatment variables (e.g., blood pressure, cholesterol, blood types, germ theory, etc.).

In comparison, psychotherapy is simply a mess. Every therapist will tell you that the range of variability in psychotherapy is infinite. Our clients usually present with vague goals ("I want to feel better," or "I want to be less nervous"). Furthermore, these vague goals often change session to session ("Last week I felt depressed, but today I can't stop thinking about my new boyfriend"). One of the challenges I found with using deliberate practice for specific skills is that my clients keep changing their goals!

On top of this, we work in a field where the science is, to put it politely, poorly defined. Our diagnostic system is based on broad categories of symptoms, with little if any etiology or prognoses. We don't have the advantages that basic science offers our medical colleagues, like understanding etiology (e.g., germ theory) or specific assessment measures (e.g., blood types or cholesterol levels). This lack of basic science in our field may be why adherence to specific treatment models has not been associated with better outcomes in actual practice, and strict adherence has been associated with poorer outcomes (see Chapter 11 for more on this topic).

Further complicating matters, psychotherapy involves frequent disagreement with our clients. In fact, disagreements are so predictably common that whole models of therapy and entire research programs are focused on successfully navigating alliance ruptures (e.g., control mastery therapy, Weiss, 1993; alliance-focused training, Eubanks-Carter, Muran, & Safran, 2015). Whether it's called client resistance or therapist countertransference, everyone agrees that maintaining an open, collaborative, and productive relationship in psychotherapy is often hard. A musician doesn't have to negotiate each note with the audience, and a surgeon doesn't have to maintain eye contact with the patient during surgery.

In comparison, music and medical practitioners have the luxury of consistency. When they learn a technique (playing an A-flat or performing a pap smear), they can do it *the same way, every time.* In contrast, psychotherapy has zero skills that can be used robotically the same way, every time; all skills must be used flexibly, in the context of an infinitely complex range of clinical presentations.

This challenge of infinite variability brings us back to the value of clinical experience—what Hendlin calls "clinical wisdom." Decades of work experience offer therapists a deep well of pattern recognition, so they are more comfortable with variability: "Over years of practice, the experienced psychotherapist develops not only a varied skill set but also the wisdom to know how to approach and deal with certain types of clients with certain types of problems" (Hendlin, 2014, p. 11).

The idea that clinical experience leads to clinical wisdom is just common sense. However, if decades of clinical experience help therapists become experts, then why has a large body of psychotherapy research consistently found that therapist experience is *not* related to client outcomes?

I knew I was missing something, but I didn't know what. This dilemma made me curious to go back to the expertise literature. Specifically, I wondered, what does the research on expertise have to say about expertise in fields where there is so much complexity and poorly defined goals? Fortunately, there is a whole domain of research that focuses specifically on this problem: natural decision making.

DECISION MAKING IN DIFFICULT SITUATIONS

Natural decision making is a field of study that examines *how experts* make decisions in difficult situations (Klein, 2008). The goals of natural decision making are to (a) better understand the processes involved in effective decision making, and (b) improve methods for teaching professionals how to make better decisions in complex situations. Natural decision making got its start in the military (a field rife with difficult decisions) but has since expanded to a wide range of fields, including nursing, nuclear power plant operation, anesthesiology, airline piloting and engineering (Klein, 2008).

"Difficult" situations include six factors that relate to psychotherapy (Klein, Calderwood, & Clinton-Cirocco, 2010):

1) Ill-structured problems (not artificial, well-structured problems).
2) Uncertain, dynamic environments (not static, simulated situations).
3) Shifting, ill-defined, or competing goals (not clear and stable goals).
4) Action/feedback loops (not one-shot decisions).
5) Time stress (as opposed to ample time for tasks).
6) High stakes (not situations devoid of true consequences for the decision maker).

Sound familiar?

Prior to the discovery of natural decision making, training in decision making emphasized a systematic, comprehensive evaluation of many options before picking the option with the highest utility. For example, military commanders were encouraged to systematically consider every available option and weigh the pros and cons before making a decision. This logical, orderly process is called a "utility estimate" and assumes that the decision maker has plenty of time and comprehensive knowledge of the options.

While utility estimates were easy to teach and worked well in the classroom, researchers in the field discovered that experts in difficult situations rarely have sufficient time or information to complete a thorough utility estimate:

> It was fairly clear how people didn't make decisions. They didn't generate alternative options and compare them on the same set of evaluation dimensions. They did not generate probability and utility estimates for different courses of action and elaborate these into decision trees. Even when they did compare options, they rarely employed systematic evaluation techniques.
>
> (Klein, 2008, p. 456)

The military started funding research in natural decision making in 1988, after a U.S. Navy Aegis Cruiser got caught in a very challenging, fast-paced situation on the coast of Iran that involved poor communication between the U.S. and Iranian militaries. A series of mistakes was made by U.S. naval commanders that culminated in the tragic shooting down of an Iranian commercial airliner, killing 290 passengers. This disaster highlighted the need for better training methods for making tough decisions in challenging situations where there is limited time and information: "Unfortunately, the training methods and decision support systems [at the time] … did not improve decision quality and did not get adopted in field settings. People found these tools and methods cumbersome and irrelevant to the work they needed to do" (Klein, 2008, p. 456). After this incident, the military hired researchers to reapproach the science of decision making from the ground up by (a) identifying top-performing experts in the field, and (b) finding out how they actually make effective decisions. From this, natural decision making was born.

Research on top performers in the field revealed that when experts are faced with difficult situations, they actually use "a blend of intuition and analysis" (Klein, 2008, p. 457) to make decisions. In sharp contrast to a lengthy utility analysis, experts use a mixture of rapid unconscious recognition with conscious decision making, based largely on their experience. This process is called the Recognition-Primed Decision Model (RPD). "The RPD Model states that when it comes to high-stakes, time-pressured decisions, people do not use 'rational choice' or utility analysis; instead, they rely on their experience" (Ross, Shafer, & Klein, 2006, p.

406). "The recognition-primed decision (RPD) model describes how people *use their experience* in the form of a repertoire of patterns ... The patterns highlight the most relevant cues, provide expectancies, identify plausible goals, and suggest typical types of reactions in that type of situation" (Klein, 2008, p. 457, emphasis added).

Ross and colleagues (2006, pp. 405–6) provide a long list of benefits from experience, three of which seem particularly salient to the practice of psychotherapy:

- Perceptual skills: Experts have the ability to make fine discriminations. They see more in a situation than a novice by noticing cues a novice does not.
- Mental models: Experts have rich internal representations of how things work in their domain of practice ... These mental models allow them to learn and to understand situations more rapidly.
- Self-monitoring or metacognition: Understanding one's own strengths and limitations.

All this research might seem to support the assumption of many therapists about the sufficiency of clinical experience to achieve expertise, so clearly summarized by Hendlin: "Clinical wisdom ... comes only with the ripeness of time and experience" (2014, p. 11). But remember: a large body of psychotherapy research has found that senior psychotherapists do not have reliably better outcomes than junior therapists, or sometimes even trainees (Goldberg et al., 2016; Tracey et al., 2015).

So why does experience help all these other fields, but not ours? What are we missing? Feedback.

PLEASE TELL ME WHAT I'M DOING WRONG

Research in natural decision making didn't discover that experience was solely sufficient for expertise. Rather, expertise comes from "obtaining feedback that is accurate and diagnostic" (Ross et al., 2006, p. 412). Ericsson and colleagues noted this back in their original (1993) study on deliberate practice: "In the absence of adequate feedback, efficient learning is impossible and improvement only minimal even for highly motivated subjects. Hence mere repetition of an activity will not automatically lead to improvement in, especially, accuracy of performance" (p. 367).

Professionals in all the fields studied by natural decision making researchers—military commanders, neonatal intensive care nurses, chess players, design engineers, electronic warfare technicians, offshore installation managers—*get constant performance feedback* (Ross et al., 2006). In contrast, psychotherapists work largely in secret and isolation, sheltered from any performance feedback besides our own self-perceptions (Tracey et al., 2015). It's notable that a few of those professions listed above work under high levels of confidentiality or even secrecy, such as military commanders or medical professionals, demonstrating that confidentiality is not a good excuse for a lack of continuous performance feedback.

Based on their studies, researchers have developed a four-step model for decision skills training to "accelerate the transition toward expertise" (Ross et al., 2006, p. 412).

1) Explore and reveal the limits of the mental models.
2) Practice seeing and assessing cues and their associated patterns.
3) Receive feedback on what is not being recognized or accounted for in the mental models.
4) Compare perceptions and decisions with others when the training is done in a small group setting.

Most psychotherapists receive plenty of 1 and 2 on this list. However, virtually all therapists receive precious little of 3 and 4—feedback.

"But wait!" many therapists may say. "I get feedback from my clients every day." Sure, our treatment successes might tell us what we're doing right or wrong, but those aren't the cases where feedback is so crucial. The most important skill development occurs when I get feedback from my treatment failures and dropouts. Otherwise I can just repeat the same mistakes again and again.

Unfortunately, my clients who are stalled, deteriorating, or about to drop out—the cases I need to learn from—are the least likely to provide me with honest feedback. In a recent study of 547 clients by Matt Blanchard and Barry Farber (2016) at Columbia University, 93% of the clients reported having lied to their therapist. Negative reactions to therapy was one of the most common topics clients did not disclose to their therapist, including "pretending to find therapy effective" and "not admitting to wanting to end therapy."

The lack of accurate feedback in routine psychotherapy has been cited as one of the fundamental problems underlying an overall lack of expertise in psychotherapy (Tracey et al., 2014). Notably, each of the prominent researchers who made this claim—Terence Tracey, Bruce Wampold, James Lichtenberg, and Rodney Goodyear—has over 40 years of experience in psychology. They implore therapists to address this issue: "It is crucial that therapists obtain quality information about both client and therapist outcomes if they are to establish expertise" (2014, p. 226).

Not one of my dropouts left me a detailed note saying exactly what I did wrong that caused them to leave. None of my treatment failures identified my skill deficiencies before they left treatment. When a client deteriorates or drops out, my memory and notes about what happened are usually not sufficient to learn from that case. To learn from these cases I need videos or other perspectives outside my own biased and incomplete memory.

I can't think of any other field where professionals are cloistered in such isolation and secrecy, going decades without exposure to any professional external feedback on their mistakes and failures. Imagine a writer who went decades without anyone reading his or her work, a musician or dancer who went decades without performing for others, or an athlete who went decades without competing. How good could they expect to become? Without external data (e.g., video, client feedback, outcome data, expert consultation, follow-up data), case consultations are like an artist describing one of their paintings to a friend and then asking for an art review based on the verbal description.

Doctors can usually find out pretty reliably whether a procedure worked or where it went wrong.[1] Musicians know whether they are on key or not. Unfortunately, I don't have the luxury of having reliable and specific feedback handed to me. I have to strive for every bit of it.

Haggerty and Hilsenroth (2011, p. 193) described the limits of memory well:

> Suppose a loved one has to undergo surgery and you need to choose between two surgeons, one of whom has never been directly observed by an experienced surgeon while performing any surgery. He or she would perform the surgery and return to his or her attending physician and try to recall, sometimes incompletely or inaccurately, the intricate steps of the surgery they just performed. It is hard to imagine that anyone, given a choice,

would prefer this over a professional who has been routinely observed in the practice of their craft.

Are there excellent psychotherapists who don't use videotape? Of course. However, imagine how much better they could be if they analyzed their own session videos, and in particular their treatment failures?

Here's how I explain videotaping to my clients:

> Everyone has blind spots and makes mistakes. That is human and happens in any field. My strategy is to get continual feedback from clinical experts to help me spot my mistakes and address them. It's kind of like getting a routine audit. If anyone goes long enough without an audit, problems will develop. Getting feedback on my work from experts helps me help you.

It's time to make videotaping a standard of practice for psychotherapy.[2] To help, I've included more information on how to videotape psychotherapy sessions in the Appendix.

NOTES

1 Within medicine, the impact of experience on effectiveness has been tied to the amount of feedback doctors receive. For example, radiologists work in conditions that limit the feedback they receive, which has been identified by research as a primary reason that their accuracy does not improve with years of experience or number of diagnoses they have performed (Ericsson & Pool, 2016).

2 I'm speaking particularly to my psychodynamic colleagues who have historically put up the greatest resistance to videotaping. I'm not alone in calling for videotaping. Prominent psychodynamic clinicians and researchers are now encouraging the use of videotaping for training and routine practice in psychodynamic models (e.g., Abbass., 2004; Alpert, 1996; Briggie, et al., 2016; Eubanks-Carter et al., 2015; Friedlander et al., 2012; Haggerty & Hilsenroth, 2011; McCullough, Bhatia, Ulvenes, Berggraf, & Osborn, 2011).

CHAPTER 8

EXPERTISE IN SPIRITUAL PRACTICES

Addressing Experiential Avoidance

In this part of the book we have been exploring what we can learn from the science of expertise in other fields. So far:

- From the field of medicine, we've learned to increase our focus on the clinical outcomes of each patient and each practitioner.
- From the field of performing arts, we've learned to identify specific incremental skills just beyond the practitioner's current ability and repetitively practice those skills.
- From the field of emergency work, we've learned to make years of experience more productive and learn from our failures by using continuous feedback.

In this chapter I'd like to explore an aspect of psychotherapy that is, in my opinion, almost unique among fields: how we deal with our clients' emotional pain and anxiety. Are we able to tolerate our clients' painful feelings, or do we avoid them?

This is a particularly personal and vulnerable subject. It's less about skill acquisition and more about emotional growth. To be honest, as I wrote this chapter I worried that I might risk losing some readers because of the vulnerable nature of the topic. However, this topic is simply too important to ignore. This isn't just my opinion. Leaders from psychotherapy models across the spectrum agree.

I will start with an illustrative case example.

EXPERIENTIAL AVOIDANCE: A CASE EXAMPLE

My client was an eight-year-old boy who had recently been referred for therapy at the community mental-health clinic where I was doing my internship. He was referred by his school for pervasive anxiety and trouble focusing. He had also recently developed vocal and motor tics. The boy lived with his mother, who was developmentally delayed and depressed. She had been in a long series of physically abusive relationships throughout the boy's life. Most recently, she had started corresponding with a man in prison for child abuse with the intention of marrying the felon when he left prison in a year. The mother was currently in therapy at our clinic, and her therapist was trying desperately to help her set healthy boundaries so she wouldn't lose her son to the foster-care system.

The boy originally attended Catholic school, but his steadily increasing anxiety symptoms had caused the school to kick him out. He had recently been transferred to a public school, which is when he developed the vocal and motor tics.

The overall treatment plan was to provide social support for the family, help the mother develop healthier boundaries, and then bring the mother and son together for family therapy. My role in this plan was to help the boy with his anxiety symptoms in the meantime, knowing that his situation wasn't going to improve immediately. The other adults in the boy's life, his mother and teachers, were unable to respond to his anxiety, so it had just grown to the point of turning into physical symptoms. He was a bright boy and could sense that his mother was not able to provide a safe environment for him.

WHAT TO DO WITH ANXIETY

My supervisor said,

> I'm going to teach you some anxiety-regulation techniques that can help the boy. However, these will only work if he trusts you. And he'll only trust you if he knows you can hear and accept what he is feeling, unlike all the other adults in his life. So your first learning task is internal: learn to hear and accept the anxiety that he will express through his play, without compulsively trying to "solve" it. Give him some time to show you how he feels and prove to him that you can handle his feelings. Only then will he be receptive to the anxiety-regulation techniques.

My supervisor explained to me that because the boy's distress stemmed from very real safety concerns (in contrast to maladaptive thoughts), we couldn't aim to extinguish his anxiety. Rather, my first job was to help him *tolerate* his anxiety. This meant that *I* had to tolerate the boy's anxiety before he could learn to tolerate it himself, something other adults in his life had been unable to do. (Recall that he had recently been expelled of Catholic school due to his anxiety symptoms.) If I couldn't tolerate the boy's anxiety, then he would simply hide his feelings and probably get worse. The scientific term for this is *experiential avoidance*, "attempts to reduce distressing thoughts, feelings, or other negative subjective experiences even when doing so is ineffective and causes problems" (Scherr, Herbert, & Forman, 2015, p. 22).

The task of working with a child's feelings was eloquently described by seminal child psychologist Virginia Axline, who counseled, "Accept the child exactly as he is ... so the child feels free to express his feelings completely" (Axline, 1947, p. 73). The goal is to form a positive relationship that is characterized by warmth and acceptance. The therapist is emotionally available while not imposing his or her own emotional needs on the child: "The therapist does not patronize the child, hurry him, or, in impatience, quickly do things for him that implies a lack of confidence in his ability to take care of himself" (p. 62). These words should also fully apply to psychotherapy with adults. Sounds easy, huh?

THE HARDEST LESSON

Unfortunately, it is not. In fact, this learning task—hearing and accepting anxiety without compulsively trying to solve it—requires that the therapist have sufficient emotional strength and low levels of experiential avoidance. This has been the single most difficult lesson I have struggled with in my training, probably because I have a problem with my own experiential avoidance. I have struggled with anxiety throughout my life and at the time I worked with this boy was still mired in unproductive long-term therapy. There was simply no way that I could help the boy tolerate his anxiety while I was so averse to my own. It actually wasn't until some years later that I was finally able to tolerate higher levels of anxiety in my clients, and even to this day I struggle when faced with psychotic levels of anxiety.

My experiential avoidance was clearly demonstrated in one of our therapy sessions. We met in a typical play-therapy room filled with toys, games, and craft materials. I started every session with the same words, "We can use this time for whatever you want. This is your time and space." This had been a particularly hard week for the boy. Before our session I heard from the mother's therapist that she had been receiving letters from the convict she was hoping to marry and had been showing the letters to the boy. This, of course, meant that child-protective service was one step closer to taking the boy away from the mother.

The boy started this session by gathering all the toys from around the room and putting them on the floor. He then said, "There's a lot of rain." He made water motions with his hands and looked at me. "The water is rising fast, really fast!" He took one of the toy soldiers that was on the floor and stood it up. "This guy is drowning. He's trying to swim, but he can't." He then dropped that soldier and picked up another. "This guy too. Dead!" He then repeated this with a doll, a stuffed animal, more toy soldiers. He had each try to swim to safety but then drown. While he did this, he looked me straight in the eye.

Throughout this process I felt my own anxiety steadily rise. By the time the eighth or tenth toy drowned, I intervened. I took one of the toys from the floor and said, "This toy can swim to safety. He can live." I placed that toy up high on a chair.

The boy walked over to the chair and pushed it over. "Nope, he drowned too. Look, the water is still rising!"

My anxiety spiked. I grabbed another toy from the floor. "But this guy can make it; he's a good swimmer!" I placed that toy on a table.

The boy knocked the toy from the table, and it fell back to the floor. "Nope. Drowned."

We repeated this process a few times. I kept trying to save the toys while the boy kept drowning them. Each time my anxiety spiked higher.

I pleaded, "Can't any of the toys swim to safety?"

The boy raised his hands above his head. "The water is so high, it's drowning everyone!" He climbed onto the chair and raised his hands above our heads. "Look how high the water is. Everyone's dead. Look!"

I replied, with a desperate tone in my voice, "But someone has to live, right?"

I was just another adult in the boy's life who couldn't tolerate his anxiety. As Jon Frederickson once noted in my supervision, I was relating to the client I *wanted* to have rather than the one who showed up.

COLLABORATIVE SUPERVISION TO THE RESCUE?

Luckily, I had a supervisor who was able to spot my emotional blind spot and address my experiential avoidance in a gentle, collaborative manner. She said, "You have to give the boy space to show you how anxious he is. He'll do this through his play. Don't try to redirect his play. This is just your attempt to deny his anxiety. Until he sees that you can tolerate his anxiety, he can't trust you." Fortunately, my supervisor was able to tolerate *my* anxiety, or else we would have ended up in parallel process in supervision (Bernard & Goodyear, 2014).

I really wanted to provide the boy with more patience and acceptance than the other adults in his life. However, despite my best intentions, I just simply couldn't do it. I had an emotional training block. Although my head believed the value of the theory and intended to do it, my heart wasn't emotionally ready to put it into action. I told the client that all of his experience was welcome in the play-therapy room, and although I really intended that to be true, I simply was unable to tolerate his higher levels of anxiety. I couldn't even tolerate his high anxiety in symbolic play.

To help me understand this problem, my supervisor recommended that I read Axline's book on play therapy. One section stood out to me in particular:

> A therapist is not ready to go into the playroom with a child until she has developed self-discipline, restraint, and a deep respect for the personality of the child. There is no discipline so severe as the one which demands that each individual be given the right and opportunity to stand on his own two feet and to make his own decisions.
>
> (Axline, 1947, p. 64)

My first reaction to my supervisor was indignation. I thought I already had developed "self-discipline, restraint, and deep respect for the personality of the child." However, as I observed my own work with this client and others over the next few weeks, I began to see evidence that I was actually redirecting all of my clients, including the adults, away from their painful feelings.

Part of the knotty problem with experiential avoidance is that there is usually a cognitive justification or rationalization for it. "I can't let him drown" or "I need to show him how to stay positive," or "My job is to help him, not let him suffer." I thought I was trying to help my client, but I was actually unconsciously avoiding my own anxiety. And like most therapists, I'm pretty good at coming up with clinical rationalizations. This is the opposite of what Axline and my supervisor said was necessary for therapy with children.

As I came to accept my own emotional training block, a question emerged in my mind: How could I learn "self-discipline, restraint, and deep respect for the personality of the child"? I had clearly already broken Axline's rule of their being a prerequisite for going into the therapy room! I reread Axline's book and found no guidance on how to develop the emotional strength she insisted that I have as a prerequisite for being a therapist.

Axline is not alone in emphasizing the dangers of experiential avoidance. Most psychotherapy textbooks and training manuals set a high level of emotional self-awareness and nonreactivity as an essential component for providing psychotherapy (also called empathic attunement; Kohut, 1977; for a review, see Rowe & Isaac, 2000). The importance of psychotherapists tolerating clients' anxiety has been stressed in many schools of therapy, starting with Freud (1958 [1910]), and including Gestalt (Perls, 1973), client-centered therapy (Rogers, 1961), logotherapy (Frankl, 1988), existential therapy (Yalom, 1980), emotion-focused therapy (Greenberg, 2010), among many others. More recently, the cognitive and behavioral camps have also recognized the problem of experiential avoidance in therapists, most notably third-wave CBT therapy models like dialectical behavior therapy, mindfulness-based cognitive therapy, functional analytic psychotherapy, acceptance and commitment therapy, integrative behavioral couple therapy, and others (e.g., Hayes et al., 2004; Hembree, Rauch, & Foa, 2003; Öst, 2008; Scherr, Herbert, & Forman, 2015; Segal, Williams, & Teasdale, 2002).

In other words, our personal emotional capacity serves as a glass ceiling that limits our professional effectiveness: "The therapist effect lies at the intersection between psychotherapists' professional and personal functioning" (Nissen-Lie et al., 2015, p. 1).

While it is clear that a high level of emotional self-awareness is essential for providing psychotherapy, it isn't at all clear how therapists are meant to achieve that.

THE CONSEQUENCES OF LOW EMOTIONAL SELF-AWARENESS
IN THERAPISTS

Recall what motivated my quest to learn about deliberate practice: the realization that half of my clients, the "other 50%," weren't improving. Could therapists' experiential avoidance cause problems? The psychotherapy research literature suggests so.

As we reviewed in Chapter 1, the second-largest contributor to psychotherapy outcome after client variables is the quality of the therapist (Norcross, 2011). For example, therapist variance accounts for *ten times* more of the variance in psychotherapy outcome than the model of treatment (Wampold & Imel, 2015, p. 257).

A large body of psychotherapy research has explored what characteristics make some therapists better or worse clinicians (e.g., Mohr, 1995). In a notable example, a group of prominent researchers (Castonguay, Boswell, Constantino, Goldfried, & Hill, 2010) recently published a paper titled "Training Implications of Harmful Effects of Psychological Treatments" in which they highlighted "difficulty tolerating negative emotion" as a harmful therapist trait that must be addressed in training.

Ackerman and Hilsenroth (2003) did a review of the research in this area, and the results are not good, to put it politely. They dismissed "the notion that therapists are well adjusted individuals with little negative contribution to the therapeutic process" (p. 173), and summarized their findings in this way:

> These findings underscore the *potentially adverse impact therapists' personal attributes can have on the therapeutic relationship and process*. Whether or not therapists can be taught to be empathic and warm, it is of critical importance that they vigilantly work toward conveying a respectful, flexible, accepting, and responsive attitude toward their patients.
>
> (p. 173; emphasis added)

LIMITED SOLUTIONS

While there is widespread agreement across models that therapists' experiential avoidance can cause problems, there is also unfortunately a very limited range of strategies for dealing with it. Specifically, there are two: get therapy, or get out.

The original way psychotherapy training addressed experiential avoidance was requiring trainees to their own therapy (Freud, 1958 [1910]). While I am an enthusiastic supporter of therapy for trainees—my own therapy saved my butt and was an essential part of my development—requiring therapy is problematic for a few reasons.

First, therapy only works if the client (the therapist in this case) is highly motivated for personal introspection. Sending therapists off to therapy can give the message that experiential avoidance is an illness or pathology, something that should be fixed rather than a universal human trait that we all should continually attend to via skill development. Furthermore, it is important for therapists to address experiential avoidance that arises specifically from their own work, which may not be addressed in their own therapy.

The second way psychotherapy training addresses experiential avoidance is through *gatekeeping*, the euphemistic term for kicking out trainees who are deemed inappropriate for the profession.

What we really need in our field are training methods to directly address experiential avoidance as a core part of training—something more than get therapy, or get out.

There are some promising leads. Although dynamic communities were the first to propose the importance of therapist emotional development, more recently the third-wave CBT models are leading the charge. For example, acceptance and commitment therapy emphasizes the importance of addressing experiential avoidance in therapists, and there is some preliminary evidence that this improves therapist effectiveness (Hayes, Bissett et al., 2004).

However, our field really needs to address this more seriously. It is curious that we have a problem acknowledged so widely across the field and yet don't have a good solution. Simply put, how can we use deliberate practice to develop the capacity to tolerate painful feelings?

I will propose an answer to that question in the following sections. But first, let's take a moment to consider some easier methods of handling client distress.

THE SIMPLE WAY TO HANDLE CLIENT DISTRESS

Before going to graduate school, I spent a summer doing a scuba divemaster internship at a dive shop in Honduras. One of the lessons taught was how to rescue panicking divers. The key to the lesson is learning that when someone is panicking in the water their first instinct is to flail around and climb on top of anyone who tries to rescue them. This desperate instinctual impulse will, of course, drown the rescuer and thus also the person who is panicking.

Scuba schools have developed a reliable system for addressing this problem. The trick is to swim around the panicking diver and grab his scuba tank from behind. You can then drag him to safety while staying out of his reach so he can't drown you. If the panicking diver won't let you swim around him, you should dive under him and back up behind him. This works because a panicking diver will never intentionally put his face back under the water.

Scuba schools teach this skill using simulation-based mastery learning with deliberate practice. They break the overall task into discrete component skills, show you how to practice each skill in simulation with a buddy, and have you repetitively practice each skill until you master them all. The training process is fun (especially when you're paired with a dive buddy twice your size who gets a kick out of enthusiastically trying to drown you, as I was). Most trainees can get it within a few hours.

One of the more colorful characters at the dive shop was Hans, a tough, gruff man who had recently retired after three decades working as a rescue diver for the German Navy. (One of his favorite games was showing new scuba instructors how to perform CPR under water.) One night at the bar on the dive-shop roof Hans explained that his unit had a special procedure for rescuing panicking women with babies from a sinking ship. He said in his strong German accent, "Saving a mother with a baby is a particular challenge because the mother can unintentionally drown the baby. You don't have time to swim around or under her. You have to save them fast." The simple system developed to do this is pretty shocking, if efficient: drop out of a helicopter on top of them, punch out the woman first, then load both the mother and baby onto a life raft and helicopter them to safety. "If the mother is unconscious then she can't resist," he explained, logically.

This is a very straightforward way of handling patient anxiety. Punch out the client, then helicopter to safety. No muss, no fuss. I must admit, I'm a bit jealous.

Most other fields are similar in their simplistic approach to anxiety: maintain a focus, show no fear, and don't let them see you sweat. Pilots don't have to sit with their passengers' fear; they've got a locked door separating them. Surgeons don't have to relate emotionally to their patients during surgery; the patient is unconscious. Musicians and dancers get to be in their own emotional world. In competitive fields like athletics and chess, you actually want your opponents to be intimidated by you.

In psychotherapy, it's like we're a pilot but the most terrified passenger is sitting in our lap. Or we're like a surgeon, but the patient is not sedated and we have to maintain eye contact and keep asking her how she's feeling during the surgery. Or like we're a dancer or musician, but we have to maintain eye contact with the person in the audience who has the worst agoraphobia.

Nissen-Lie and colleagues (2015, p. 2), a team of psychotherapy researchers in Norway, noted this challenge:

> It may be difficult to compare the work of psychotherapy with other professions because of its specific requirement that, to be of help to clients, the therapists must succeed in integrating their professional capacities and expertise with their personal attributes in a way that almost blurs the distinction between them.

We are the only field that has to sit eye to eye with someone else's pain and be emotionally open as we try to help while simultaneously withholding the instinctual urge to immediately do whatever we can to make it stop. Could deliberate practice help therapists develop the emotional resiliency needed to balance helping with accepting?

I returned to my ever growing library of books on expertise. Looking through books on deliberate practice for other fields, I found nothing that would help with experiential avoidance. Pulling out the big guns, I opened up the *Handbook of Expertise and Expert Performance* (Ericsson et al., 2006). This tome contains 900 pages exploring expertise and deliberate practice spanning dozens of fields. Unfortunately, I still couldn't find any other field that has to train professionals to build emotional awareness and address experiential avoidance.[1]

Is there any field like ours? As luck would have it, the answer to my search was actually just a few feet down the bookshelf, in the religion section.

THE FIRST DELIBERATE PRACTICE: SPIRITUAL PRACTICES

In college I wanted to study psychology. However, my college's psychology program had an emphasis on behaviorism, and my mind was too restless for the rigorous patience needed for scientific experiments. So, instead of psychology, I studied comparative religions.

One of my favorite professors was John Newman. John had lived and practiced at both Buddhist and Christian monasteries. Spirituality wasn't just academic for him. Tall, thin, and bursting with energetic knowledge, he lives in the middle of Indiana corn fields on a farm that feels like a spiritual retreat. When he wrote on the chalkboard his fingers crackled, like the electricity of ancient wisdom was flowing through his hands onto the board.

The year I graduated he published a book called *Disciplines of Attention* that examines the use of spiritual practices, like Theravada Buddhist meditation and Ignatian Christian exercises, and psychotherapy to "alter fundamental emotional dispositions" (Newman, 1996, p. 2).

As I was paging through the books on deliberate practice, the word "Discipline" in the title of John's book caught my eye, and I opened it up. Paging through it, I realized that people have actually used deliberate practice to address experiential avoidance not just for decades or centuries, but for millennia. In fact, addressing experiential avoidance was possibly one of the first applications of deliberate practice.

In the book, John specifically explores how spiritual practices aim for the same goal as psychotherapy, helping the practitioner gain meta-awareness of her own emotions. In spiritual practices, this is called *disidentification*. We become aware of our emotions as something that flows through us, rather than something that *is* us: "meditation ... promotes a kind of general disidentification with, or objectification of, current emotional states" (p. 31), which in turn "aims at seeing that the idea of a self increased or decreased by the present pain or pleasure was an illusion" (Newman, 1996, p. 33). Disidentification, known more commonly as mindfulness, helps us resist our human "tendency to cling to what is pleasurable and avoid what is painful and the correlate belief that present pain is bad for me, present pleasure is good" (p. 33). Bingo.

MINDFULNESS

Mindfulness is a form of deliberate practice with the goal of building *"awareness* of *present experience* with *acceptance"* (Germer, 2013, p. 7, emphasis in original).

> In a state of mindfulness, thoughts and feelings are observed as events in the mind, without over-identifying with them and without reacting to them in an automatic, habitual pattern of reactivity. This dispassionate state of self observation is thought to introduce a "space" between one's perception and response. Thus mindfulness is thought to enable one to respond to situations more reflectively (as opposed to reflexively).
>
> (Bishop et al., 2004, p. 232)

Mindfulness builds self-awareness of one's experience in each moment: "waking up from a life on automatic ... being aware of aspects of the mind itself" (Siegel, 2007, p. 5). The practice of mindfulness has the goal of helping us accept our experience, as opposed to the natural bias people have towards positive feelings or against painful feelings: "to take each moment as it comes—*pleasant or unpleasant, good, bad or ugly*—and then work with that because it is present now" (Kabat-Zinn, 1994, p. 23; emphasis added).

Mindfulness has been used as a deliberate practice for millennia by a broad range of spiritual practices, including Buddhism, Christianity, Judaism, Islam, and Taoism (Underhill, 2002). The founder of Buddhism, Siddhārtha Gautama, achieved enlightenment due to his unwavering commitment to meditation practice. In Buddhism practice is all-encompassing. Every moment is an opportunity for deliberate practice: "Zazen practice is the direct expression of our true nature. Strictly speaking, for a human being, there is no other practice than this practice; there is no other way of life than this way of life" (Suzuki, 1970, p. 22).

The promise of mindfulness for psychotherapy was first recognized by William James at the turn of the twentieth century, as reported by Epstein (1995, pp. 1–2):

> While lecturing at Harvard in the early 1900s, James suddenly stopped when he recognized a visiting Buddhist monk from Sri Lanka in his audience. "Take my chair," he is reported to have said. "You are better equipped to

lecture on psychology than I. This is the psychology everybody will be studying twenty-five years from now."

Although it took a bit longer than he envisioned, James' predictions have come true. Over the past 100 years mindfulness has been increasingly embraced by psychology. Today an entire branch of psychotherapy, third-wave CBT, is based on mindfulness. There are over 60 treatment and research centers in the United States focused on using mindfulness to benefit clients (see Germer, 2013, for a review).

Because mindfulness has clear benefits for clients, it's only natural to expect it may have benefits for therapists as well (Germer, Siegel, & Fulton, 2013; Hick & Bien, 2008; Shapiro & Carlson, 2009). Since therapists are the second-largest contributor to psychotherapy outcome (Wampold & Imel, 2015), it is reasonable to ask whether mindfulness training for therapists could improve their effectiveness (Davis & Hayes, 2011).

Recent research suggests this is true. For example, research has found that mindfulness training may promote therapists' capacity for empathy (Walsh & Shapiro, 2006), compassion (Shapiro, Brown, & Biegel, 2007), improved skill acquisition (Schure, Christopher, & Christopher, 2008), decreased stress and anxiety (Waelde et al., 2008), heightened self-efficacy (Greason & Cashwell, 2009), improved self-insight (Rothaupt & Morgan, 2007), and improved ability to respond less defensively to clients with negative affect (Gelso & Hayes, 2007; for a review of the research on mindfulness and psychotherapy training, see Davis & Hayes, 2011; Fulton, 2013; Williams, Hayes, & Fauth, 2007).

While there is substantial research on the impact of mindfulness training for trainees, very little research has been done to specifically examine whether that training impacts client outcome. This gap goes well beyond mindfulness training and is unfortunately representative of a broader problem in psychotherapy research on supervision and training (Ellis & Ladany, 1997; see Chapters 1 and 5). A notable exception is a recent study in Germany that showed trainees who engaged in Zen meditation had better client outcomes than trainees who did not (Grepmair et al., 2007).

Research programs have been integrating mindfulness as a core component of their psychotherapy-training models. For example, psychodynamic researchers John Muran and Jeremy Safran use mindfulness with the specific goal of helping trainees repair ruptures to the therapeutic alliance: "Our hope is that mindfulness training will enhance trainees' abilities to attend to the here and now with an attitude of curiosity and nonjudgmental acceptance. In other words, mindfulness training will help therapists to decenter, to observe their thoughts and feelings as temporary mental events rather than unalterable truths" (Eubanks-Carter et al., 2014, p. 4).

Noah Bruce and colleagues summarized this perspective and spoke for researchers and supervisors across the spectrum of psychotherapy models:

> We believe that the ability to attune with others can be learned, and that this ability is at the heart of a healing, empathic relationship. We propose that through mindfulness practice, a psychotherapist comes to increasingly know and befriend himself or herself, fostering his or her ability to know and befriend the patient. We further believe that the psychotherapist's ability to form an attuned, empathic relationship with the patient can lead to improvement in the patient's ability to self-attune, and that this ability can, in turn, diminish suffering, promote greater well-being, and increase the patient's ability to form and maintain interpersonal relationships. Ultimately, we posit that a greater focus on the impact of psychotherapists' mindfulness may contribute to the field's understanding of ways in which psychotherapists can be trained to foster positive relational experiences in psychotherapy.
>
> (Bruce, Manber, Shapiro, & Constantino, 2010, pp. 83–4)

CLINICAL MINDFULNESS

Researchers Daphne Davis and Jeffrey Hayes (2011) suggested that mindfulness become a "necessary specific competency" for trainees (p. 205). However, I propose that we go a step further. Psychotherapy doesn't require a general mindfulness. Rather, it demands a specific form of mindfulness, emotional self-awareness and nonreactivity in the face of our clients' most painful affects—their rage, guilt, grief, and longing— traumas so unbearable that they are avoided to the point of self-destruction. I call this *clinical mindfulness*—the ability to be emotionally self-aware and nonreactive specifically in the face of our clients' pain. It is a core component of my deliberate practice routine. I see clinical mindfulness for psychotherapy similar to physical fitness for athletics: an essential, core element of professional performance that promotes or inhibits my effectiveness. Deliberate practice exercises for developing this skill are discussed in Chapter 10.

NOTE

1 Although other fields have begun to notice. For example, there are efforts to provide emotional-attunement training for dentists after a recent study (Sherman & Cramer, 2005) revealed that levels of empathy in dentists go down over their training.

Part III

Developing Your Own Deliberate Practice Routine

In Chapters 1–4, we reviewed the path that brought me to deliberate practice: seeing my clinical failures (the "other 50%") and wanting a more effective method of clinical training. When I first heard about deliberate practice from Scott Miller, I was immediately excited. The idea just made intuitive sense: if every other field uses deliberate practice for training, then why don't we? I spent the next few years experimenting with deliberate practice myself, and researching how it is used in other fields.

Part II of this book was about that research. In Chapters 5–8, we reviewed the highlights of the research I found that promise to be particularly helpful for psychotherapy.

The next part of this book is about you. My hope is that you are now curious if deliberate practice can help your clinical training, as I was when I first heard about it from Scott Miller. The goal of the following part of this book is to help you start to experiment with developing your own deliberate practice routine. In these chapters I will describe what I have learned from my own experiments with deliberate practice, including what has worked, what hasn't, and some challenges I've encountered.

I want to emphasize the word *experiment*. This is virgin territory for psychotherapy. Take what works for you, and leave what doesn't. While much of the advice in the following chapters is based on empirical research, the ideas and exercises themselves have not been empirically tested for psychotherapy. There are promising lines of research in this area (e.g., Chow et al., 2015; Miller, Hubble, Chow, & Seidel, 2015), but that will take some years to produce. Until that time, we are each our own

N of 1 trial case study. I will provide suggestions and advice, but let your curiosity and—most importantly, your results—be your guide.

Chapter 9 describes the fundamental principles that guide my deliberate practice routine.

Chapter 10 describes exercises for basic psychotherapy skills that I have found helpful. These are:

Exercise 1:   Clinical mindfulness: developing experiential self-awareness and addressing experiential avoidance
Exercise 2:   Improving attunement with the client, part 1: what you see
Exercise 3:   Improving attunement with the client, part 2: what you hear
Exercise 4:   Improving attunement with the client, part 3: what you feel
Exercise 5:   Psychotherapy warm-ups
Exercise 6:   Building psychotherapy endurance

Chapter 11 presents exercises for specialized skills from specific treatment models. These are:

Exercise 7:   Psychotherapist activity/model assessment
Exercise 8:   Studying expert videotapes
Exercise 9:   Specific model exercises

The prominent Jazz instructor Jerry Coker (1990) wrote in his book *How to Practice Jazz*:

> Practicing music, of itself, is a skill, and a skill so important as to directly affect the end result of virtually every effort we make to study music performance. Having a great teacher helps, as does acquiring the best method books, texts, and collections of music, records, tapes, etc. But the one, most important, aspect of your study (PRACTICE) is the very activity which no teacher or book can accomplish for you. You must acquire the ability to practice well, or be forced to forego your aspirations to achieve the fullest development of your musical ability (p. I, emphasis in original).

CHAPTER 9

THE PRINCIPLES OF PRACTICE

At the same time that I started graduate school in psychology, I also picked up rock climbing. I'm not a natural athlete, but I found the mix of physical challenge and adrenalin fun. In retrospect, I also think I liked climbing because it is so much simpler than psychotherapy. Like therapy, climbing presents a never-ending series of incremental challenges. However, unlike therapy, the results of climbing are very easy to assess: you either make it to the top, or you don't. There is never debate or confusion about success or failure.

I started climbing in the gym. After a year of climbing indoors, I ventured to climbing outdoors. After a few years of that, I was looking for the next challenge. At that time, my climbing partner heard of a route up El Capitan, the largest vertical rock face in Yosemite National Park. I had previously considered El Capitan to be the sole territory of professional rock climbers. However, my friend described a route up the face that is accessible, called the Salathé Wall. "The technical climbing is actually pretty easy," he said. "It's just really, really tall."

On one of our training days, we met an old, gruff climber at the base of the mountain. His clothes were torn, his hands were callused, and he wore climbing gear two decades old. I asked if he had any advice for climbing El Capitan. He said, "Over the years I've seen hundreds of teams attempt El Cap with all kinds of fancy new gear and techniques. Half of them fail. Why? It's not the gear or technique. Getting to the top of this big hunk of rock just comes down to one simple principle: don't ask and don't tell." I asked what he meant. He replied, "Don't ever ask if your partner wants to give up. And don't tell when you want to give up. Just keep going. If you don't give up, you get to the top."

Don't give up—a basic principle. Most fields rely on basic principles to guide practice. In this chapter, I will review my initial experiments with developing my own basic principles for the deliberate practice of psychotherapy. As discussed earlier, these principles are experimental. Although based on empirical research, they have not been empirically tested themselves. Like everything in this book, use what works for you and leave what doesn't. In the end, all that counts is your results helping clients have better outcomes.

A Note about Terminology

Because this deliberate practice routine applies to psychotherapists at all career stages, the term "therapist" is used to designate the person practicing (who may be a trainee or licensed clinician), and the term "coach" is used to designate the person providing feedback and guidance (who may be a supervisor, consultant, professor, etc.).

Deliberate Practice: Basic Principles

My deliberate practice routine is based on five processes:

1) Observing our own work via videotape.
2) Getting expert feedback from a coach or consultant.
3) Setting small incremental learning goals just beyond our ability.
4) Repetitive behavioral rehearsal of specific skills.
5) Continuously assessing our performance via client-reported outcome.

These processes are repeated throughout a career, starting at the beginning of graduate school and continuing through licensure into middle and later career (Figure 9.1).

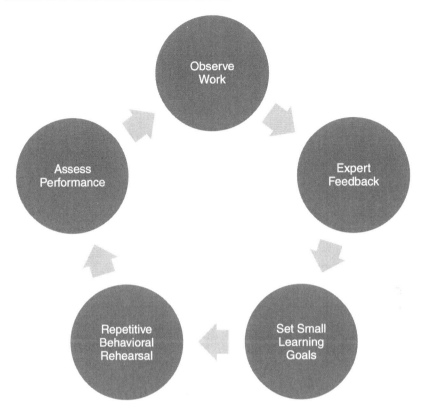

Figure 9.1 Career-long repetition

Additionally, my routine includes learning principles gleaned from how other fields (e.g., medicine, performing arts, and emergency management) use deliberate practice:

- We use the clinical outcomes of our individual clients as the most valid empirical basis for our work (see Chapter 5).
- We learn best by focusing on specific incremental skills just beyond our current ability and repetitively practicing those skills (see Chapter 6).
- We maximize learning from our clinical experience, particularly from our clinical failures, by reviewing our own work via videotape (see Chapter 7).
- We address our own experiential avoidance by developing emotional self-awareness and nonreactivity (see Chapter 8).

115

How Is This New and Different?

First, let's review what parts of this routine are *not* new.

The goals of training (development of clinical skills and emotional self-awareness) are not new. In fact, these goals are as old as psychotherapy itself and are shared by most psychotherapy models. Formal training programs in *helping skills* date back to at least the 1960s (Hill & Lent, 2006; Hackney & Bernard, in press).

The methods of training (videotape and clinical role play) are not new. Clinical role play has been in use since at least the days of psychotherapy pioneer Jacob Moreno (1932). Videotape has been used for supervision since at least the early 1960s (Abbass, 2004).

This routine's focus on experiential exercises is not new. Psychotherapy training has incorporated behavioral skill rehearsal since the days of early behaviorism. More recently, a growing body of research has investigated the use of experiential exercises for skill development across a wide range of psychotherapy models (e.g., Crits-Christoph et al., 2006; Davis & Hayes, 2011; Hilsenroth et al., 2015).

What are we aiming for that is new and different? Lessons from the science of expertise incorporating training methods that are considered essential for training in most other fields but are currently very rare or nonexistent in psychotherapy training. These include the following.

Difference 1: Smaller, More Incremental Skill Components

We try to isolate the smallest components of skills, microskills, that are just beyond our ability. For example, in traditional training a coach may suggest that a therapist "listen more carefully" to a client. In this routine, the coach will isolate a microskill within listening carefully, such as "Watch the video of this client and count how many times you talk over the client" or "Watch the video and count how many seconds you allow to pass after the client stops talking before you respond" or "Watch this video and carefully note your internal experience when the client is expressing anger. Write down how often that makes you feel uncomfortable."

Difference 2: Maximizing Time Spent on Simulation-Based Behavioral Rehearsal

In this routine we spend as much time as possible practicing skills in simulation rather than teaching theory or talking about skills. We recognize that unless a therapist is actually practicing a skill the learning is theoretical, not behavioral. For example, if in a one-hour class 20 minutes is spent explaining a technique, 10 minutes watching a demonstration of the skill, 10 minutes in discussion, and another 20 minutes in role play of the skill (with each therapist doing five minutes), then we consider each therapist to have had five minutes of substantive skill development.[1] This stands in contrast to traditional psychotherapy training, where passive learning (lecture) or theoretical learning (discussion) are paramount.

Difference 3: Repetition and Effort

This routine emphasizes skill development and maintenance through career-long repetition of basic and advanced exercises. Just as musicians, athletes, chess masters, and pilots practice the same basic skills throughout their careers, we never stop practicing. Furthermore, our practice is not mindless repetition, but a constant attempt to push ourselves—to upset our own homeostasis. We aim for continual improvement rather than automaticity. If it doesn't feel hard, then you're not advancing your skills.

Difference 4: Solitary Deliberate Practice

Like many other fields, we recognize that expert performance comes from many hours of solitary deliberate practice. Meeting with coaches or consultants is essential for feedback and performance appraisal, but logistical variables (notably, money) limit how much expert feedback we can access. The good news is that solitary deliberate practice is free! The bad news is that it requires considerably more effort and willpower than practice with an expert.

SIMULATION-BASED TRAINING

Deliberate practice requires behavioral skill rehearsal in simulations of actual psychotherapy. This is primarily done via two methods: videotape and role-play.

Videotape Review

The therapist watches videos of his or her own therapy sessions. While watching the video, the therapist does an exercise assigned by the coach (sample exercises are described later in this chapter). For advice on videotaping psychotherapy see the Appendix, and for a review of the literature, see Haggerty and Hilsenroth (2011).

Example

A coach and therapist identify a video of a session in which the client and therapist have a poor working alliance. The coach directs the therapist to watch this videotape while doing Exercises 2, 3, and 4 (see below).

Advantages of Videotape Review

Videos expose therapists to their own work with their own clients. This can be more effective for addressing therapists' experiential avoidance. Also, video review can be done solo by the therapist in solitary deliberate practice. Note that this is much more effortful than deliberate practice with a coach or peers.

Role play

The coach picks a challenging part of psychotherapy to simulate. First, the coach demonstrates the skill by role playing the therapist. Then they switch and the coach role plays the client and the therapist plays the therapist. The therapist repeats a specific skill in the role play until she attains mastery of the skill. Role play can also be done with peers or paid actors. Some universities use volunteer students from the drama department.

Example

A coach and therapist identify a video of a session in which the client is shutting down because the therapist is talking over him. The coach sets up a role play in which she plays the client and the therapist practices specific skills involved in listening more carefully. They repeat the role play until the therapist demonstrates mastery of the skills.

Advantages of Role Play

Because role play is artificial, the coach has much more control over the content and focus of the training. For example, the coach can limit the role play to one specific learning problem or skill. Or the coach can role play the exact same client with multiple therapists. This is called "standardized" role playing. Therapists can role play their clients. This often gives therapists a better understanding and emotional "feel" for their clients.

How Practice Feels

For deliberate practice to be viable, we have to acknowledge how it feels. Deliberate practice is the opposite of coasting. We face our own limits, focus on our failures, reveal our weaknesses. No one inherently enjoys this. It often feels somewhere between frustration and boredom. The effort and struggle are immediate while the gain and rewards are in the future.

However, there is a paradoxical result from this hard work of deliberate practice. As we practice and improve our skills, we get closer to our original goal in becoming therapists: more effectively helping our clients. This taps into our inherent motivation and delivers rewards that far exceed the effort required for practice. See Chapter 12 for more information on sustaining motivation for deliberate practice.

What to Practice

My deliberate practice routine focuses on two categories of skill: (a) exercises for basic psychotherapy skills, also called *facilitative interpersonal skills* (Anderson, Ogles, Patterson, Lambert, & Vermeersch, 2009; see Wampold, in press), and (b) exercises for specialized skills from specific treatment models. Both are essential for effective practice, similar to how musicians must practice both universal notes and specific arrangements or pieces. The exercises for basic psychotherapy skills that I have found helpful are described in Chapter 10, and those for specialized skills from specific treatment models in Chapter 11.

HOW TO PICK CASES FOR DELIBERATE PRACTICE

One of the underlying principles of my deliberate practice routine is to focus on cases that are stalled, deteriorating, or at risk for deterioration. These can be identified through a variety of methods listed below. It is important to note, however, that none of these methods is 100% reliable; they all have blind spots. Thus, it is recommended that multiple methods be used for each case. Ideally you will have at least three different sources of data, so you can triangulate toward a more reliable assessment.[2] The most common are (1) client report, (2) coach/therapist judgment, (3) routine outcome monitoring (ROM) data, (4) qualitative data from the client, and (5) collateral information from other people who know the client.

Client Report

I aim to do verbal check-ins with clients regarding treatment progress every session. When asked, clients will sometimes report if they are stalled, deteriorating, or considering terminating treatment. However, getting detailed and accurate feedback is challenging. Simply asking "How was today's session?" as many therapists do is rarely sufficient. Many clients will not disclose when treatment is going poorly or they are at risk of dropping out (Blanchard & Farber, 2016). Using short structured feedback forms every session can help, such as the Session Rating Scale (Miller et al., 2003). For detailed guidance on how to facilitate accurate and helpful feedback, see Miller, Prescott, & Maeschalck (in press).

Coach/Therapist Judgment

Clinical judgment is another valuable tool for determining which cases may be at risk of deterioration and dropout. You may get a hunch or intuitive feeling that something isn't right. Note, however, that recent research has raised significant doubts about clinicians' ability to predict their own cases at risk of deterioration (Walfish et al., 2012), so clinical judgment should not be considered sufficiently reliable without additional sources of information.

ROM Data

Routine outcome monitoring is a process of giving a short outcome or therapeutic alliance measure to your client at each session throughout treatment as a "check-in" regarding their well-being, clinical progress, and the quality of the therapeutic relationship. ROM has been shown by a large body of research to be a good way to identify clinical cases at risk of deterioration or dropout (Miller et al., 2013). Note, however, that ROM data is not sensitive to change or reliable with some clients (McLeod, in press). For example, some clients do not understand or express themselves in the language used by ROM measures (e.g., Elliott et al., 2009; Stephen, Elliott, & Macleod, 2011). Other clients may have reasons to understate or overstate their distress, such as those in mandated treatment or in legal proceedings. For detailed instructions and case examples on how to use ROM, see Miller et al. (in press).

Qualitative Data

In contrast to ROM data, which is typically numerical, qualitative data refer to more contextual, nuanced, and subtle methods of assessing client outcome that aim to more accurately capture each client's idiosyncratic self-concept and manner of expression (Hill, Chui, & Baumann, 2013; Levitt, 2015; McLeod, 2010, 2013, 2016). These include questionnaires, structured interviews, or semi-structured conversations about what is changing or not changing in the client's life. Studies have shown that some clients do not assess their progress via symptom change (McLeod, 2010). For these clients, there is a risk that "the feedback from quantitative measures may be misleading (and therefore not a helpful source of information in relation to deliberate practice) because it is too far removed from the client's own way of making sense—it may not be asking the right questions" (McLeod, in press). For detailed advice on how to use qualitative data with deliberate practice, see McLeod (in press).

Collateral Information

This includes conversations with significant people in the client's life (their employers, teachers, family, etc.) and consultations with the client's other treatment providers.

HOW TO PICK EXERCISES FOR DELIBERATE PRACTICE

There are two ways I determine which exercises to practice:

1) One of my coaches assigns me deliberate practice exercises, based on his analysis of my work and potential areas of development.
2) I pick deliberate practice exercises myself, based on my own judgment about my clinical weaknesses and areas of growth that interest me.

I recommend that you try all of the exercises presented in this book at least two or three times just to get a feel for them. This may help you identify which exercises could be of benefit for your skill development.

LOGISTICS

- *Location*: I've found that I need to do deliberate practice in a location that is private and quiet, where I will not be disturbed by colleagues, children, etc.
- *Scheduling*: It is often best to schedule the days and times that you will do deliberate practice and put them on your calendar. If you don't schedule deliberate practice but instead wait for an opportunity each day, you may often find that the whole day has gone by without doing it.
- *Timing*: The best time of day to do deliberate practice is when you will be most mentally alert. For many people this is the morning. Deliberate practice may be one of the hardest things you will do all day, and should be scheduled as such.
- *Duration*: At first aim to do one hour per week of deliberate practice in three 20-minute blocks. This will give you a good taste of the experience. It's important to keep your initial expectations modest and bank some successes or else you may get demoralized. When you have successfully done an hour of deliberate practice for a few weeks, step it up to two hours a week, in four 30-minute blocks. Over time you can adjust your routine to meet your training goals and schedule. See Table 9.1 for a sample of practice routines.[3]

Table 9.1 Sample deliberate practice routines

	Beginner	Intermediate	Advanced
Monday	20 minutes	40 minutes	60 minutes
Tuesday		20 minutes	60 minutes
Wednesday	20 minutes	60 minutes	60 minutes
Thursday		20 minutes	60 minutes
Friday	20 minutes	40 minutes	60 minutes
Saturday			60 minutes
Sunday			

DELIBERATE PRACTICE JOURNAL

Therapists should keep a deliberate practice journal (Ericsson et al., 1993; Chow et al., 2015) to record their training activities. A journal will help track which exercises have helped, so you can continuously refine and improve your practice routine. It will also help to answer logistical questions, such as the best time and days for practicing.

The journal should contain the date/time, duration, focus, and notes (see Table 4.1 for an example). The notes area is for any experiences, observations, or insights that may help the therapist over time to improve his or her own learning process. For example, I use the notes area to record:

- My response to practice (e.g., did it feel helpful or not?).
- My energy level during practice.
- Any issues in my personal life that may have affected practice.
- Emotional responses or experiential avoidance.

ASSESSING THE EFFECTIVENESS OF DELIBERATE PRACTICE

The effectiveness of deliberate practice should be continually assessed. As discussed in Chapter 5, this assessment must be based on client outcome (in contrast to fidelity or adherence to a model). In other words, therapists and coaches should continually ask themselves, "Is deliberate practice actually helping me help my clients?" Good methods for assessing the impact of practice on client outcomes include the same methods discussed previously:

- client reports;
- coach/therapist judgment;

- ROM data;
- qualitative data;
- collateral information.

Assessing the effectiveness of deliberate practice can be tricky for a few reasons. First, there are many moderating variables that can influence the effectiveness of psychotherapy, such as the client's family, employment, physical health, housing, etc. In fact, the majority of the variance in outcome in therapy is due to factors in clients' lives that are outside therapists' influence (Bohart & Wade, 2013). These factors can make it challenging to isolate the impact of the therapist's deliberate practice on the client's well-being. For example, deliberate practice may help a therapist become incrementally more skilled at building a working alliance with a client, but the client may still deteriorate because of losing his or her employment, housing, or a primary relationship. In this scenario, the clinical goal may be to help reduce the degree of deterioration.

Additional reasons why assessing the effectiveness of deliberate practice can be tricky is that therapist judgment is not very reliable (Walfish et al., 2012), and clients are not always forthright or consistent when reporting their symptoms or the impact of therapy on their well-being (Blanchard & Farber, 2016).

An additional challenge is that the impact of psychotherapy may take some time to appear or may diminish over time. For these reasons, Ericsson (2015) emphasizes the importance of long-term follow-up to assess the effectiveness of deliberate practice. For more information on assessing the effectiveness of deliberate practice, see Ericsson & Pool (2016).

NOTES

1 All of the non-behavioral components of learning are of course essential (e.g., explaining techniques, watching demonstrations, discussion, etc.) However, they can easily consume most of the time in class or supervision. In many fields, the majority of behavioral rehearsal is done during solitary deliberate practice as homework. Supervision/ coaching time is largely seen as a tool for guiding that solitary deliberate practice.

2 The current standard in the field is just two sources of data (client report and therapist judgment), which results in 40–60% of clients not benefiting from treatment (Lampropoulos, 2011).

3 Note that top performers in many fields including music, athletics, etc. typically practice for two to three or more hours per day, six days per week.

Chapter 10

DELIBERATE PRACTICE EXERCISES FOR BASIC SKILLS

When I first told Jason Whipple about my plans to write a book on using deliberate practice for psychotherapy, he responded, "Beware the fad." When I asked what he meant, he replied,

> Be careful where you focus the deliberate practice. Research consistently shows that the majority of the variance in psychotherapy outcome is in the client, and then second in the therapist. The treatment model (CBT, etc.) matters far less. This means that deliberate practice should focus on the basic interpersonal skills first. Otherwise deliberate practice could simply devolve into another fad: a "model" or "myth" for how to do psychotherapy that ends up explaining 1% of the outcome variance like all the other existing models.

Jason's advice is smart. Most of my clinical failures have stemmed from limits in my basic psychotherapy skills, such as not accurately attuning with my clients, failing to build a solid therapeutic working alliance, or not managing my own experiential avoidance. Early in my training, I had hoped that learning the right psychotherapy model would improve my effectiveness. However, I now see that the most important step is building these basic skills. Without the basic interpersonal skills, I can't be effective in any psychotherapy model.

Thus, my first experiments with deliberate practice focused on basic psychotherapy skills that are common to all models. Called *facilitative interpersonal skills* (Anderson et al., 2009), *basic therapy-related interpersonal skills* (Schöttke, Flückiger, Goldberg, Eversmann, & Lange, 2016), and *relational skills* (Boswell & Castonguay, 2007), this skill set includes empathy, verbal fluency, emotional expression, persuasiveness, and problem focus. For a review of the research in this area, see *Psychotherapy Relationships that Work: Evidence-Based Responsiveness* (Norcross, 2011) and *The Great Psychotherapy Debate* (Wampold & Imel, 2015).

This chapter presents deliberate practice exercises I have found to be helpful for acquiring and maintaining some of these essential psychotherapy skills. These exercises are appropriate for all mental-health practitioners, including every stage of development (beginner to advanced); every treatment population (e.g., individual psychotherapy, marriage and family therapy, school counseling, substance abuse counseling, etc.); and every theoretical orientation (e.g., CBT, dynamic, etc.). These exercises are based on Bruce Wampold's *Contextual Model* of how psychotherapy works (Wampold, in press).

The exercises in this chapter are:

Exercise 1:   Clinical mindfulness: developing experiential self-awareness and addressing experiential avoidance

Exercise 2:   Improving attunement with the client, part 1: what you see

Exercise 3:   Improving attunement with the client, part 2: what you hear

Exercise 4:   Improving attunement with the client, part 3: what you feel

Exercise 5:   Psychotherapy warm-ups

Exercise 6:   Building psychotherapy endurance

Exercise 1: Clinical Mindfulness: Developing Experiential Self-Awareness and Addressing Experiential Avoidance

The overall goal of this exercise is to help develop *clinical mindfulness* (see Chapter 8), awareness of your internal experiences while being exposed to your clinical work via videos of your psychotherapy sessions. More specifically, the exercise focuses on two areas of internal experience that are particularly relevant for delivering psychotherapy:

1)   The first area is building your *experiential self-awareness*, the inner processes and experiences that occur during your psychotherapy sessions. These include your thoughts, feelings, bodily sensations, anxieties, hopes, fears, etc. In actual therapy sessions, your focus is

usually on your client, so these processes often occur in the background, out of your conscious awareness. However, these processes can still restrict your ability to communicate and empathize with your clients. Thus, the goal of these exercises is to bring these processes and experiences up to your conscious awareness.

2) The second area is noticing your own *experiential avoidance*, the urge to avoid uncomfortable experiences like anxiety, fear, doubt, sadness, anger, guilt, etc. While it is natural to have an urge to avoid unpleasant experiences, if you are not aware of your experiential avoidance, you will have a harder time helping your clients with their painful experiences. In surgery, it is important for the surgeon to have a clean scalpel. In psychotherapy, your mind and heart are the scalpel.

Research Base

The importance of experiential self-awareness and problems with experiential avoidance have been discussed by most major models of psychotherapy, starting with Freud and leading up to modern third-wave CBT models (see Chapter 8 for a review). Even more recently, there has been a growing awareness of the potential value of therapists developing mindfulness skills to improve their psychotherapy (Germer et al., 2013; Hick & Bien, 2008; Shapiro & Carlson, 2009; Siegel, 2007; for a review see Davis & Hayes, 2011 and Bruce et al., 2010).

This exercise is similar to interpersonal process recall (Kagan & Kagan, 1997), an older method of supervision that uses videotape to help explore supervisees' experiences and reactions to their clients. However, one important difference is that this exercise focuses on the supervisees' experience in the present moment while watching the video, not recalling their experience from the actual therapy session. Focusing on experiences in the present moment is more effective for addressing experiential avoidance.

Instructions

1) Read through all of the instructions before starting the exercise. Set aside at least 30 minutes for watching your own videos in a private place where you will not be disturbed. Keep notes during the exercise on a pad of paper or on your computer.

2) Pick any video of your work. Before you start the video, pause for a moment and notice your interior state. Write down anything you notice. For example, are there

   a. any sensations in your body?
   b. any thoughts in your mind?
   c. any anxiety or feelings?
   d. any urges to avoid watching the video?
   e. any other experiences (e.g., hesitancy, eagerness, optimism, self-doubt, etc.)?

3) Start the video and listen to what you and the client say. Try not to think about your psychotherapy technique in the video. Instead, just focus on noticing your internal experiences while watching the video.

4) If a section of the video causes strong sensations that you want to explore further, pause or rewind the video to watch these parts again. However, do not fast forward or skip parts; this can be unconscious experiential avoidance.

5) Write down any sensations you have in your body while watching this video. Below are some questions that can help guide you in the process.

   a. Write down anything you notice. For example, are there
      i. any sensations in your body?
      ii. any thoughts in your mind?
      iii. any anxiety or feelings?
      iv. any urges to avoid watching the video?
      v. any other experiences (e.g., hesitancy, eagerness, optimism, self-doubt, etc.)?

   b. Where in the video do you notice the most tension, anxiety, or defenses (e.g., urges to stop, take a break, avoid, etc.)? Note that many people (including me) have all these experiences in the first ten seconds, or even before the video starts.

   c. What was the client's presentation when you got most tense? For example, were they being passive, avoidant, reaching out to you for help, or arguing? What were they talking about?

   d. Write down when you notice your body shifting while watching the tape (crossing legs, shifting in chair, foot tapping, crossing arms, frowning). Make a list then go back and see what happened immediately before—e.g., what topics, interactions, etc. preceded the movement.

6) As you watch the video, notice and write down the following:
   a. Does time seem to move faster or slower than usual?
   b. Does this process feel difficult or easy?
   c. Is this process enjoyable or unpleasant or both?
   d. Do you have any urges to avoid any parts of this experience?

Personal Observations

This was the first deliberate practice exercise I did. For the first few weeks almost everything I noticed when watching the video was unpleasant: tension, anxiety, self-attacking thoughts, urges to avoid the exercise, etc. This gradually gave way to breakthroughs of strong feelings: grief, anger, hope, longing, guilt, love. Over time this exercise has gotten easier. But I always notice at least some tension or avoidance urges, and sometimes those experiences are still dominant.

This deliberate practice exercise has the added benefit of improving my personal life. I usually feel clearer, calmer, and more centered after doing it. To this day it continues to be the most challenging and rewarding exercise I practice.

Notes

1) The goal of this exercise is to notice all internal experiences (or urges to avoid) that are aroused by watching your case videos. Some of these experiences may have nothing to do with the client or even psychotherapy, which is okay. For example, you may have thoughts or feelings about your past or other people in your life. The session video is only the stimulus. Let yourself notice whatever experiences it evokes. (This is in contrast to Exercise 4, which focuses on your internal experiences in direct relation to the client.)

2) Remember that the goal is not to change your experience but to be aware of it and tolerate it. Experiential avoidance is a very natural human reaction. In my experience, this is often the hardest thing for a therapist to learn about this exercise. Common responses are that therapists wants to avoid the exercise, thinking they are supposed to be super relaxed and trying to force themselves to feel that way, feeling ashamed of and criticizing themselves for their experiential avoidance, and not wanting to acknowledge their avoidance to

coaches or colleagues. If you notice any of these responses in yourself, just write them down and continue the exercise.

3) Many people find this exercise to be more challenging than they originally thought it would be. Just sitting and noticing sounds so easy! If you, like most, find it to be actually very hard, try to not get demoralized. You are in good company. It took the Buddha a few decades to achieve self-awareness, so it might take you a few years, too.

4) As with all of these exercises, one of the big challenges is to keep yourself from automatization and its mindless repetition. Deliberate practice only works if you are alert and seeking new information. This is exhausting!

Exercise 2: Improving Attunement with the Client, Part 1: What You See

The goal of this exercise is to develop your ability to better attune with your clients, a necessary component of building a therapeutic working alliance (Elliott, Bohart, Watson, & Greenberg, 2011; Norcross, 2011; Safran, Muran, & Eubanks-Carter, 2011). This exercise is part of a set of three exercises that build necessary skills for accurate attunement: noticing what you *see* the client doing, what you *hear* from the client, and what you *feel* internally while sitting with the client. These exercises work by artificially isolating each of these skills, so you can focus on each skill individually. This exercise focuses on the first specific component of attunement: what you see.

Research Base

One of the most robust findings from psychotherapy research over the past few decades is that the quality of the therapeutic relationship strongly predicts the success or failure of psychotherapy (Horvath, Del Re, Flückiger, & Symonds, 2011). Elements of the therapeutic relationship that have been identified as important include empathy, congruence, and the ability to work collaboratively with clients. These skills require deep and accurate awareness of the client's experience, including nonverbal and unconscious communication (Siegel, 2007). Notably, each of these variables accounts for the variance in psychotherapy outcome ten times more than therapist adherence and competence in a model (Norcross, 2011; see also Wampold & Imel, 2015, p. 257).

This exercise draws on research about *microexpressions*: very brief facial expressions of emotion that last a fraction of a second (Ekman, 1972). Microexpressions often convey thoughts and feelings that a person is suppressing (concealing on purpose) or repressing (unconsciously avoiding so they are not even aware of the feeling). Microexpressions often contrast with the content of a person's words. For example, a client may say, "I only feel love for my husband" while displaying a microexpression of disgust. In contrast, macroexpressions last longer (between a half-second and four seconds) and generally fit with the content of what someone is saying.

Research has suggested that training in microexpressions can help clients become more aware of other people's emotions (e.g., Russell, Green, Simpson, & Coltheart, 2008). Being able to accurately observe and understand microexpressions will also help therapists attune better with our clients. (See Paul Ekman's website at www.paulekman.com for more information and training resources on microexpressions.)

Instructions

1) Read through all of the following instructions before starting the exercise. Set aside at least 30 minutes for watching your own videos in a private place where you will not be disturbed. Keep notes during the exercise on a pad of paper or on your computer.

2) Pick a video of one of your recent psychotherapy sessions. This exercise works best if you use the same video for Exercises 2, 3, and 4.

3) When you start the video, turn the sound off. Watch the client very carefully. Notice his posture and any movements he makes. Try to watch his face very carefully and see if you can catch any fleeting microexpressions. Also try to notice any unconscious body movements the client makes (e.g., momentarily making a fist or clenching his hands). Consider these questions while you watch the video.

   a. What is your overall impression of the client's body? Is she tense, relaxed, shrinking back, assertive, etc.?

   b. Does the impression you get from watching the video with the sound off match your previous impression of the client, or does the client seem different with the sound off? For example, does the client seem more/less confident, more/less emotional, more/less motivated, etc.?

c. What do you see with the sound off that you might have missed if the sound had been on?

d. What kind of relationship with you is the client's body language expressing? Is it collaborative, afraid, receptive, domineering, passive, enthusiastic, etc.?

e. Do you have any new questions for the client that you haven't thought of previously?

f. If you can also see yourself in the video, notice any similarities or contrasts between your body language and the client's. For example, the client may be shrinking back in their seat while you lean forward.

g. Try mimicking the client's expressions with your own body. For example, mimic their facial expressions, body posture, etc. Notice any feelings you have when you do so. What does this tell you about the client's experience?

4) At the end of the exercise, write down a summary of your new perceptions, insights, or questions about the client.

Personal Observations

One weakness that frequently appears in my clinical work is failing to notice my clients' ambivalence about making changes in their lives. A common consequence of this is falling into an active/passive relational dynamic with my more ambivalent clients, in which I provide the will for change in therapy, thereby unconsciously colluding with the client's passivity. In other words, I proceed as if they were 100% on board, while they might actually be more like 50% or even 10%. I am especially prone to this mistake with clients who are women or from cultures that do not value self-assertiveness as much as American culture (e.g., Asian cultures).

I've used this exercise to help address this weakness by focusing on clients' body language that expresses their level of engagement or ambivalence. Whenever I have a case that is stuck, I use this exercise to reassess the client's engagement and frequently discover that clients who verbally express being fully engaged are also actually expressing considerable ambivalence with their bodies. Over time I've learned that our bodies often express our true feelings more accurately than our words.

Note

Most people know how to attune with others prior to receiving any clinical training, just from their upbringing. So the primary challenge of this exercise is keeping yourself out of automaticity (mindless repeating) and making yourself learn new, more accurate methods of observing your clients. Deliberate practice only works if you are alert and seeking new information. (This is exhausting!)

EXERCISE 3: IMPROVING ATTUNEMENT WITH THE CLIENT, PART 2: WHAT YOU HEAR

This exercise, part of a set of three exercises that build necessary skills for accurate attunement, focuses on the second specific component of attunement: what you hear.

Research Base

Like the other two exercises in this set on improving attunement with the client, this exercise is based on one of the most robust findings in psychotherapy research: the quality of the therapeutic relationship strongly predicts the success (or failure) of psychotherapy (Horvath et al., 2011; Norcross, 2011; Wampold & Imel, 2015).

Instructions

1) Read through all of the following instructions before starting the exercise. Set aside at least 30 minutes for watching your own videos in a private place where you will not be disturbed. Keep notes during the exercise on a pad of paper or on your computer.

2) Use the same video that you used in Exercise 2. When you start the video, turn the screen off so you can concentrate on the conversation. Listen very carefully to the client. Notice not just what she says, but how she says it: the tone of voice, the pace of speech, and any changes therein. Some questions to consider:

   a. Does the client talk a lot or leave a lot of space?

   b. Does the client make sense, or are her thoughts scattered or illogical?

    c.   Do the client's words pull you in closer or keep you at a distance?

    d.   Do the client's words match her tone? For example, if the client says she is sad, does she actually sound sad, or instead detached, or angry?

    e.   Do you get a different impression of the client from listening just to her verbal communication? For example, does the client seem more/less active or passive, more/less intelligent, more/less distant, etc.?

    f.   What might you miss if you were watching the client as well as listening?

    g.   Do you have any new questions for the client that you haven't thought of previously?

3)   Now start the video again and repeat the previous process while focusing on yourself, what you said during the session. Ask yourself all of the same questions listed above.

4)   At the end of the exercise, write down a summary of your new perceptions, insights, or questions about the client.

Personal Observations

The value of listening very carefully became clear to me in a consultation group I attended a few years after I graduated from my doctoral program. The group was run by my friend and mentor Victor Yalom. One day Victor taught us the skill of therapeutic authenticity. We role played one of my cases where therapy was stuck, with Victor playing the client and myself as therapist. Victor pointed out that that my voice sounded different. He asked, "Do you talk to your friends like that?" I realized that I had inadvertently adopted a therapist tone of voice—I was trying to be empathic rather than just responding authentically. Victor agreed and said, "Let's try again, and this time respond to me in a voice that is natural for you—how you would talk with a friend."

Note

As with the other two exercises from this group on attunement, the major challenge is keeping yourself from automaticity. Every time you do this exercise, try to hear something new or different from the client or yourself in the videotape. Deliberate practice only works by pushing yourself to the point of strain. If it feels easy or comfortable, then you're not advancing your skills.

EXERCISE 4: IMPROVING ATTUNEMENT WITH THE CLIENT, PART 3: WHAT YOU FEEL

This exercise focuses on the third specific component of attunement: what you feel. Like the other two exercises in this set, it focuses on building attunement skills, in this case the third specific component of attunement: what you, the therapist, feel.

Research Base

One important source of information for attuning with clients is your internal experience while sitting with the client—in other words, your feelings of empathy or lack of empathy (see Eisenberg & Eggum, 2009; Elliott et al., 2011). The importance of therapists developing awareness of their internal experience while sitting with their clients, also called *experiential reflection*, has been recognized across the spectrum of psychotherapy models, from psychodynamic psychotherapy (e.g., Safran et al., 2011) to third-wave cognitive behavioral models (e.g., Hayes, Follette et al., 2004; Wilson & Dufrene, 2008).

This exercise is supported by a large body of research on mirror neurons, parts of our brain that mirror or replicate the experience of people with whom we are interacting (Preston & de Waal, 2002). Mirror neurons have been hypothesized to be the neural substrate underlying empathy (Lamm, Batson, & Decety, 2007). By practicing tuning in to our internal experience, we can learn to better understand and attune with our clients: "our internal emotional state—generated via automatic mirroring processes—can become our intuitive 'theory' of the internal state of another" (Cozolino, 2010, p. 189).

Instructions

1) Read through all of the following instructions before starting the exercise. Set aside at least 30 minutes for watching your own videos in a private place where you will not be disturbed. Keep notes during the exercise on a pad of paper or on your computer.

2) Pick the same video that you used for Exercises 2 and 3. As you watch and listen to the client, try to tune out any thoughts you may have about psychotherapy technique, theory, or models. Instead, try to focus your attention on your own emotional and physical reactions that arise as you watch the tape. For example, do you get tense or relaxed? Do you feel detached, sad, angry, happy? Do your feelings stay steady or is there a rapid fluctuation of feelings? Some questions to consider:

   a. Is it easy or hard to tune in to your own feelings and bodily sensations while watching the video?

   b. What is your emotional stance towards the client in the video? For example, do you feel warmth, aversion, closeness, anger, disgust, or fear?

   c. Do you feel like you are accurately attuning with the client, or do you feel disconnected or lost while trying to attune with him or her?

   d. Do you feel any emotional pull to assume a certain role with the client? For example, do you feel like you want to be a savior, friend, romantic partner, or take any other role?

   e. Do you notice any emotions or physical sensations that are particularly uncomfortable like anxiety, stress, or any other unpleasant feelings? If so, are these clearly connected to what the client is communicating, or is it unclear why you have these experiences while sitting with the client? (Exercise 1 can be helpful for further exploring this area.)

   f. Do you have any new questions for the client that you haven't thought of previously?

3) At the end of the exercise, write down a summary of your new perceptions, insights, or questions about the client.

Notes

1) This exercise works best by focusing on your feelings that arise in the moment while you are watching the video instead of remembering feelings you may have had in the actual therapy session.

2) While this exercise is similar to Exercise 1, there is a key difference. The goal of this exercise is to notice what you experience *in relation to the client* in your video, while the goal of Exercise 1 is to simply notice

what you experience overall, which may be completely unrelated to the client.

3) Like the other two exercises in this set, the primary challenge of this exercise is keeping yourself from automaticity and making yourself learn new, more accurate methods of observing your clients.

EXERCISE 5: PSYCHOTHERAPY WARM-UPS

Unlike the other exercises in the book, this exercise does not aim at skill development. Rather, the goal is to get you warmed up for doing psychotherapy before your actual work starts. This includes getting you into the right frame of mind for psychotherapy, remembering your therapeutic role, your psychotherapy model, etc. This exercise warms up the skills that are fundamental for psychotherapy: observation/ attunement, intervention technique, and self-awareness. Use this exercise at the beginning of the day, before you see any clients. It is meant to be kept short (15 or 20 minutes), so it can be accessible for busy practitioners.

Research Base

The concept of warm-ups has not been used in psychotherapy, with the exception of drama therapy (Dayton & Moreno, 2004), although many other professional fields involve warm-ups as part of professional practice. Psychotherapy requires a frame of mind and relational stance that is distinctly different than any other we might use during the day, so there is reason to think that psychotherapy could benefit from warm-ups as much as any other profession. (Indeed, one could argue that psychotherapists do actually warm up, but do it during the first part of their first session of the day.) Empirical support for this exercise is provided by one recent study, which found that therapists who performed a brief centering exercise prior to seeing clients had better outcomes (Dunn, Callahan, Swift, & Ivanovic, 2013).

Instructions

1) Read through all of the following instructions before starting the exercise. Set aside at least 20 minutes for this exercise in a private place where you will not be disturbed. You do not need to keep notes

for this exercise. Ideally you will use a video of a client you will see today.

2) This exercise requires the use of a timer, set for five-minute intervals. Rotate through the following four skills in five-minute segments until you have done as many minutes as you have available for this exercise (e.g., if you do the exercise for 20 minutes, then you will rotate through each skill one time).

a. Skill 1: Attunement to the client's body language: Watch the client very carefully, noticing posture and any movements. Observe the client's face very carefully to see if you can catch any fleeting microexpressions. Also try to notice any unconscious body movements the client makes (for example, momentarily making a fist or clenching his hands). Some questions to consider:

- What is your overall impression of the client's body (tense, relaxed, shrinking back, assertive, etc.)?
- What kind of relationship with you is the client's body language expressing (collaborative, afraid, receptive, domineering, passive, enthusiastic, etc.)?

b. Skill 2: Attunement to the client's verbal language: Listen very carefully to the client. Notice not just what is said but how it is said—the client's tone of voice, pace of speech, and any changes therein.

- Do the client's words pull you in closer or keep you at a distance?
- Do the client's words match his tone? For example, if the client says he is sad, does he actually sound sad or instead detached, or angry?

c. Skill 3: Attunement to your experience: Try to focus your attention on your own emotional and physical reactions that arise as you watch the tape. For example, do you get tense or relaxed? Do you feel detached, sad, angry, happy? Do your feelings stay steady or do they fluctuate rapidly?

- What is your emotional stance towards the client in the video (e.g., warmth, aversion, closeness, anger, disgust, or fear)?
- Do you feel like you are accurately attuning with the client, or do you feel disconnected or lost while trying to attune with him?

d. Skill 4: Psychotherapy model: Run the tape until you make an intervention (when you say or do anything). Then answer these questions:

- What is your intervention called according to your model (e.g., "reflecting the client's feelings", "inquiring about the client's goal" or "making an interpretation")? If your activity did not fit the model, then note that.
- Was your intervention appropriate according to your model?
- If your intervention was not correct according to your model, try saying the correct intervention out loud to the video.

Personal Observations

I've found this exercise to be especially helpful when something in my life has affected me psychologically (e.g., I am sick, having arguments at home, just back from a vacation, etc.) For this exercise I try to focus on cases where I am stuck and clients whom I will see that day.

Notes

1) This exercise can be hard the first few times. The point isn't to get it perfect but to get your brain into the rhythm of paying attention to all of these different variables.
2) Don't overdo it. Just do enough to get warmed up.
3) Advanced students can shorten the length of each skill segment to four minutes, or one minute per skill.

Exercise 6: Building Psychotherapy Endurance

The goal for this exercise is to build your capacity to stay attuned and engaged for a 50-minute session. Anyone can sit in a chair and talk for 50 minutes, but psychotherapy involves a lot more than that. It is emotionally and intellectually taxing. This exercise builds your endurance and capacity for performing three broad domains of psychotherapy skills for 50 minutes:

- Staying emotionally attuned and engaged with the client.
- Remaining aware of your internal experience and how it may be affecting the treatment.

- Increasing meta-awareness of your psychotherapy model.

Because building endurance requires strain, it is essential to do this exercise for a sufficient period of time: at least ten minutes longer than your usual psychotherapy session. For example, if your usual session length is 50 minutes, do this exercise for 60 minutes. More time is better, as long as you don't overtax yourself.

Research Base

Deliberate practice can help build your capacity to attune and engage by straining your capacity, which activates a metabolic tear-and-rebuild process:

> When the human body is put under exceptional strain, a range of dormant genes in the DNA are expressed and extraordinary physiological processes are activated. Over time the cells of the body, including the brain ... will reorganize in response to the induced metabolic demands of the activity by, for example, increases in the number of capillaries supplying blood to muscles and changes in metabolism of the muscle fibers themselves. These adaptations will eventually allow the individual to execute the given level of activity without greatly straining the physiological systems.
>
> (Ericsson, 2006, p. 695)

Instructions

1) Read through all of the following instructions before starting the exercise. Try to do this exercise on a day when you are not seeing clients. Otherwise it will exhaust you and risk lowering the quality of your work. Likewise, don't do it at the end of a long work day when you are depleted. Do this exercise for at least ten minutes longer than your typical therapy session in a private place where you will not be disturbed. Keep notes during the exercise on a pad of paper or on your computer.

2) This exercise requires the use of a timer, set for five-minute intervals. Rotate through the following skills in five-minute segments. Keep rotating through the different skills until you have done as many minutes as you have available for this exercise (e.g., if you do the exercise for 60 minutes you will rotate through each skill 15 times).

3) You will inevitably lose focus during one or more of the skills (maybe all of them!). When you do, take note of which skill you were doing and what the client was doing at the time. Losing track can be a result of many variables: getting tired, an emotional or avoidance response to the client in the video, or some other internal process.

a. Skill 1: Attunement to the client's body language. Watch the client very carefully. Notice his posture and any movements he makes. Try to watch the client's face very carefully to see if you can catch any fleeting microexpressions. Also try to notice any unconscious body movements the client makes, for example, momentarily making a fist or clenching his hands. Some questions to consider:

- What is your overall impression of the client's body (tense, relaxed, shrinking back, assertive, etc.)?

- What kind of relationship with you is the client's body language expressing (collaborative, afraid, receptive, domineering, passive, enthusiastic, etc.)?

b. Skill 2: Attunement to the client's verbal language. Listen very carefully to the client. Notice not just what is said but how it is said, as well as the client's tone of voice, pace of speech, and any changes therein.

- Do the client's words pull you in closer or keep you at a distance?

- Do the client's words match his tone? For example, if the client says he is sad, does he actually sound sad or instead detached or angry?

c. Skill 3: Attunement to your experience. Try to focus your attention on your own emotional and physical reactions that arise as you watch the tape. For example, do you get tense or relaxed? Do you feel detached, sad, angry, happy? Do your feelings stay steady or rapidly fluctuate?

- What is your emotional stance towards the client in the video, for example, warmth, aversion, closeness, anger, disgust, or fear?

- Do you feel like you are accurately attuning with the client, or do you feel disconnected or lost while trying to attune with her?

    d. Skill 4: Psychotherapy model. Run the tape until you make an intervention. Then answer these questions:
- What is your intervention called according to your model? For example, "reflecting the client's feelings, inquiring about the client's goal," or "making an interpretation"? If your activity did not fit the model, then note that.
- Was your intervention appropriate according to your model?
- If your intervention was not correct according to your model, try saying the correct intervention out loud to the video.

4) When the exercise is complete, review your notes to see if there are any patterns in the times that you lost track of doing the skills.

Personal Observations

My model of therapy (ISTDP) specializes in doing three-hour initial sessions for new clients. When I first thought of doing this it terrified me! However, with practice I've built my endurance to the point where I can really use the time well. It now feels like a luxury to have three hours for the initial session. We can hit the ground running and get a lot done right away, which helps clients feel more confident and optimistic about our work together.

Notes

1) This exercise is quite challenging. It is very common to frequently lose track of doing the skills. Sometimes just staying aware of whether you are on track or not can itself be challenging. Feeling challenged is a good sign. It means you are stretching your capacity!

2) Like all exercises in this book, the goal is to gradually build awareness and capacity. Try not to criticize yourself when you notice yourself losing track. Don't be surprised if you tune out a lot more than you expected.

3) Try to keep persisting for the full 60 minutes even if you lose track a lot.

4) This exercise may feel very different than staying attuned with a real client. It's actually harder because you don't have a real client in front of you. This added challenge will improve your endurance.

Chapter 11

DELIBERATE PRACTICE EXERCISES FOR SPECIFIC MODELS

In the previous chapter we reviewed exercises to develop basic psychotherapy skills. Those basic skills are necessary for effective psychotherapy. However, they are often not sufficient. A case I had a few years ago illustrates this point with painful clarity.

My clients were a lesbian couple trying to repair their marriage. One was a veteran with depressive symptoms; the other had frequent panic attacks. They had been arguing increasingly over the past year. Their fights had recently escalated to yelling at each other, and the client with anxiety was starting to throw household objects at the wall. They came to marriage counseling because they wanted to learn better communication techniques and were worried about the impact of their fights on their teenage daughter.

Therapy seemed to start well. Both were eager for help. They were open about their problems and each was eager to discover her own contribution to the arguments. I connected quickly with the two of them. Therapy focused on helping them observe and understand their relational dynamics. In particular, we focused on the complex interplay of feelings and behavioral reactions they each had in their arguments, which often occurred during our therapy sessions.

The therapy appeared to work at first. Both clients left every session with new insights about their internal emotional processes that contributed to their problems as a couple. The veteran learned that she would shut down and withdraw to protect her partner from her anger, which she viewed as dangerous. Her partner learned that her anxiety was caused by sharp spikes in guilt, and that when her anxiety crossed a threshold she would lose control of her behavior and throw things. Both clients recognized that they were scared to express their love and longing for each other during and after their arguments, which inhibited them from reconnecting and repairing. In the first session they expressed hope and optimism for therapy to help. "You understand us," they told me.

However, red flags appeared early on. Despite their increasing insight and hope, every week the clients reported that their fights were worse. The routine outcome management data I gathered from them each week signaled that both were at risk of deterioration.

My therapeutic approach with this couple was based on two models of couples therapy I had studied: emotion-focused therapy (Greenberg, 2010; Johnson, 2002) and the psychobiological approach to couples therapy (Tatkin, 2012). Both are effective models for helping couples. However, my experience with these models was limited to reading textbooks and attending a few weekend workshops. I had not received any ongoing supervision in either model, I had not shown videotapes of my work with couples to an expert for feedback, and I had not practiced specific skills for either model. Thus, while my knowledge about these models was good, my actual skill in using the models was very limited, especially in challenging, high-arousal situations. I knew the "opening moves"—how to start therapy. These are pretty simple. But when the clients' feelings and anxiety got activated, things got complicated quickly, and I didn't understand the therapy models sufficiently to keep our work within the model. So, instead I reverted to my model for individual therapy. I switched back and forth between the two clients, like I was doing individual therapy for two people rather than treating a couple.

This pattern repeated each week: I would start the session using a model for couples therapy, but when the couple started arguing I got lost and switched to doing individual therapy with each partner. And each week the couple told me that therapy was helpful while their symptoms simultaneously got worse. This deterioration was confirmed by the ROM data. After a half-dozen sessions, we talked about their worsening symptoms and the option of transferring them to another therapist. Both clients wanted to continue with me. "You understand us so well," they said. "We learn so much in here. We just need to try harder at home."

We finally crossed the line around session 10. The veteran came to therapy alone. She said that her partner had been hospitalized for a

Figure 11.1 The therapeutic relationship
© Victor Yalom, www.psychotherapy.net

suicide attempt after one of their fights. Their daughter was staying with a grandparent who was trying to have the girl removed from the home.

The next week, after the partner left the hospital, I met with both clients and explained that I was going to refer them to a colleague who specialized in helping high-conflict couples. They resisted the transfer. "But you get us!" they said. When they left, all three of us were disappointed. While I had sufficient basic skills to attune with each client as an individual, I did not have the specialized skills to help them as a couple.

A musician needs to know more than just how to be on key; he also needs to learn each piece in perfect detail. A basketball player needs to know more than just how to dribble and shoot; she also needs to learn the plays for challenging situations. Therapists need more than basic facilitative interpersonal skills; we also need to learn specialized techniques for specific clinical situations.

The delicate balance between basic facilitative interpersonal skills and specific psychotherapy models is termed *appropriate responsiveness* (Stiles, Honos-Webb, & Surko, 1998). It is defined by Hatcher (2015):

> The therapist exercises flexible and astute judgment in the conduct of the
> session, anchored in perception of the client's emotional state, needs, and

goals, and integrates techniques and other interpersonal skills in pursuit of optimal outcomes for the client. *Appropriate responsiveness involves knowing what to do and when to do it.*

(p. 23, emphasis added)

This chapter presents exercises I have used to hone psychotherapy skills from specific models. The exercises in this chapter are:

Exercise 7: Psychotherapist activity/model assessment
Exercise 8: Studying expert videotapes
Exercise 9: Specific model exercises

Exercise 7: Psychotherapist Activity/Model Assessment

The goals of this exercise are to: 1) assess your *awareness* and *control* over your activity in session with your clients; 2) assess your *adherence* to your psychotherapy model; and 3) assess the *effectiveness* and *fit* of your psychotherapy model with your clients.

This exercise helps you develop more fine-grained control of what you do in your sessions. This is not to suggest that spontaneity is bad. On the contrary, being flexible, authentic, and adaptive is actually very important for psychotherapy (Hatcher, 2015). However, simply "winging it" throughout therapy sessions is not helpful. Like jazz, therapy works best from a balanced blend of spontaneity and deliberate control. The more awareness and control you can develop over your activity, the more you will be able to intentionally decide when to let yourself be spontaneous or deliberately adhere to a model.

Even seemingly can't-fail activities such as expressing empathy or positive regard can be experienced as intrusive, inauthentic, or incongruous by some clients if used at the wrong time or in the wrong way. Kazdin (2009) wrote that "the best patient care will come from ensuring that the optimal variation of treatment is provided" (p. 426). Thus, it is important for therapists to develop awareness and control of their activity in session.

This exercise will also deepen your understanding of your model, including how much you are adhering to your model and how well your model works for each particular client. This is called "metaknowledge" or "metacompetency" in your model (Hatcher, 2015).

Because this exercise requires a more advanced level of knowledge about a model, it is only appropriate as independent practice for more advanced students who already understand their model and have some experience using it. However, this exercise can be used by beginning students if they do it with their coach, which can be a good way to learn more about a psychotherapy model.

Research Base

This exercise is based on the large body of research showing that psychotherapy should be customized for each therapist and client (Beutler, 1999; Bohart & Wade, 2013; Hill & Knox, 2013; Owen & Hilsenroth, 2014). Regardless of which psychotherapy model is being used, research has suggested that a number of therapist activities can be either helpful or harmful, depending upon how and when they are used (Krause & Lutz, 2009; Stiles 2009). For example, therapist self-disclosures and interpretations should be used carefully and deliberately in psychotherapy (Barnett, 2011; Hatcher, 2015).

Instructions

1) Read through all of the following instructions before starting the exercise. Set aside at least 30 minutes for watching your own videos in a private place where you will not be disturbed. Keep notes during the exercise on a pad of paper or on your computer.
2) Start the video. Pause the video after you say or do anything (you probably won't get very far into the video). With the video paused, write down the following:
   a. Domain 1: Assess your *awareness* and *control* over your activity in session with your clients.
      - Can you understand what you did and why you did it? Or are you not sure? Note this.
      - Try to determine from the video whether you used your intervention deliberately or spontaneously. In other words, were you using forethought and planning when you acted, or was it unplanned or impulsive?
   b. Domain 2: Assess your *adherence* to your psychotherapy model.

- What is your intervention called according to your model? For example, "reflecting the client's "feelings", "inquiring about about the client's goal," or "making an interpretation"? If your activity did not fit the model, then note that.
- Was your intervention appropriate according to your model?
- If your intervention was not correct according to your model, try saying the correct intervention out loud to the video.

c. Domain 3: Assess the *effectiveness* and *fit* of your model for you with this client.
- What was the client's response to your intervention?
- Did the intervention seem helpful or not helpful for the client, or is it unclear, which is frequently the case in the immediate moment with a client?
- Did the client seem to understand why you used that intervention?
- Did the client seem to feel that it was helpful for achieving his goals?
- How comfortable did you feel using the intervention? Did it feel correct at the moment or forced?
- Do you think the intervention was the right thing to do at that time, regardless of the model?

3) When you are finished, review your notes from this video. See if you can determine any patterns. For example, what was your ratio of impulsive to deliberate actions? Were there any trends in the client's responses?

Personal Observations

One of the hardest challenges I've had in learning psychotherapy has been simultaneously holding confidence in my psychotherapy model and openness and flexibility to see where the model is inaccurate or lacking for each individual client. On one hand, using my model has enabled many of my clients to experience life-transforming changes and breakthroughs. On the other hand, the worst mistakes I've made as a therapist, the sessions that make me cringe in retrospect, were when I prioritized adherence to my model over attunement with my client (termed "overzealous transfer" by Schwartz, Chase, & Bransford, 2012).

I think this challenge comes from a fundamental misunderstanding of how psychotherapy works: thinking that it works because of something I do to the client (my effort and responsibility) rather than something the client does (her effort and responsibility). Early in my training a particularly observant client helped me understand this problem when she said to me, "Tony, you're doing fine. Relax!"

Notes

1) Although most clinical training is done through psychotherapy models, it is important to remember that, despite considerable effort, psychotherapy research has yet to find robust links between skills in specific models (termed "specific components") and client outcome (Wampold & Imel, 2015). This can be challenging for psychotherapists to hear, so it bears repeating: although we know that therapy generally works for about half of our clients, we don't know why. Of all those fancy therapy techniques we've learned—cognitive interweaves, interpretations, reframing, exposure with response prevention, Socratic dialogue, two-chair technique, thought diaries, systematic desensitization—not one has been identified by research as an essential ingredient for successful therapy. Furthermore, there is no evidence-based explanation of how and why they work (Kazdin, 2009). Thus, as therapists we must balance confidence in our models with humility about the limits of our knowledge.

2) This exercise is designed for advanced students who already understand their model and have some experience using it. However, it can be used by beginning students if they do it with their coach. Doing this exercise with a coach can be a good way to learn more about a psychotherapy model.

3) Some awkwardness is to be expected when learning a new psychotherapy model. This is not necessarily a bad sign. However, if the awkwardness or unease lasts a long time, that may be a sign to try a different model.

Exercise 8: Studying Expert Videotapes

Professionals in many fields train by studying the work of masters. For example, chess students study the transcripts of chess masters' games move by move. This exercise is how I study the sessions of expert therapists. Following the principles of deliberate practice (see Chapter 9), this exercise emphasizes active learning through behavioral rehearsal. Rather than just watching a videotape of a therapy session, I actively engage with it line by line.

Research Base

This exercise is based on the large body of research that shows active engagement to enhance skill acquisition (e.g., McGaghie & Kristopaitis, 2015; Taylor & Neimeyer, 2015).

Instructions

1) Read through all of the following instructions before starting the exercise. Set aside at least 30 minutes for watching a video in a private place where you will not be disturbed. Keep notes during the exercise on a pad of paper or on your computer.
2) Pick a session video by an expert therapist who works in the model you are trying to learn. Session videos by master therapists are available for purchase or rent. For example, www.psychotherapy.net has a large library of videos available for online streaming. Alternately, ask your supervisor or coach for one of their videos to study.
3) Start the video. Pause the video after the client says or does anything. With the video paused, write down what you would do next. Consider these questions:
    a. What would you say, do, or not do at this point? (Staying silent is an option.)
    b. What is your rationale for what you would say, do, or not do?
    c. Is your activity based on your psychotherapy model, or not?
4) Play the video. Note what the expert therapist does and then pause the video again. Answer these questions:
    a. How did the expert's activity compare or contrast with yours?
    b. Do you understand what they did and why they did it?
5) When you are finished, review your notes from this video. See if you can determine any patterns. Keep a list of questions to ask your supervisor or coach.

EXERCISE 9: SPECIFIC MODEL EXERCISES

Ideally, someday soon the developers of each psychotherapy model will publish collections of deliberate practice exercises specific to their models, similar to books on how to practice different musical instruments or different sports. Examples of specific skills for different psychotherapy treatment models are:

- CBT: Explaining an intervention plan, making links between the plan and the clinical formation (Roth, 2016).
- Psychodynamic psychotherapy: Making interpretations, identifying transference or countertransference (McWilliams, 1999).
- Client-centered psychotherapy: Active listening, expressing congruence (Rogers, 1961).
- Emotion-focused therapy: Experiential focusing, two-chair dialogue (Greenberg, 2010; Johnson, 2002).
- Motivational interviewing: Engaging, focusing, planning (Miller & Rollnick, 2012).

Until that day, it is up to each coach to develop exercises for the specific psychotherapy model used. There is a potentially limitless range of exercises that include the five deliberate practice components listed above. Following are three examples of model-specific exercises. I encourage you to experiment with creating your own.

Example 1: CBT

Step 1: Observing your own work via videotape. The therapist and coach identify a case that is stuck. To identify the case they use a combination of clinical judgment, routine outcome monitoring data, and the client's verbal report to the therapist. The therapist picks a video of a recent session.

Step 2: Getting expert feedback from a coach or consultant. The coach identifies a communication problem in the session—the therapist and client are having frequent disagreements about which of the client's problems are cognitive distortions versus unchangeable situations. When they disagree, the therapist starts lecturing the client, and the client becomes defensive. This is causing a rift in the working alliance and stalling the client's progress.

Step 3: Setting small incremental learning goals just beyond the clinician's ability. The coach teaches the therapist some techniques to help her more deeply explore the client's circumstances and beliefs. The coach keeps the teaching portion of the supervision short to allow more time for simulated behavioral rehearsal in the next step.

Step 4: Repetitive behavioral rehearsal of specific skills. The coach demonstrates the skill by role playing the therapist. Then they switch and the coach role plays the client while the therapist practices the new techniques. The coach continues the role play for 30 minutes, with increasingly more challenging dialogues, until the therapist has demonstrated that she has mastered the new techniques. Throughout the supervision, the coach aims to maximize the amount of time the supervisee is performing behavioral rehearsal, rather than talking about the skills. At the end of the hour, the coach assigns the following homework to the therapist:

> Spend an hour watching the video of this session with this client again. Pause the tape every time the client or you get defensive. Then say your new interventions to the video. Repeat this process for the entire video. This way you will be more prepared the next time you see this client.

Step 5: Continuously assessing performance via client outcome. In the next supervision session, the coach and therapist review a video of the following session with the client along with the client's ROM data. They try to assess the outcome of the previous training based on three different data sources: ROM data, the coach's clinical judgment, and the therapist's clinical judgment. Based on that assessment, they restart this process at Step 1.

Example 2: Emotion-Focused Therapy

Step 1: Observing your own work via videotape. The therapist and coach identify a case that is stuck. To identify the case they use a combination of clinical judgment, ROM data, and the client's verbal report to the therapist. The therapist picks a video of a recent session.

Step 2: Getting expert feedback from a coach or consultant. The coach identifies one of the therapist's skill deficits—when the client expresses grief, the therapist does not acknowledge or reflect her feelings, but instead tries to convince the client to stay more positive.

Step 3: Setting small incremental learning goals just beyond the clinician's ability. The coach teaches the therapist some techniques to help her reflect and explore the client's feelings. The coach keeps the teaching portion of the supervision short to allow more time for simulated behavioral rehearsal in the next step.

Step 4: Repetitive behavioral rehearsal of specific skills. The coach demonstrates the skill by role playing the therapist. Then they switch and the coach role plays the client while the therapist practices the new techniques. The coach continues the role play for 30 minutes, with increasingly more challenging dialogues, until the therapist has demonstrated that she has mastered the new techniques. Throughout the supervision, the coach aims to maximize the amount of time the supervisee is performing behavioral rehearsal, rather than talking about the skills. At the end of the hour, the coach assigns the following homework to the therapist:

> Spend an hour watching the video of this session with this client again. Pause the tape every time the client shows some feelings. Then practice your new techniques to the video. Repeat this process for the entire video. This way you will be more prepared the next time you see this client.

Step 5: Continuously assessing performance via client outcome. In the next supervision session, the coach and therapist review a video of the following session with the client along with the client's ROM data. They try to assess the outcome of the previous training based on at least three different data sources (see Chapter 9). Based on that assessment, they restart this process at Step 1.

Example 3: Short-Term Dynamic Psychotherapy

Step 1: Observing your own work via videotape. The therapist and coach identify a case that is stuck. To identify the case they use a combination of clinical judgment, ROM data, and the client's verbal report to the therapist. The therapist picks a video of a recent session.

Step 2: Getting expert feedback from a coach or consultant. The coach identifies a problem in the session—the client has not stated a clear and specific goal for therapy, so the therapy has been aimless and unproductive.

Step 3: Setting small incremental learning goals just beyond the clinician's ability. The coach teaches the therapist some techniques to help the client identify a clear and specific goal. The coach keeps the teaching portion of the supervision short to allow more time for simulated behavioral rehearsal in the next step.

Step 4: Repetitive behavioral rehearsal of specific skills. The coach demonstrates the skill by role playing the therapist. Then they switch and the coach role plays the client while the therapist practices the new techniques. The coach continues the role play for 30 minutes, with increasingly more challenging dialogues, until the therapist has demonstrated that she has mastered the new techniques. Throughout the supervision, the coach aims to maximize the amount of time the supervisee is performing behavioral rehearsal, rather than talking about the skills. At the end of the hour, the coach assigns the following homework to the therapist:

> Spend an hour watching older videos of sessions with this client. Notice when the client is vague or ambiguous about his goal for therapy. At that moment pause the video and practice asking the client about his specific goal for therapy, using your new techniques. Repeat this process using videos of a few different sessions. This way you will be more prepared the next time you see this client.

Step 5: Continuously assessing performance via client outcome. In the next supervision session, the coach and therapist review a video of the following session with the client along with qualitative outcome data obtained from the client after the previous session. They try to assess the outcome of the previous training based on at least three different data sources. Based on that assessment, they restart this process at Step 1.

Part IV

Sustaining Deliberate Practice

> The journey to truly superior performance is neither for the faint of heart nor for the impatient. The development of genuine expertise requires struggle, sacrifice, and honest, often painful self-assessment.
>
> *(Ericsson, Prietula, & Cokely, 2007, p. 2)*

I run deliberate practice groups for psychotherapists at all career stages. One of the universal comments that I hear from all participants in these groups is that deliberate practice is hard.

From beginning trainees to licensed psychotherapists with a few decades of experience and full private practices, everyone agrees that solitary deliberate practice is one of the most, if not the most, challenging and effortful activities they do during the day.

Why is it hard? A few of the reasons are:

- Deliberate practice requires considerable time and energy.
- Deliberate practice costs money (for expert feedback).
- Deliberate practice is emotionally challenging because it focuses on your uncomfortable learning edges, your clinical challenges and failures—the "other 50%."
- Deliberate practice in mental health is generally not encouraged, recognized, acknowledged, rewarded, or compensated.

This raises the question: How can we help psychotherapists sustain deliberate practice?

In the following chapters we'll review research and advice for encouraging and sustaining deliberate practice. These chapters include:

- The inner game: grit, self-regulation, and harmonious passion.
- Advice for supervisees: finding your path to expertise.
- Advice for supervisors: how to integrate deliberate practice into supervision.
- Advice for mid- and later career: lifelong learning.

CHAPTER 12

THE INNER GAME

Self-Regulation, Grit, and Harmonious Passion

> Nothing in the world can take the place of persistence. Talent will not; nothing is more common than unsuccessful men with talent. Genius will not; unrewarded genius is almost a proverb. Education will not; the world is full of educated derelicts. Persistence and determination alone are omnipotent.
>
> *(Calvin Coolidge)*

It is 10am and I am sitting at my desk. This is the time that I have scheduled in my calendar for deliberate practice. I have everything I need: videos of sessions of clients who are stalled or at risk of deterioration and exercises assigned by my coach. I'm in a quiet place where I won't be disturbed, and I've got a cup of hot coffee. Then the thoughts start.

"I wonder if I should check my email one last time?"

"I'm tired today. Maybe I should go to the gym before practicing, just to pick my energy up."

"I don't have enough focus to benefit from practice right now."

"I need to confirm if those checks I deposited have cleared yet."

"I should probably do some writing before I practice, just to make sure I meet that deadline."

"I'm really distracted by what my wife/daughter/friend/etc. said this morning, I probably can't practice right now."

"I'll just read the news first for a few minutes."

"The coffee is getting cold, I should go heat it up."

157

Deliberate practice is a war, and the battlefield is inside us. On one side is our motivation, our ambition to succeed, and our desire to help the other 50% of clients who are beyond our reach. On the other side is our fear, laziness, insecurity, procrastination, tension, boredom, doubts—our human weakness. This conflict has been called the *inner game* (Gallwey, 1997).

Since the turn of the twentieth century, psychologists have recognized the gap between what people are capable of doing and what they actually do. William James (1907) noted, "As a rule men habitually use only a small part of the powers which they actually possess and which they might use under appropriate conditions" (p. 14). Charles Darwin said, "Men did not differ much in intellect, only in zeal and hard work, and I still think this is an eminently important difference" (Ericsson & Charness, 1994). John Watson, the founder of behaviorism, said that "practicing more intensively than others ... is probably the most reasonable explanation we have today not only for success in any line, but even for genius" (Watson, 1930, p. 212).

For over 100 years, psychologists have endeavored to understand what drives human motivation: What characteristics and habits enable some to persevere, while most of us stop short of our potential?

One of the more prominent studies of this subject was conducted in the 1980s by Benjamin Bloom, a psychologist at the University of Chicago. Bloom and colleagues (1985) identified 120 experts across a broad range of fields—musicians, scientists, athletes, artists—and examined how these top performers achieved their success. They found that innate talent or natural ability was insufficient for the highest levels of accomplishment:

> The child who "made it" was not always the one considered to be "most talented." Many parents described another one of their children as having more "natural ability." The characteristics that distinguished the high achiever in the field from his or her siblings, most parents said, was a *willingness to work and a desire to excel.*
>
> (*p. 473, emphasis added*)

Recent research has shed light on this topic. In this chapter we will review three areas of research that offer the potential to improve our inner game: self-regulation, grit, and harmonious passion.[1]

SELF-REGULATION

The study of self-regulation was born from the pioneering work on self-efficacy by psychologist Albert Bandura in the 1970s at Stanford University. While studying how people overcome phobias, Bandura (1977) noticed that those who successfully overcame their phobias had different thoughts, attitudes, and beliefs about themselves when compared to people who couldn't overcome their phobias. Most notably, people who overcame their phobias had better *expectations* of themselves. They believed that they had the capacity or potential to succeed.

In the decades since, psychologists have drilled down in this area and discovered a host of mental processes that underlie and facilitate self-efficacy. Taken together, these mental processes are called *self-regulation*: "the self-generated thoughts, feelings, and actions that are strategically planned and adapted to the attainment of personal goals" (Zimmerman, 2006, p. 705).

Put simply, self-regulation is the collection of strategies that successful people use to win the inner game. Psychologists have identified three main variables of self-regulation (Bandura, 1986):

1) *Personal self-regulation.* These are the thoughts, attitudes, and beliefs we have about ourselves. For example, our self-confidence, self-acceptance of our mistakes, and patience with ourselves when learning a difficult skill.
2) *Environmental self-regulation.* This is how we adjust our environment to help us achieve our goals. For example, changing the temperature in an office or playing soft music in the background.
3) *Behavioral self-regulation.* These are the behavioral adjustments we make to improve our performance. For example, not checking email or Twitter while practicing.

These three forms of self-regulation create positive or negative feedback loops that either support or interfere with progress.

One of the ways to improve our self-efficacy is to better understand and control our self-regulation. Specifically, researchers have found the following to be helpful (Zimmerman, 2006):

1) Using positive self-talk and imagery of success.

2) Using time management (e.g., determining the best time of day to practice).
3) Actively managing your environment (e.g., only practicing in a location where you will not be disturbed).
4) Self-monitoring your practice (e.g., keeping a deliberate practice journal; see Chapter 9).
5) Attributing your success or failure to your practice rather than your personal traits or luck.
6) Aiming to improve the quality of your practice more than the quantity.
7) Constantly assessing and adapting practice strategies to address new life challenges (e.g., the birth of a child or a new job).

Another component of self-regulation is effective goal setting (Locke & Latham, 2002). Researchers (Zimmerman, 2006) have found that:

1) Experts set more specific goals, while amateurs tend to set more general goals.
2) Experts use goals that involve both process and outcome (e.g., "My goal is to practice smarter and thus do better"), while amateurs use goals that just focus on outcome ("My goal is just to do better").
3) Experts use strategic planning to achieve their goals, while amateurs focus mostly on effort.
4) Experts set goals that are realistic, while amateurs often set goals that are too high or too low.

GRIT

Research on the inner game has recently become the focus of psychologists in the field of positive psychology. A relatively new domain of psychology born at the turn of the twenty-first century, positive psychology turns the traditional focus of psychological research (pathology, diseases, and symptoms) on its head and instead uses scientific methods to study strengths that lead to achievement, satisfaction, and well-being (Seligman, 2012).

Angela Duckworth and colleagues (Duckworth, Peterson, Matthews, & Kelly, 2007), researchers in the field of positive psychology, reviewed a century of psychological research on achievement along with the findings of more recent studies, looking for any notable traits or characteristics that uniquely predicted success. In their review, they found one particular characteristic that is uniquely important for success: *grit*, which they defined as "perseverance and passion for long-term goals. Grit entails working strenuously toward challenges, maintaining effort and interest over years despite failure, adversity, and plateaus in progress" (p. 1087).

Grit is different than other traits that have traditionally been credited with success. While intelligence, hard work, conscientiousness, and self-control are sufficient for winning the battle, grit is necessary for winning the war. Grit is about long-term perseverance and focus, also known as follow-through: "The gritty individual approaches achievement as a marathon; his or her advantage is stamina. Whereas disappointment or boredom signals to others that it is time to change trajectory and cut losses, the gritty individual stays the course" (Duckworth et al., 2007, p. 1087).

One of the larger studies in this area was conducted by Lauren Eskreis-Winkler, one of Duckworth's graduate students, and colleagues. Their study found strong evidence linking grit with success across a wide range of endeavors: "Grittier soldiers were more likely to complete an Army Special Operations Forces selection course, grittier sales employees were more likely to keep their jobs, grittier students were more likely to graduate from high school, and grittier men were more likely to stay married" (Eskreis-Winkler, Duckworth, Shulman, & Beal, 2014, p. 1).

DEVELOPING GRIT

After discovering grit, the next step was to study whether it could be cultivated. In other words, is it possible to help students develop the ability to persevere and maintain focus through hard challenges?

To examine this question, Eskreis-Winkler and colleagues (in press) ran a series of studies that tested whether "nonexperts" could be encouraged to engage in sustained deliberate practice. In one study, grade school and college students were given a series of increasingly difficult math problems on a computer. The students were divided into two groups. The first group was instructed to simply do the problems. The other group of students was given a series of interventions that emphasized the necessity and benefits of deliberate practice. For example, one statement was, "If you are frustrated or confused *while practicing* ... it can mean you are working on your weaknesses." Another statement was, "when you practice and everything goes perfectly, it may feel good, but it's probably a sign that you're not challenging yourself." Another said, "Many people think talent is all that matters ... actually scientific evidence suggests that *deliberate practice* is incredibly important to improvement and success" (p. 3). To emphasize the potential for distractions, all students in the study were given the freedom to use YouTube, Facebook, and Instagram on their computers during the study. (In retrospect, it's amazing that even one math problem was completed!)

The results of the study were clear: students who received the interventions encouraging deliberate practice had both improved attitudes about deliberate practice and better academic achievement. Notably, the interventions targeting motivation for deliberate practice were crucial for the results: "Students who were taught the tenets of deliberate practice without an accompanying motivational lesson (targeting self-relevant expectancies and values) did not improve their deliberate practice behavior or their achievement" (Eskreis-Winkler et al. 2016, p. 14).

HARMONIOUS PASSION

So far the gist of this chapter has been "no pain, no gain." And I have to admit that for many readers this may not feel terribly uplifting. With all this talk of conflict, combat on an inner battlefield, self-regulation, and grit, it would be understandable to ask yourself, "Why follow your passion if it feels like misery?"

The short answer: you shouldn't ... not if it feels like misery, at least. This finding comes again from the field of positive psychology. Robert Vallerand, a positive psychology researcher in Canada, has studied the relationship people have with their work, their subjective experience of passion. Through a series of studies involving amateurs and experts from a wide range of fields, Vallerand and colleagues (2003) have found that people have two broad types of passion: harmonious passion and obsessive passion. Together, these are termed the *dualistic model of passion*.

Harmonious passion occurs when you are internally aligned with your work, when you are using it, rather than it using you. Vallerand, Houlfort, & Forest (2014, p. 87) describe this as:

> autonomous internalization of the activity into the person's identity and
> self ... when individuals have freely accepted the activity as important for

them without any contingencies attached to it ... a motivational force to engage in the activity willingly and engenders a sense of volition and personal endorsement about pursuing the activity.

As the term suggests, harmonious passion feels good. It "allows the person to fully partake in the passionate activity with a secure sense of self-esteem, flexibility, and an openness to experience the world in a nondefensive, mindful manner" (p. 90). Harmonious passion is characterized by being able to take breaks or leave the work for a time when necessary, without guilt or remorse. It protects against depression and anxiety and facilitates flow and satisfaction (Vallerand et al., 2014).

In contrast, obsessive passion is forced on oneself. It is something we feel that we *need* to do in order to maintain a positive self-image or acceptance by others. Obsessive passion is motivated by a lack of sufficient self-esteem rather than a desire to engage in work. As you may guess, obsessive passion feels bad, like a bitter pill you have to take but don't enjoy. "With obsessive passion, internally controlling rather than integrative self-processes are at play leading the person to engage in the activity with a fragile and contingent sense of self-esteem" (Vallerand et al., 2014, p. 90). Research has shown that obsessive passion can lead to emotional problems like exhaustion, burnout, and frustration or rumination at work (Vallerand et al., 2014). Furthermore, it is less effective at improving performance (Bonneville-Roussy, Lavigne, & Vallerand, 2011; Vallerand et al., 2008).

Although willpower clearly plays an important role in deliberate practice, it must be done in a loving and constructive way, like the willpower a loving parent uses to take care of a child rather than how a stern prison guard forces a prisoner to comply. Engaging in deliberate practice requires navigating a delicate internal balance: on one hand, harnessing your self-regulation and grit to repeatedly face your failures and seek out new skills, while on the other hand cultivating a compassionate and loving relationship with yourself regarding your learning.

Deliberate practice must be a constructive, nonpunitive learning experience, something you want to do, rather than are forced to do by others or yourself. Nissen-Lie and colleagues (2015) summarized this point succinctly: "Love yourself as a person, doubt yourself as a therapist" (p. 1).

NOTE

1 Note that the inner game is not the only challenge in engaging in deliberate practice. Situational, social, and cultural variables can help or hinder achievement, including insufficient time, money, childcare, etc. These factors are discussed further in Chapter 16.

CHAPTER 13

ADVICE FOR SUPERVISEES

Finding Your Path to Expertise

This book is about using deliberate practice to improve your clinical effectiveness, across your entire career span. In this chapter I will discuss some challenges and opportunities that pertain specifically to the beginning stage of your career. This chapter presents advice for trainees: therapists who are in graduate school, not yet licensed for independent practice, and still under formal supervision. (Chapter 15 is for clinicians at later stages of their career.)

However, before we get to my advice, I'd like to start this chapter by recognizing a major problem with the whole idea of using deliberate practice in graduate school. If you are a graduate student, this problem has undoubtedly already occurred to you so far while reading this book.

WHY DELIBERATE PRACTICE DOES NOT WORK FOR EVERYONE

Deliberate practice takes time, energy, and focus. Here's the problem: we all know that in graduate school, these are three things you don't have a surplus of.

Graduate school is full of tasks you *have* to do, like being pulled in 20 directions at once. On any given week you have an exam on Monday, a paper due on Tuesday, a new client on Wednesday, an internship application to complete by Thursday, and a research thesis proposal due on Friday.

You must complete these assignments, or else you will be kicked out of your graduate program.

Because you *must* do these tasks, the question of whether you *want* to do them is largely irrelevant. All of the tasks listed above can be accomplished through begrudging compliance. You are graded on ability to complete papers, exams, and research; not how much heartfelt desire you felt while doing them.

Because of this, graduate students usually quickly figure out that the best way to successfully navigate graduate school is what I call the strategy of *smart compliance*: figuring out whom you have to please, what they want, and how to comply with the least amount of time and energy.

Unfortunately, smart compliance doesn't work for deliberate practice.

Deliberate practice is totally different than pretty much everything else in graduate school: it only works if you put your heart into it. Deliberate practice requires intentionally straining your own learning capacity; simply going through the motions of practice doesn't help. As Ericsson and Pool (2016) say, "It isn't enough to simply follow a teacher's or coach's directions" (p. 99).

Deliberate practice only helps if you *want to push yourself*. Winner (1996) called this a "rage to master" a skill; I suggest simply a strong desire to improve is sufficient. Otherwise, it's just a waste of time and energy.

The truth is that you don't *need* to use deliberate practice or aim for expertise. Competency is sufficient for a successful career in mental health, and the vast majority of trainees achieve competency in graduate school without any deliberate practice.

For this reason, I advise you to take a moment and consider two things. First, do you really *want* to try using deliberate practice? Put aside the compliance and obligation, and take a moment to be selfish: How much do you desire skills beyond competency? How much do you crave expertise? How much are you willing to sacrifice to be at the top of your field in 10 or 20 or 30 years?

Second, after you have assessed whether you want to use deliberate practice, take a look at your life circumstances to see if you *can* use deliberate practice. How much time, energy, and focus can you dedicate to skill improvement? Most graduate students go through significant periods of time where they are maxed out. Graduate students who have young children at home may find themselves stretched particularly thin. If this is the case for you, then consider keeping your experiments with deliberate practice small, or possibly waiting until you have more resources. Telling yourself that you have to practice when you do not have the resources is a recipe for burnout. Aim for competence now, and leave advanced skill development for later. You have your whole career ahead of you.

If and when you choose to take this path, here is some advice.

DELIBERATE PRACTICE REQUIRES A GOOD COACH

The process of deliberate practice requires effective coaching (Ericsson, 2015). Coaches provide essential components of skill development that are very difficult or impossible to do on your own. These include:

1) Performance feedback: coaches tell you what you're getting right and where you're off track.
2) Guidance on skill development: coaches identify skills just beyond your current ability, and show you how to learn them.
3) Morale: coaches help you with your *inner game*: sustaining your morale when times are tough, through the inevitable failures, frustrations, and boredom that accompany skill development.

You might be thinking, "Doesn't my supervisor fill the role of my coach?"

Yes, helping you develop skills is one of your supervisor's jobs. However, it is unfortunately not their highest priority. While there is considerable overlap between clinical supervision and coaching, there is one crucial difference: the goal of a coach is to help you master specific skills, while your clinical supervisor's primary responsibility is to ensure your clinical *competence*.

YOUR SUPERVISOR'S TOP PRIORITY

Clinical supervision is widely recognized as having two broad and overlapping goals: ensuring client welfare and aiding supervisee professional development (Bernard & Goodyear, 2014; Falender & Shafranske, 2004). These two goals of course have considerable overlap— helping your professional development should, ideally, line up nicely with improving your client's welfare.

Unfortunately, the reality of clinical supervision is not so ideal: a lot of your supervisor's time and attention is consumed by activities that are essential components of *competent* health-care delivery, but are unrelated to developing your clinical skills (for example, checking your paperwork, billing, and scheduling).

Take a look at the biannual formal evaluations your supervisor must complete about you for your graduate program. These typically have a long laundry list of different criteria important for *competency in health-care delivery*, such as professionalism, record keeping, collegiality with staff and peers, openness to supervision, knowledge about psychotherapy theory, etc. These criteria are essential for competent work in health care. However, attending to all of them in supervision simply leaves less time, energy, and focus for skill development.

I recently gave a presentation at the annual meeting of the Association of Psychology Training Clinics. In the audience were about 100 directors and supervisors from clinical training sites. At the beginning of the talk I asked the audience, "If you ever have to choose between the two responsibilities of clinical supervision—ensuring client welfare and aiding supervisee professional development—how many of you would choose the first (client welfare)?" Every hand in the room shot up.

Your supervisor will never be fired or disciplined by the board of licensing if you fail to develop your skills a step beyond competence. However, she (or her boss) could get in serious trouble if your client deteriorates and the licensing board finds out that you don't complete your notes, treatment plans, and other paperwork correctly.

Before I come across as negative about clinical supervision, I want to emphasize two things here: first, your supervisor almost certainly *wants very much* to help your skill development (that's why most supervisors take the job). Second, helping you provide competent care is an *important step towards* clinical excellence. It just often isn't sufficient, due to the scope of the job and logistical limits beyond your supervisor's control.

For this reason, if you really want to push your skill development with deliberate practice, I recommend that you find coaching to supplement your clinical supervision.

HOW TO CHOOSE A COACH

Choose a coach[1] with care! Your coach can have a profound influence on your life, both professionally and personally. Their job is to get under your skin: to know your blind spots, weaknesses, and anxieties; your passions, what motivates you, and drives your quest for improvement.

The experience of good coaching feels very intimate, but must of course also respect professional boundaries (for a thorough discussion of this topic, see Barnett, 2008). This is a tough balancing act for the coach, and not everyone can do it.

Don't assume that just because someone is an expert therapist they are also a good coach—providing psychotherapy and teaching psychotherapy are two very different skills. Many excellent therapists are poor at providing training.

When you are considering a training program or coach, ask to observe a class first. Here is a list of positive and negative traits to look for while you observe the class.

Recommended:

1) Coaches who use videotapes of your work with real clients to assess your learning challenges and opportunities.
2) Coaches who focus on teaching skills at each trainee's threshold of learning.
3) Coaches who teach skills using active, experiential learning methods such as role plays (also called behavioral rehearsal).
4) Coaches who assign deliberate practice homework customized to each student.
5) Coaches who show videotapes of their own work with real clients.
6) Coaches who use ROM, qualitative methods of assessing outcome (McLeod, in press), and/or follow-up data from clients.
7) Coaches who teach you how to collect client feedback and use it in their coaching (for example, with the Session Rating Scale; Miller et al., in press).
8) Coaches who earnestly collect feedback from their trainees.
9) Coaches who establish a non-hierarchical, collaborative, and open atmosphere in their trainings.
10) Coaches who are open and respectful of other psychotherapy models and teachers.
11) Coaches who are mindful of avoiding harmful dual roles with their trainees (Barnett, 2008).
12) Coaches who make a systematic effort to track their own clinical outcomes and make that data available to the public (unfortunately this is currently very rare, but hopefully will soon become standard for the field).

Questionable or concerning:

1) Coaches who create hierarchical or closed atmospheres in their training.
2) Coaches who insist that their psychotherapy model is best, or denigrate other models.
3) Coaches who cultivate a cult-like community (a signal of this is that their students will refer to them in exclusively glowing terms and denigrate other teachers).
4) Coaches who provide psychotherapy for their trainees.

Where to Find Coaching

The most common venues for clinical training are:

1) Psychotherapy Training Programs.
2) Consultation Groups.
3) Individual consultation.
4) Peer consultation.

Psychotherapy Training Programs

The most common venue for clinical training outside of graduate school is in training programs for the major psychotherapy models. For example, there are training programs for CBT, DBT, emotion-focused therapy, eye movement desensitizing and reprocessing, psychodynamic psychotherapy, etc. These are often called "post-graduate" or "continuing education" programs, because they are geared towards licensed therapists seeking continuing education. (While you do not need continuing education credit as a graduate student, the training can still be very valuable.)

Many of these programs offer deeply discounted rates for graduate students. They are also good for networking and setting up a referral base if you will be going into private practice after graduate school.

Some of these programs offer certificates in their psychotherapy models. Note that getting a certificate typically represents attaining a baseline level of competency in a psychotherapy model, and is itself insufficient for advancing your clinical skills. Rather, what will really help you improve your effectiveness is engaging in long-term continuous training (see below).

Consultation Groups

Another common venue for training is consultation groups. These are typically run by a senior clinician and have three to eight students, making them cost effective. They are also good for networking and building a referral base. The best way to find a consultation group is to approach a senior clinician you respect and ask them if they offer one, or would consider starting one. In my experience, many senior clinicians are eager to pass on what they have learned, and are very responsive when approached about starting consultation groups.

Individual Consultation

Perhaps the ideal form of coaching is a long-term, one-on-one relationship. This format provides the most time for the coach to review the learner's work, offer feedback, teach skills, and guide deliberate practice. The downside to this format is cost: experienced psychotherapy supervisors/consultants are expensive. For this reason, most learners use a combination of consultation groups combined with less frequent individual coaching.

Peer Consultation

The most cost-effective method of coaching is peer consultation, in which a group of learners gather together regularly to watch each other's videos, provide feedback, and practice skills. The advantages of this format are cost (it's usually free) and the opportunity for building comradery and supporting morale. The disadvantage is that the absence of an expert coach can limit skill acquisition. Some peer-consultation groups will occasionally bring expert coaches in periodically to teach skills. Like other coaching formats, peer consultation works best in a long-term relationship, so group members get to know each other's strengths and opportunities for growth.

Following are some additional suggestions for psychotherapy training.

1) Aim for long-term training relationships and avoid short-term or sporadic training. The best training occurs in a long-term relationship in which the coach has sufficient opportunity to provide training and then see how you respond to it over time by watching videos of your work (for example, meeting weekly for at least a year). This time allows them to really get to know your weaknesses and growth edges. Attending a few weekend intensives sporadically can be fun and exciting, but is not effective for skill acquisition: it is actually more like psychotherapy tourism than solid clinical training.

2) Engage in individual or small-group training. This is necessary for personalized performance feedback, an essential component of deliberate practice. It also allows the coach to better assess your learning needs and learning style. Being one of many people in a workshop or lecture audience can be sufficient for learning theory, but doesn't help with skill acquisition.

NOTE

1 The term "coach" refers to anyone teaching you psychotherapy skills. Other common terms for this include "consultant," "trainer," etc. I use the term coach to emphasize the importance of teaching skills.

CHAPTER 14

ADVICE FOR SUPERVISORS

Integrating Deliberate Practice into Supervision

> No matter what the initial characteristics (or gifts) of the individuals, unless there is a long and intensive process of encouragement, nurturance, education, and training, the individuals will not attain extreme levels of capability.
>
> *(Bloom, 1985, p. 3)*

This chapter offers some advice for supervisors who want to experiment with integrating deliberate practice in their supervision. The term "supervisor" in this chapter refers to a formal training relationship in which the supervisor is legally responsible for the supervisee's work.

Incorporating deliberate practice into supervision involves the following changes:

1) Increasing the focus on skills (primary challenge: time).
2) Using active versus passive learning (primary challenge: restraint).
3) Working at the threshold of strain (primary challenge: maintaining collaboration).
4) Using sufficient repetition (primary challenge: effort).
5) Making homework an integral part of learning (primary challenge: culture).
6) Assessing performance through client outcome (primary challenge: not getting caught in the model).
7) Addressing experiential avoidance (primary challenge: navigating boundaries).

8) Supporting trainees' inner game for career-long deliberate practice (primary challenge: cultivating harmonious passion).

Additional guidance on integrating deliberate practice into clinical supervision can be found in Goodyear & Rousmaniere (in press).

CHANGE 1: INCREASING THE FOCUS ON SKILLS

Deliberate practice works by focusing on specific, discrete skills. This is different than traditional supervision, which is typically structured around monitoring cases. However, the two can be compatible. You can use a case review (watching a videotape of a recent session with the trainee) to identify specific skills for the trainee to practice.

The primary challenge is making sure to set aside sufficient time (e.g., 15–30 minutes per skill) to practice specific skills after you review each case. If you are responsible for more than a few of the trainee's cases, you probably won't have sufficient time to review all the cases and practice skills. In this instance, it is recommended that you assign the trainee deliberate practice homework to practice specific skills, and schedule a separate time for the trainee to practice skills with you or someone else who can serve as a skills coach (e.g., a more advanced student).

CHANGE 2: USING ACTIVE VERSUS PASSIVE LEARNING

"Passive experience has no place either for therapists or teachers in a deliberate practice environment" (McGaghie & Kristopaitis, 2015, p. 224). Deliberate practice only occurs when a trainee is actively practicing a skill (behavioral rehearsal). This stands in contrast to traditional supervision, where passive learning (discussion with the supervisor) is paramount.

Ericsson and Pool (2016) call this the difference between learning knowledge versus learning a skill: "The traditional approach has been to provide information about the right way to proceed and then mostly rely on the student to apply that knowledge. Deliberate practice, by contrast, focuses solely on performance and how to improve it."

The primary challenge in focusing on skills is self-restraint. It can be tempting to spend more time talking about psychotherapy theory than focusing on skills (e.g., talking about case conceptualization, treatment planning, nuances of the psychotherapy model, similar cases, etc.). Supervisors have an abundance of knowledge about psychotherapy and can easily fill the allotted supervision time sharing their knowledge. This is contraindicated in deliberate practice.

Talking about theory is tempting because it feels better and is much easier than deliberate practice. The supervisor gets to sound smart, while the trainee doesn't have to struggle with a skill at her learning edge. Furthermore, the supervisor doesn't have to struggle to develop more effective role-play exercises based on assessing the therapist's need. Here's a simple rule of thumb: if the supervisor is talking, the trainee is not practicing.

CHANGE 3: WORKING AT THE THRESHOLD OF STRAIN

Deliberate practice works by working at optimal strain, which involves practicing skills just beyond the trainee's current skill threshold, so he or she can learn incrementally without becoming overwhelmed (Ericsson, 2006). The challenge presented by this level of effort is maintaining a collaborative relationship with the trainee, where the trainee feels personally invested in maximizing his or her effort, rather than passively obeying the supervisor. This challenge is exacerbated by the involuntary, hierarchical, and evaluative nature of the supervisory relationship. Trainees don't have the option of opting out of supervision (Ellis et al., 2014; Ladany et al., 1996). This can lead to an invisible problem of compliance without effort, in which the trainee simply goes through the motions of deliberate practice but doesn't push him or herself to the point of strain. Mere compliance is ineffective for deliberate practice. The rewards you get are directly proportional to the effort you put in.

Supervisees must feel some collaborative ownership of the process, or else they risk falling into passive compliance. Because of the hierarchical and evaluative nature of supervision, it is the responsibility of the supervisor to start these discussions and invite collaboration in supervision (Ellis et al., 2014). Supervisors should involve supervisees collaboratively in supervision, so they feel invested in the process. Supervisors should explicitly talk with trainees about their goals for supervision, their preferences for how it is conducted, and the quality of the bond between the trainee and the supervisor (Rousmaniere & Ellis, 2013; for detailed advice on this topic, see Ladany, Friedlander, & Nelson, 2016).

Change 4: Using Sufficient Repetition

Deliberate practice only works if there is sufficient repetition of behavioral rehearsal for trainees to consolidate their skill acquisition. This requires significant effort by both the trainee and supervisor. Repetitively practicing skills beyond a trainee's threshold is simply more exhausting than teaching and discussing psychotherapy theory. Having the trainee attempt the same skill again and again can feel boring for the supervisor and frustrating for the trainee. Thus there is a natural tendency for both coaches and trainees to drift back into teaching or discussions about psychotherapy models or theory, which is much more comfortable and enjoyable than skill rehearsal. The primary challenge in having sufficient repetition is maintaining a high level of effort throughout supervision.

Change 5: Making Homework an Integral Part of Learning

In the first study on deliberate practice, Ericsson and colleagues (1993) discovered that the only variable that predicted the skill of violinists was the amount of time they spent in solitary deliberate practice: "There is complete correspondence between the skill level of the groups and their average accumulation of practice time alone with the violin" (p. 379).

Unfortunately, solitary deliberate practice is much harder than deliberate practice with a coach or peers. The trainee is alone, without others to provide encouragement or discipline. This poses a significant challenge for psychotherapy because unlike music, athletics, and many other disciplines we don't have a culture of solitary practice. In these other fields it would be unthinkable to train without solitary deliberate practice, but for psychotherapy that is the norm. Thus, for deliberate practice to work, supervisors must create a culture of solitary practice by emphasizing the importance of skill-focused homework. This can be done by assigning homework after every supervision and then taking a few minutes during the next supervision to review the trainee's experience from doing the homework. Ask trainees to keep a deliberate practice journal (see Chapter 9) and review the journal with trainees in supervision.

Change 6: Assessing Performance through Client Outcome

Traditional supervision, and especially supervision of empirically supported treatments, have used trainees' adherence and fidelity to treatment models as criteria to evaluate trainee performance. Deliberate practice is different. Client outcome is the bottom-line evaluative criterion for assessing performance.

This can be disorienting for many supervisors, who were trained with a focus on adherence and fidelity. However, psychotherapy research has shown little connection between adherence to a model and client outcome (Branson et al., 2015; Webb et al., 2010). Furthermore, strict adherence to a model without flexibility has been shown to negatively impact outcomes (Hatcher, 2015). However, use of a model is essential for psychotherapy (see Chapter 11). Thus, the primary challenge in assessing client outcome is avoiding getting caught up in the psychotherapy model. There is a tricky balance between using a model to provide psychotherapy and retaining sufficient freedom from the model to stay flexible and not get caught in blind spots.

Coaches should use at least three different data sources for evaluating client outcome to triangulate toward a more reliable assessment. The most common are (1) client report, (2) coach/therapist judgment, (3) ROM data, (4) qualitative data from the client, and (5) collateral information from other people who know the client (e.g., their spouse, boss, teacher, etc.). See Chapter 9 for more on outcome assessment.

Change 7: Addressing Experiential Avoidance

The problem of experiential avoidance predates deliberate practice. It has been recognized as an impediment to training in a wide range of psychotherapy models (see Chapter 8 for a review). However, the repetitive focus on behavioral rehearsal (active learning) in deliberate practice is emotionally evocative and thus exposes or highlights experiential avoidance in a way that traditional supervision does not. In fact, in traditional supervision it is possible never to encounter experiential avoidance because the focus is on passive learning (talking about theory or models), which is simply less emotionally evocative than active behavioral rehearsal.

The emotionally evocative nature of deliberate practice can serve to "flush out" experiential avoidance and thus offers a good opportunity for learning and growth if the supervisor is able to be aware of the process and guide trainees through exercises to help them become aware of their own process. An example exercise for this is presented in Chapter 10. This is not possible if the supervisor's own experiential avoidance is strong enough to make him or her blind to the process.

The primary challenge in addressing experiential avoidance is navigating boundaries. Focusing on experiential avoidance is deeply personal and vulnerable. Thus it is important to keep a clear line between supervision and psychotherapy. Because supervision is involuntary, hierarchical, and evaluative, it is simply not an appropriate place for supervisees to share deeply vulnerable memories, thoughts, or feelings as they would in their own psychotherapy (e.g., memories of abuse, etc.).

To maintain clear boundaries, supervisors should explicitly clarify the difference between supervision and psychotherapy with their trainees. For example, a supervisor could say,

> We are going to do an exercise where we will watch a video of your session, and I will ask you to reflect on any aversive emotional reactions you may feel regarding your client. We are doing this because it is important for you to learn to become aware of your own experiential avoidance. However, because this is supervision and not psychotherapy, I will not ask you to identify the aversive emotions, thoughts, or reactions you may have. Instead, just write them down in your personal notes. Your own psychotherapy can be a good, safe place to explore those emotions, thoughts, or reactions. In psychotherapy you have full control of the process and don't have to worry about judgments or evaluations.

For a thorough discussion on this topic and advice for navigating the tricky boundaries of supervision, see Barnett (2008).

Change 8: Supporting Trainees' Inner Game for Career-Long Deliberate Practice

Deliberate practice forces trainees to face their mistakes and failures much more than traditional supervision does. As discussed in Chapter 9, there is a risk of this process being overly frustrating or demoralizing for trainees. Thus, supervisors using deliberate practice need to attend more to trainees' inner game than happens in traditional supervision.

The challenge here is helping trainees develop harmonious passion, which allows them to pursue their passion with openness and mindfulness. Signs that trainees are experiencing harmonious passion include their ability to take breaks or leave the work for a time when necessary without guilt or remorse, feeling good about themselves even when they fail or make mistakes, and experiencing flow and satisfaction from their work (Vallerand et al., 2014). If these experiences are not present, supervisors should help guide trainees toward a better relationship with themselves and their work.

One of the goals of this model of training is to help trainees develop the attitude and skills necessary for engaging in deliberate practice across their entire career span. In the literature on expertise, this process is called becoming a self-regulated therapist: "When medical students, interns, and residents have acquired the necessary set of mental representations, they will have become self-regulated therapists—that is, members of the medical community who have the tools to improve their and their team members' performances over their entire professional careers" (Ericsson, 2015, p.13).

Chapter 15

ADVICE FOR MID- AND LATER CAREER

Lifelong Learning

Achieving and maintaining expertise is a "lifelong quest" (Ericsson, 2004, p. S79). Top performers in music and athletics engage in daily deliberate practice throughout their entire careers.

One of the most robust findings from decades of research on expertise across a wide range of fields is that work experience itself is not sufficient for advancing beyond competence. Rather, continuous deliberate practice is required for achieving and maintaining expert performance (Ericsson, 2006). Ericsson (2008) summarized this finding, "Once a professional reaches an acceptable skill level, more experience does not, by itself, lead to improvements" (p. 992).

What about in psychotherapy? All mental-health professional associations acknowledge the importance of continual training throughout one's professional career. This *lifelong learning* (Webster, 1971) is defined by Lichtenberg & Goodyear (2012) as "a continuously supportive process which stimulates and empowers individuals to acquire the knowledge, values, skills and understanding they require throughout their professional lifetimes and to apply them with confidence, creativity, and enjoyment in their various professional roles, circumstances, and environments" (p. 3).

In the United States, lifelong learning is typically done through a continuing education (CE) format (called "further education" in the United Kingdom). Unfortunately, most CE classes use a format that is not effective for building or even maintaining skills (Scherr et al., 2015). In their review of the field, psychologists Greg Neimeyer and Jennifer Taylor found that current CE formats have little impact, if any, on helping

Table 15.1 Training formats

Works well for skill development	Doesn't work well for skill development
Active learning (behavioral rehearsal via role play, etc.)	Passive learning (lectures about theory)
Personal relationship with a coach	Being one of many in an audience
Direct observation of your work (live or via video)	No observation of your work
Continual learning over a long period of time (years)	Training that is sporadic or short term (occasional weekend workshops)
Weekend intensives or immersions with follow-up consultation and performance review	Stand-alone weekend workshops without follow-up consultation and performance review

psychotherapists actually improve client outcome: "A central concern follows from the field's failure to produce reliable evidence that CE translates into discernibly superior psychotherapy or outcomes, which serves as the cornerstone of the warrant underlying CE and its related commitment to the welfare of the consumer" (2010, p. 668).

Three major problems with current CE formats stand out. First, CE classes typically use a passive learning format, in which a large audience listens to a lecture or watches a demonstration. Research has shown passive learning formats to be "the least effective educational methods for promoting lifelong learning" (Taylor & Neimeyer, 2015, p. 2; see also Taylor & Neimeyer, in press).

Second, CE classes are typically taken sporadically, an evening lecture here and a weekend workshop there. Sporadic learning is not sufficient for skill acquisition or maintenance (Ericsson, 2006). Third, CE classes typically include little or no observation of the participant's work and thus cannot provide performance feedback, two essential components of skill acquisition and maintenance (Ericsson, 2006; see Table 15.1 for a summary of training formats).

IMPROVING LIFELONG LEARNING

How can psychotherapists engage in more effective lifelong learning? By using the principles of deliberate practice throughout their careers. Following are nine suggestions for improving lifelong learning.

1) Focus on stalled or deteriorating cases.
2) Use active learning methods.
3) Develop a long-term relationship with a coach.
4) Use homework to consolidate learning.
5) Assess performance through client outcome.
6) Work at your threshold of strain.
7) Address your experiential avoidance.
8) Use performance feedback loops.
9) Develop your inner game.

1: Focus on Stalled or Deteriorating Cases

Skill acquisition works best if we focus on our growth edges, our weaknesses, skill deficits, and blind spots. "Only when people face failures of their entrenched procedures do they actively engage in learning and modification of their skills" (Johnson et al., 2006).

Luckily, most of us have sufficient blind spots for a lifetime of learning. Recall that 50% of the average psychotherapist's cases do not respond well to treatment (Lampropoulos, 2011). Even if you consider yourself to be a top-performing psychotherapist, you still have blind spots. (Most of us do consider ourselves to be top performers. In a recent study, the average therapist rated his/her own work performance in the 80th percentile; Walfish, et al., 2012.) Research has shown that psychotherapists have particularly strong blind spots when it comes to their own cases that are at risk of deterioration (Hannan et al., 2005; Hatfield, McCullough, Frantz, & Krieger, 2010).

As one accrues experience and status within the field, it can become more difficult to acknowledge or recognize your own blind spots. In comparison, it is easier for trainees to focus on their failures because they don't have a self-image or reputation to protect. For more experienced psychotherapists, it is especially important to maintain a professional modesty and wariness about overconfidence, termed "defensive pessimism" (Norem & Cantor, 1986) and "professional self-doubt" (Nissen-Lie, Monsen, & Rønnestad, 2010).

2: Use Active Learning Methods

Traditional continuing education focuses largely on knowledge acquisition via passive learning such as lectures. Knowledge acquisition is important for some domains of psychotherapy like learning about new laws, regulations, or ethical issues. However, it has not been proven effective for skill acquisition or improved clinical effectiveness (Taylor & Neimeyer, 2015). Furthermore, research shows knowledge gained via passive learning is largely forgotten relatively quickly (termed "professional obsolescence"; Wise et al., 2010, p. 289).

Thus, when selecting a continuing education program, it is valuable to first assess how much of the time is spent in active learning methods such as practicing skills through role play. This is the amount of time that you should consider to be actual skill acquisition. According to Ericsson and Pool (2016), "The most effective forms of practice are doing more than helping you learn to play a musical instrument; they are actually increasing your *ability* to play" (p. 43, emphasis in original). In other words, how you learn matters as much as what you learn.

3: Develop a Long-Term Relationship with a Coach

Discovering your personal blind spots and growth edges requires training with someone who knows you and your work well. This is best done in a long-term relationship with a coach. Seeing your work over time will help your coach customize deliberate practice exercises specifically for your learning needs and style of learning. This simply cannot be accomplished through occasional weekend workshops.

4: Use Homework to Consolidate Learning

Looking at other fields, we see that most of the learning occurs in solitary deliberate practice where the student can spend time repeating lessons learned from his or her coach. To improve your gains from continuing education, select programs that will assign you homework to consolidate your learning.

5: Assess Performance through Client Outcome

There is a cautionary saying in medicine, "The operation was a great success; unfortunately, the patient died." The bottom line of continuing education must be improved work performance as assessed through client outcome. Select continuing education programs that emphasize client outcome as the primary method of assessment. Assessing client outcome can be tricky, so it is recommended that a variety of methods be used (see Chapter 9).

6: Work at Your Threshold of Strain

Skill acquisition is like going to the gym: if you're not sweating, it isn't helping. This is true for both time spent at CE programs and time spent on your own solitary deliberate practice homework.

7: Address Your Experiential Avoidance

We all have experiential avoidance; it is a universal human trait (see Chapter 8). Whatever experiential avoidance you aren't aware of will likely serve as a glass ceiling that will limit your psychotherapy skill development. Choose CE programs that help you identify and address your experiential avoidance.

8: Use Performance Feedback Loops

Deliberate practice works through a performance feedback loop. You practice a skill, perform it with real clients, review the results with a coach who gives you feedback, which then informs the next skill to practice. In contrast, most CE offerings are stand-alone knowledge dumps, without the opportunity for follow-up performance feedback. This is why sporadic training does not develop clinical skills or impact clinical outcomes (Taylor & Neimeyer, 2015). Ericsson (2015) noted that "workshops or even a four-day training will be insufficient for attaining substantial improvement in everyday performance" (pp. 12–13).

9: Develop Your Inner Game

Arguably the toughest aspect of achieving expertise is the inner game: using self-regulation, grit, and finding harmonious passion in your work (see Chapter 12). Choose CE programs that help you improve your inner game. Atul Gawande (2011), a surgeon who encourages getting feedback as part of lifelong learning for medical professionals, noted the amount of personal courage required for true learning later in a career:

It will never be easy to submit to coaching, especially for those who are well along in their career. I'm ostensibly an expert. I'd finished long ago with the days of being tested and observed. I am supposed to be past needing such things. Why should I expose myself to scrutiny and fault-finding?

Chapter 16

CHALLENGES TO DELIBERATE PRACTICE

The science of expertise is a relatively young field; the concept of deliberate practice was first identified only a few decades ago (Ericsson et al., 1993). Although these ideas have been generally well received, questions and challenges have also been raised about the importance of deliberate practice for attaining expertise. In this chapter we will review these questions.

THE GREAT EQUALIZER?

A significant question focuses on the *accessibility* of deliberate practice. Part of the appeal of deliberate practice is that it seems egalitarian: everyone is as good as the effort they invest. However, this is only true if a host of other variables are equal, and unfortunately life is rarely so fair.

Deliberate practice requires time, money, attention, and energy: resources that many people simply do not have a lot of. For example, a graduate student who is a single parent of young children may find it significantly more challenging to engage in deliberate practice than a graduate student who does not have children.

In their study of 120 experts across a broad range of fields, Bloom and colleagues (1985) noted that many of their subjects were able to achieve expertise only because of significant situational advantages, such as growing up in a family with sufficient resources to make coaching available from an early age.

Furthermore, demographic variables such as gender, race, ethnicity, and economic class may affect the accessibility of deliberate practice. Research has shown that children in some minority communities face disadvantages from an early age that result in challenges throughout their education (Cook, 2015), including unequal access to school resources, academic opportunities, teacher quality, and fair discipline (Annie E Casey Foundation, n.d.). Many families do not have the economic resources necessary to support their children in deliberate practice. Likewise, discrimination and bias by teachers and peers can impact students' self-identity at early sensitive periods (Dee, 2004), which may discourage students from having the confidence needed to pursue a challenging career or engage in deliberate practice. Individuals' social environment can have a strong impact on supporting the pursuit of deliberate practice, particularly at a young age (for example, the extent of encouragement provided by parents and teachers; Ericsson & Pool, 2016).

Is Deliberate Practice Necessary or Sufficient for Expertise?

Ericsson and colleagues' (1993) proposal that deliberate practice is valuable for skill acquisition is widely accepted with little debate. However, researchers have questioned whether deliberate practice is necessary or sufficient for attaining expertise, and the relative importance of other variables.

In their paper titled "Deliberate practice: Is that all it takes to become an expert?", Hambrick and colleagues (2014) noted that other variables may be important for the development of expertise, such as genetic intelligence, personality, and the age at which one starts practicing. They analyzed performance data by chess and music experts, and concluded that "deliberate practice is necessary but not sufficient to account for individual differences in performance" (Hambrick et al., 2014, p. 36).

Likewise, Ackerman (2014) discussed the genetic and environmental variables that contribute to or interfere with the development of expertise, including intelligence, physical limitations, injuries, early experiences during developmental critical periods, aging, and genetic talent. Ackerman (2014) concluded that a "significant amount of practice is necessary, but not sufficient for expert/elite performance" (p. 8).

Other researchers have questioned the amount of deliberate practice required to achieve expertise. In their review of data from chess experts,

Campitelli and Gobet (2011) found "strong evidence that abundant DP is necessary (but not sufficient) and estimated that the minimum requirement to achieve master level is 3,000 hours of DP" (p. 280). Similar to other researchers who have raised questions about deliberate practice, Campitelli and Gobet (2011) suggested that a number of other genetic and environmental variables are important for achieving expert performance, including general intelligence, handedness, season of birth, and experiences during developmental critical periods.

THE PROBLEMATIC DEFINITION OF "PRACTICE"

Ericsson and colleagues have published extensive rebuttals to these arguments (e.g., Ericsson, 2014, 2016; Ericsson & Moxley, 2012). One of the main underlying issues involves the definition of the word "practice." Merriam-Webster's dictionary defines the word practice as "to do something again and again in order to become better at it." Unfortunately, research shows that this definition is problematic. While doing something again and again can lead to basic competency in a skill, after that point simple repetition does not improve proficiency, and rarely leads to expertise (Ericsson, 2006).

A recent study by Macnamara, Hambrick, and Oswald (2014) provides an example of this problem. The authors compared the results of 157 studies on deliberate practice across five fields: music, games, sports, professions, and education. Their analysis of these studies concluded that "deliberate practice is important, but not as important as has been argued" (p. 1). Notably, their analysis found that deliberate practice explained less than 25% of the variance in music and sports. However, their analysis had a major flaw: the authors' use of the term "deliberate practice" included a wide range of activities that have not necessarily been shown to improve performance. For example, some of the studies included time spent competing in games. Competition is performance, not deliberate practice, and may not improve skill proficiency beyond a level of basic competency (Ericsson, 2006, 2014, 2016).

Many of us think we are already doing deliberate practice because we define it the same way the dictionary defines practice: "doing something again and again in order to get better at it." This problem is especially pertinent for psychotherapy because we have a tradition of assuming that work experience itself leads to improved performance. In fact, we use the term "psychotherapy practice" to describe our work, not efforts to improve our effectiveness. This blurring of the definition of practice can impede our efforts to improve.

In an attempt to address this problem of vague definitions, Ericsson and Pool (2016) redefine deliberate practice in their recent book that was published shortly before this book was completed. They reserve the term deliberate practice for fields that are "reasonably well developed" (p. 98), which are defined by two conditions. First, there must be wide agreement on "objective criteria for superior performance," (p. 98) and a rank of top performers who have achieved that level of expertise. Second, there must be training methods that reliably improve performance, and teachers who know how to apply these methods to help students learn. To borrow a term from the psychotherapy research literature, these might be called empirically supported training methods. Ericsson and Pool (2016) use the term *purposeful practice* to describe practice activities that would have previously met the criteria for deliberate practice, but are in areas that do not meet the criteria of a well-developed field. They reserve the term deliberate practice to only apply to "practice that is both purposeful and *informed* ... guided by the best performers' accomplishments and by an understanding of what these expert performers do to excel" (p. 98, emphasis in original). Ericsson and Pool (2016) summarize the difference between the two as "Deliberate practice is purposeful practice that knows where it is going and how to get there" (p. 98).

To avoid confusion, I have retained the original (Ericsson et al., 1993) definition of deliberate practice for this book. However, I think Ericsson and Pool's (2016) points are particularly important for the field of mental health. First, we very much do need to develop broad consensus on what constitutes expert psychotherapy, which should be grounded first and foremost in client outcome (see Chapter 5). Unfortunately, assessing the effectiveness of a psychotherapist is trickier than assessing the effectiveness of an athlete or chess player. Psychotherapy has many effects that are subtle or emerge over a long period of time. We need outcome-measurement tools that can accurately and reliably capture these effects. Second, we need research to identify which methods of deliberate practice reliably result in improved effectiveness, and we need to teach clinical supervisors and coaches how to use these new training methods.

CHAPTER 17

LOOKING FORWARD

In this book we have explored how to use the science of expertise to improve the effectiveness of psychotherapy. In Part I we reviewed how this process starts: by acknowledging our challenges and failures—the "other 50%"—and by training using the principles of deliberate practice (Ericsson, 2006):

1) Observing our own work via videotape.
2) Getting expert feedback from a coach.
3) Setting small incremental learning goals just beyond our ability.
4) Repetitive behavioral rehearsal of specific skills.
5) Continuously assessing our performance via client-reported outcome.

In Part II of this book we explored what the field of mental health can learn from the science of expertise in other fields:

- We use the clinical outcomes of our individual clients as the most valid empirical basis for our work (see Chapter 5).
- We learn best by focusing on specific incremental skills just beyond our current ability and repetitively practicing those skills (see Chapter 6).
- We maximize learning from our clinical experience, particularly from our clinical failures, by reviewing our own work via videotape (see Chapter 7).

- We address our own experiential avoidance by developing emotional self-awareness and nonreactivity (see Chapter 8).

Part III of this book presented advice to help you start experimenting with developing your own deliberate practice routine.

In Part IV we explored methods to sustain morale on the hard path to expertise (the inner game) and guidance for therapists at all career stages, from trainees to seasoned, licensed psychotherapists in independent practice.

Looking Forward

For our field to make the most of deliberate practice, we need large-scale research programs to examine which particular skills reliably lead to improved client outcomes and how best to practice those skills. William McGaghie described this process for the field of medical education in Chapter 5.

Fortunately, there are already promising research developments in this direction (Chow et al., 2015; Eubanks-Carter et al., 2015; Hill et al., 2015; Hilsenroth and Diener, in press; Miller et al., 2013; Tracey et al., 2015). However, scientifically researching and developing deliberate practice programs for psychotherapy is a major endeavor and will take decades of work. In the meantime, I'd like to propose that we don't sit back and wait.

Most of the fields that use deliberate practice do so with methods developed prior to the invention of the scientific method and without the benefit of the science of expertise. For example, classical music and athletics developed effective methods for deliberate practice centuries ago, well before there was any scientific study of those fields. In fact, almost all of the fields reviewed in the *Cambridge Handbook of Expertise and Expert Performance* (Ericsson et al., 2006) developed their methods of deliberate practice without the benefit of scientific inquiry.

The Pioneers

Who developed these methods of deliberate practice? Pioneering practitioners and teachers in each field, engaging in a continuous trial-and-error process of invention and refinement. Ericsson calls these individuals "pathfinders"—people who, through extensive deliberate practice, push their personal skills to such heights that they expand and redefine what is possible for their field. "Having studied many examples of creative genius, it's clear to me that much of what expert performers do to move the boundary of their fields and create new things is very similar to what they were doing to reach that boundary in the first place" (Ericsson & Pool, 2016, p. 204).

Who will develop the first methods of deliberate practice for psychotherapy? *We will.* We are the pioneers. Each of us is a case study in how to improve clinical training. We can be the first generation of psychotherapists to integrate the principles of deliberate practice into clinical training.

If, through persistent trial and error, we are successful, future generations of psychotherapists may be more effective than we could even dream of being today. Just as has happened in so many other fields, today's top-performing clinicians could be tomorrow's baseline.

In the twentieth century our field was largely focused on determining which treatment model was best. Let's take the next step and use the twenty-first century to learn how each individual psychotherapist can become more clinically effective.

Pick a model that feels right to you, record your work, find a good coach, and *practice.*

EPILOGUE

When the first draft of this book was completed, I sent it to friends and colleagues for feedback. One of the people I sent it to was Simon Goldberg, the graduate student who performed the first large-scale longitudinal study of therapist clinical skill development based on client outcomes (Goldberg et al., 2016; see Chapter 1). A Zen practitioner, Simon has a particular gift for approaching psychotherapy research with a continually fresh perspective (the Zen term for this is *beginner's mind*). One of the questions Simon raised about the draft was particularly valuable. He asked, "What about *your* Other 50%? Has your own work with deliberate practice improved your outcomes?"

The truth is, I don't know yet. At least not empirically. This is because I have moved between different work settings frequently since I started working as a psychotherapist. Tracking clinical effectiveness over time requires seeing many clients in the same job setting over a significant period of time, and I have not had sufficient time in one location to do so. While I *feel* like I am getting better, I do not yet have the data to confirm it. As we reviewed in Chapter 1, our subjective judgment about our effectiveness is subject to strong bias and is not very reliable on its own. Thus, I am wary of trusting my subjective judgment as sufficient to confirm my improvement. I need empirical data. As I mentioned in the Prologue, this book is not the victory lap of a master therapist.

I am not alone in my lack of empirical data about my clinical skill development. As discussed in Chapter 5, scant research to date has looked at psychotherapy skill development over time, as measured by actual impact on client outcomes. Very few therapists routinely track their clinical outcomes. This is not due to avoidance; most of us want to know more about our clinical outcomes. Rather, this stems from a blind spot in the culture of psychotherapy. One of my main goals for this book is to highlight this problem. My hope is that ten years from now we will have developed methods for therapists to more accurately track their clinical effectiveness, as well as the effectiveness of their supervision and training.

As described in Chapter 9, in my early 30s I had two major goals: climb El Capitan in Yosemite Valley and become a great psychotherapist. Five years later I climbed El Capitan. Now, ten years later and despite considerably more effort, I still struggle to be a good therapist, much less great. Becoming a better therapist is the hardest thing I have ever attempted. However, it is also the most rewarding, and every day I feel incredibly fortunate to be on this quest.

APPENDIX

Videotaping Psychotherapy

Videotaping is widely acknowledged as a valuable tool to improve the effectiveness of clinical training and supervision across a wide range of psychotherapy models (e.g., Bernard & Goodyear, 2014; Briggie et al., 2016; Ellis, 2010; Friedlander et al., 2011). Notably, this includes psychodynamic supervisors, who previously were among the most cautious regarding videotape (e.g., Abbass et al., 2004; Alpert, 1996; Eubanks-Carter et al., 2015; Haggerty & Hilsenroth, 2011; McCullough, Bhatia, Ulvenes, Berggraf, & Osborn, 2011).

PICKING A VIDEO CAMERA

Economy-model digital video cameras are suitable for recording psychotherapy. They are available for less than $200. Choosing economy-model video cameras that have been for sale for more than one year is recommended because newer or premium cameras may record in newer digital formats that may not be compatible with playback devices (such as your computer). For security reasons, therapists should dedicate a specific device exclusively for videotaping psychotherapy. That camera should be used only for that purpose, and kept locked with the psychotherapy notes.

Audio

Most economy-model video cameras have sufficient sound quality for recording psychotherapy. If higher-quality sound is required, choose a video camera with ports for an external microphone.

Video Playback

Videos can be played on a wide range of devices, including computers and modern televisions. VLC Media Player software is recommended for viewing videos on a computer.

Storing Digital Videos

Videos can be stored directly on the video camera or transferred to a computer hard drive. If videos are stored on a computer, therapists should use a strong password for the computer and set the computer to auto-encrypt when not in use (see Rousmaniere & Kuhn, 2015). One good option is to save videos to an auto-encrypting portable hard drive (e.g., the Apricorn Aegis Padlock). This kind of drive requires a password for access and automatically encrypts itself when it is unplugged from a computer. This helps ensure security even if the portable drive is lost or stolen.

Picture-in-Picture Video

Therapists may wish to see both themselves and the client in the video through "picture-in-picture" video. The simplest method for doing this is to place a large mirror behind the client, in view of the camera, so the therapist's face appears in the mirror. Picture-in-picture video can also be accomplished by having multiple cameras or webcams feeding into video-processing software. This requires some additional cost and technical expertise to set up.

Videotaping on Mobile Devices

Many mobile devices (e.g., smartphones, tablets) have videotaping features. However, it is recommended that therapists avoid or be very careful when using mobile devices to record psychotherapy sessions. This is because mobile devices may pose greater threats to security and confidentiality than other recording methods. Mobile devices are common targets of theft and are easily lost. Additionally, mobile devices often include preinstalled software that automatically sends backups of videos to the internet cloud. Therapists may not realize this backup software is running or may not know how to turn it off. If a mobile device is used to videotape psychotherapy, internet connectivity on that device should be disabled, the device should be used exclusively for that purpose, device encryption should be turned on, and the device should be kept locked with psychotherapy notes.

CONSENT

Client consent should be obtained in writing before videotaping. Legal and regulatory issues may apply, depending upon your jurisdiction. More information on this topic, as well as template consent forms, are available at www.zurinstitute.com.

HOW TO INTRODUCE VIDEOTAPING TO CLIENTS

Here's how I explain it to my clients:

> Everyone has blind spots and makes mistakes. That is human and happens in any field. My strategy is to get continual feedback from clinical experts to help me see opportunities to help you better. It's kind of like getting a routine audit. If anyone goes long enough without an audit, problems can develop. Getting expert feedback on my work helps me to help you.

For detailed case examples of how videotaping can be used in supervision, see Osborn and Bhatia (2015) and Escudero and Friedlander (2015). For a discussion about the evolution of videotape in psychotherapy, see Costello (n.d.).

REFERENCES

Abbass, A. (2002). Intensive short-term dynamic psychotherapy in a private psychiatric office: Clinical and cost effectiveness. *American Journal of Psychotherapy, 56*(2), 225-32.

Abbass, A. (2004). Small-group videotape training for psychotherapy skills development. *Academic Psychiatry, 28*(2), 151-5.

Abbass, A. (2015). *Reaching through Resistance: Advanced Psychotherapy Techniques.* Kansas City, MO: Seven Leaves Press.

Abbass, A., Kisely, S. R., Town, J. M., Leichsenring, F., Driessen, E., De Maat, S., Gerber, A., Dekker, J., Rabung, S., Rusalovska, S., & Crowe, E. (2014). Short-term psychodynamic psychotherapies for common mental disorders. *Cochrane Database of Systematic Reviews, 7.* doi: 10.1002/14651858.cd004687.pub4

Ackerman, P. L. (2014). Nonsense, common sense, and science of expert performance: Talent and individual differences. *Intelligence, 45,* 6-17. doi: 10.1016/j.intell.2013.04.009

Ackerman, S. J. & Hilsenroth, M. J. (2003). A review of therapist characteristics and techniques positively impacting the therapeutic alliance. *Clinical Psychology Review, 23*(1), 1-33. doi: 10.1016/S0272-7358(02)00146-0

Ægisdóttir, S., White, M. J., Spengler, P. M., Maugherman, A. S., Anderson, L. A., Cook, R. S., Nichols, C. N., Lampropoulos, G. K., Walker, B. S., Cohen, G., & Rush, J. D. (2006). The meta-analysis of clinical judgment project: Fifty-six years of accumulated research on clinical versus statistical prediction. *Counseling Psychologist, 34,* 341-82. http://dx.doi.org/10.1177/0011000005285875

Alpert, M. (1996). Videotaping psychotherapy. *Journal of Psychotherapy Practice and Research, 5,* 93-105.

American Psychological Association (APA). (2012). *Resolution on the Recognition of Psychotherapy Effectiveness.* Retrieved on October 10, 2015 from http://goo.gl/l5zk8Z

American Psychological Association (APA). (2014). *Guidelines for Clinical Supervision in Health Service Psychology.* Retrieved on November 24, 2015 from https://goo.gl/81Jjev

Anderson, T., Ogles, B. M., Patterson, C. L., Lambert, M. J., & Vermeersch, D. A. (2009). Therapist effects: Facilitative interpersonal skills as a predictor of therapist success. *Journal of Clinical Psychology, 65*, 755–68.

Annie E Casey Foundation (n.d.). *Race Matters*. Retrieved on April 8, 2016 from http://goo.gl/Xygo5B

Association for Counselor Education and Supervision (2011). *Best Practices in Clinical Supervision*. Retrieved on November 24, 2015 from https://goo.gl/3n5qp2

Axline, V. M. (1947). *Play Therapy*. New York: Ballantine.

Baldwin, S. A. & Imel, Z. E. (2013). Therapist variables in psychotherapy research. In M. J. Lambert (Ed.), *Bergin and Garfield's Handbook of Psychotherapy and Behavior Change* (5th ed.). New York: Wiley.

Bambling, M., King, R., Raue, P., Schweitzer, R., & Lambert, W. (2006). Clinical supervision: Its influence on client-rated working alliance and client symptom reduction in the brief treatment of major depression. *Psychotherapy Research, 16*, 317–31. doi: 10.1080/10503300500268524

Bandura, A. (1977). Self-efficacy: Toward a unifying theory of behavioral change. *Psychological Review, 84*, 191–215.

Bandura, A. (1986). *Social Foundations of Thought and Action: A Social Cognitive Theory*. Englewood Cliffs, NJ: Prentice Hall.

Barnett, J. E. (2008). Mentoring, boundaries, and multiple relationships: Opportunities and challenges. *Mentoring & Tutoring, 16*(1), 3.

Barnett, J. E. (2011). Psychotherapist self-disclosure: Ethical and clinical considerations. *Psychotherapy, 48*(4), 315–21. doi: 10.1037/a0026056

Bernard, J. M. & Goodyear, R. K. (2014). *Fundamentals of Clinical Supervision* (5th ed.). Boston, MA: Merrill.

Beutler, L. E. (1999). Manualizing flexibility: The training of eclectic therapists. *Journal of Clinical Psychology, 55*(4), 399–404.

Beutler, L. E. & Howard, M. (2003). Training in psychotherapy: Why supervision does not work. *Clinical Psychologist, 56*(4), 12–16.

Beutler, L. E., Malik, M., Alimohamed, S., Harwood, T. M., Talebi, H., Noble, S., & Wong, E. (2004). Therapist variables. In M. J. Lambert (Ed.), *Bergin and Garfield's Handbook of Psychotherapy and Behavior Change* (5th ed., pp. 227–306). New York: Wiley.

Bishop, S. R., Lau, M., Shapiro, S., Carlson, L., Anderson, N. D., Carmody, J., Segal, Z., Abbey, S., Speca, M., Velting, D., & Devins, G. (2004). Mindfulness: A proposed operational definition. *Clinical Psychology: Science and Practice, 11*(3), 230–41. doi: 10.1093/clipsy/bph077

Blanchard, M. & Farber, B. A. (2016). Lying in psychotherapy: Why and what clients don't tell their therapist about therapy and their relationship. *Counselling Psychology Quarterly, 29*, 90–112.

Bloom, B. S. (Ed.) (1985). *Developing Talent in Young People*. New York: Ballantine Books.

Bohart, A. C. & Wade, A. G. (2013). The client in psychotherapy. In M. J. Lambert (Ed.), *Bergin and Garfield's Handbook of Psychotherapy and Behavior Change* (5th ed.). New York: Wiley.

Bohman, G., Blessed, E. M. E., & Ögren, M.-L. (2015). One-sided focus on CBT harms Swedish mental health. *Svenska Dagbladet*. Retrieved on March 11, 2016 from http://goo.gl/SmRXFl

Bonneville-Roussy, A., Lavigne, G. L., & Vallerand, R. J. (2011). When passion leads to excellence: The case of musicians. *Psychology of Music, 39*(1), 123–38. doi: 10.1177/0305735609352441

Boswell, J. F. & Castonguay, L. G. (2007). Psychotherapy training: Suggestions for core ingredients and future research. *Psychotherapy: Theory, Research, Practice, Training, 44*(4), 378–83. doi: 10.1037/0033-3204.44.4.378

Branson, A., Shafran, R., & Myles, P. (2015). Investigating the relationship between competence and patient outcome with CBT Highlights. *Behaviour Research and Therapy, 68*, 19–26. doi: 10.1016/j.brat.2015.03.002

Briggie, A. M., Hilsenroth, M. J., Conway, F., Muran, J. C., & Jackson, J. M. (2016). Patient comfort with audio or video recording of their psychotherapy sessions: Relation to symptomatology, treatment refusal, duration, and outcome. *Professional Psychology: Research and Practice, 47*(1), 66–76. doi: 10.1037/a0040063

Bruce, N., Manber, R., Shapiro, S. L., & Constantino, M. J. (2010). Psychotherapist mindfulness and the psychotherapy process. *Psychotherapy, 47*(1), 83–97. doi: 10.1037/a0018842

Buchanan, T. W. (2007). Retrieval of emotional memories. *Psychological Bulletin, 133*(5), 761–79. http://doi.org/10.1037/0033-2909.133.5.761

Budge, S. L., Owen, J. J., Kopta, S. M., Minami, T., Hanson, M. R., & Hirsch, G. (2013). Differences among trainees in client outcomes associated with the phase model of change. *Psychotherapy, 50*, 150–7. http://dx.doi.org/10.1037/a0029565

California Board of Psychology. (2001). *Final Statement of Reasons.* Hearing date: November 2, 2001.

Callahan, J. L., Almstrom, C. M., Swift, J. K., Borja, S. E., & Heath, C. J. (2009). Exploring the contribution of supervisors to intervention outcomes. *Training and Education in Professional Psychology, 3*(2), 72–7. doi: 10.1037/a0014294

Callahan, J. L., Aubuchon-Endsley, N., Borja, S. E., & Swift, J. K. (2009). Pretreatment expectancies and premature termination in a training clinic environment. *Training and Education in Professional Psychology, 3*(2), 111–19. http://doi.org/10.1037/a0012901

Campitelli, G. & Gobet, F. (2011). Deliberate practice: Necessary but not sufficient. *Current Directions in Psychological Science, 20*(5), 280–5. doi: 10.1177/0963721411421922

Castonguay, L. G., Boswell, J. F., Constantino, M. J., Goldfried, M. R., & Hill, C. E. (2010). Training implications of harmful effects of psychological treatments. *American Psychologist, 65*(1), 34–49. http://doi.org/10.1037/a0017330

Chabris, C. F. & Simons, D. J. (2014). Why our memory fails us. *New York Times.* Retrieved on November 19, 2015 from http://nyti.ms/1FJR0mA

Chow, D. L., Miller, S. D., Seidel, J. A., Kane, R. T., Thornton, J. A., & Andrews, W. P. (2015). The role of deliberate practice in the development of highly effective psychotherapists, *Psychotherapy, 52*(3), 337–45.

Clement, P. W. (1994). Quantitative evaluation of 26 years of private practice. *Professional Psychology: Research and Practice, 25*(2), 173–6. doi: 10.1037//0735-7028.25.2.173

Clement, P. W. (2008). Outcomes from 40 years of psychotherapy in a private practice. *American Journal of Psychotherapy, 62*(3), 215–39. Retrieved from www.ncbi.nlm.nih.gov/pubmed/18846970

Coker, J. (1990). *How to Practice Jazz.* New York: Jamey Aebersold.

Cook, L. (2015). U.S. education: Still separate and unequal. *US News and World Report.* Retrieved on April 9, 2016 from http://goo.gl/nttDUu

Costello, P. C. (n.d.). *The Influence of Videotaping on Theory and Technique in Psychotherapy: A Chapter in the Epistemology of Media.* Retrieved from www.media-ecology.org/publications/MEA_proceedings/v3/Costello03.pdf

Coughlan, E. K., Williams, A. M., McRobert, A. P., & Ford, P. R. (2014). How experts practice: A novel test of deliberate practice theory. *Journal of Experimental Psychology. Learning, Memory, and Cognition, 40*(2), 449–58. doi: 10.1037/a0034302

Coughlin, P. (2006). *Intensive Short-Term Dynamic Psychotherapy.* New York: Karnac.

Coughlin, P. (2007). *Lives Transformed.* New York: Karnac.

Cozolino, L. (2010). *The Neuroscience of Psychotherapy: Healing the Social Brain* (2nd ed.). New York: W. W. Norton.

Crits-Christoph, P., Connolly Gibbons, M. B., Crits-Christoph, K., Narducci, J., Schamberger, M., & Gallop, R. (2006). Can therapists be trained to improve their alliances? A pilot study of alliance-fostering therapy. *Psychotherapy Research, 13,* 268–81. doi: 10.1080/10503300500268557

Csikszentmihályi, M. (1990). *Flow: The Psychology of Optimal Experience.* New York: Harper & Row.

Davanloo, H. (1990). *Unlocking the Unconscious.* New York: Wiley.

Davis, D. M. & Hayes, J. A. (2011). What are the benefits of mindfulness? A practice review of psychotherapy-related research. *Psychotherapy, 48*(2), 198–208. doi: 10.1037/a0022062

Dayton, T. & Moreno, Z. (2004). *The Living Stage: A Step-by-Step Guide to Psychodrama, Sociometry and Group Psychotherapy.* New York: HCI.

Dee, T. S. (2004). The race connection. *Education Next, 4,* 53–9.

Detzer, D. (2005). *Donnybrook: The Battle of Bull Run, 1861.* New York: Harcourt.

Duckworth, A. L., Peterson, C., Matthews, M. D., & Kelly, D. R. (2007). Grit: Perseverance and passion for long-term goals. *Journal of Personality and Social Psychology, 92*(6), 1087–101. http://doi.org/10.1037/0022-3514.92.6.1087

Duncan, B., Miller, S., & Hubble, M. (2007). How being bad can make you better. *Psychotherapy Networker,* November/December, 36–45.

Dunn, R., Callahan, J. L., Swift, J. K., & Ivanovic, M. (2013). Effects of pre-session centering for therapists on session presence and effectiveness. *Psychotherapy Research, 23,* 78–85. doi: 10.1080/10503307.2012 .731713

Eisenberg, N. & Eggum, N. D. (2009). Empathic responding: Sympathy and personal distress. In J. Decety & W. Ickes (Eds), *The Social Neuroscience of Empathy* (pp. 71–83). Cambridge, MA: MIT Press.

Ekman, P. (1972). *Emotion in the Human Face.* New York: Malor Books.

Ekman, P. (2003). *Emotions Revealed.* New York: Henry Holt and Co.

Elliott, R., Partyka, R., Wagner, J., Alperin, R., Dobrenski, R., Messer, S. B., Watson, J C., & Castonguay, L. G. (2009). An adjudicated hermeneutic single case efficacy design study of experiential therapy for panic/phobia. *Psychotherapy Research, 19,* 543–57.

Elliott, R., Bohart, A. C., Watson, J. C., & Greenberg, L. S. (2011). Empathy. *Psychotherapy, 48,* 43–9. doi: 10.1037/a0022187

Ellis, M. V. (2010). Bridging the science and practice of clinical supervision: Some discoveries, some misconceptions. *Clinical Supervisor, 29,* 95–116.

Ellis, M. V. & Ladany, N. (1997). Inferences concerning supervisees and clients in clinical supervision: An integrative review. In C. E. Watkins (Ed.), *Handbook of Psychotherapy Supervision* (pp. 447–507). New York: Wiley.

Ellis, M. V., Berger, L., Hanus, A. E., Ayala, E. E., Swords, B. A., & Siembor, M. (2014). Inadequate and harmful clinical supervision: Testing a revised framework and assessing occurrence. *Counseling Psychologist*, *42*(4), 434–72. doi: 10.1177/0011000013508656

Epstein, M. (1995). *Thoughts without a Thinker*. New York: Basic Books.

Ericsson, K. A. (2003). Development of elite performance and deliberate practice: An update from the perspective of the expert performance approach. In J. L. Starkes & K. A. Ericsson (Eds), *Expert Performance in Sports: Advances in Research on Sport Expertise*. New York: Human Kinetics.

Ericsson, K. A. (2004). Deliberate practice and the acquisition and maintenance in medicine and related domains: Invited address. *Academic Medicine*, *79*, S70–S81.

Ericsson, K. A. (2006). The influence of experience and deliberate practice on the development of superior expert performance. In K. A. Ericsson, N. Charness, P. J. Feltovich, & R. R. Hoffman (Eds), *The Cambridge Handbook of Expertise and Expert Performance* (pp. 683–703). Cambridge: Cambridge University Press.

Ericsson, K. A. (2008). Deliberate practice and acquisition of expert performance: A general overview. *Academic Emergency Medicine*, *15*, 988–94. doi: 10.1111/j.1553-2712.2008.00227.x

Ericsson, K. A. (2014). Why expert performance is special and cannot be extrapolated from studies of performance in the general population: A response to criticisms. *Intelligence*, *45*, 81–103. doi: 10.1016/j.intell.2013.12.001

Ericsson, K. A. (2015). Acquisition and maintenance of medical expertise. *Academic Medicine*, *90*(11), 1–16. doi: 10.1097/ACM.0000000000000939

Ericsson, K. A. (2016). Summing up hours of any type of practice versus identifying optimal practice activities: Commentary on Macnamara, Moreau, & Hambrick (2016). *Perspectives on Psychological Science*, *11*(3), 351–4. doi: 10.1177/1745691616635600

Ericsson, K. A. & Charness, N. (1994). Expert performance: Its structure and acquisition. *American Psychologist*, *49*, 725–47.

Ericsson, K. A. & Lehmann, A. C. (1996). Expert and exceptional performance: Evidence of maximal adaptation to task constraints. *Annual Review of Psychology*, *47*, 273–305. http://doi.org/10.1146/annurev.psych.47.1.273

Ericsson, K. A. & Moxley, J. H. (2012). A critique of Howard's argument for innate limits in chess performance or why we need an account based on acquired skill and deliberate practice. *Applied Cognitive Psychology*, *26*(February), 649–53. doi: 10.1002/acp.2841

Ericsson, K. A. & Pool, R. (2016). *Peak: Secrets from the New Science of Expertise*. New York: Houghton Mifflin Harcourt.

Ericsson, K. A., Krampe, R. T., & Tesch-Romer, C. (1993). The role of deliberate practice in the acquisition of expert performance. *Psychological Review*, *100*, 363–406.

Ericsson, K. A., Charness, N., Feltovich, P. J., & Hoffman, R. R. (2006). *The Cambridge Handbook of Expertise and Expert Performance*. Cambridge: Cambridge University Press.

Ericsson, K. A., Prietula, M. J., & Cokely, E. T. (2007). The making of an expert. *Harvard Business Review*, July–August, 1–9.

Escudero, V. & Friedlander, M. L. (2015). e-SOFTA: A video-based software for observing the working alliance in clinical training and supervision. In T. G. Rousmaniere & E. Renfro-Michele (Eds), *Using Technology for Clinical Supervision: A Practical Handbook* (pp. 223–38). Alexandria, VA: American Counseling Association Press.

Eskreis-Winkler, L., Duckworth, A. L., Shulman, E., & Beal, S. (2014). The grit effect: Predicting retention in the military, the workplace, school and marriage. *Frontiers in Personality Science and Individual Differences, 5*(36), 1-12.

Eskreis-Winkler, L., Young, V., Brunwasser, S. M., Shulman, E. P., Tsukayama, E., & Duckworth, A. L. (in press). Using wise interventions to motivate deliberate practice. *Journal of Personality and Social Psychology.*

Eubanks-Carter, C., Muran, J. C., & Safran, J. D. (2015). Alliance-focused training. *Psychotherapy, 52*(2), 169-73.

Falender, C. A. & Shafranske, E. P. (2004). *Clinical Supervision: A Competency-Based Approach.* Washington, DC: American Psychological Association.

Farber, B. A., Manevich, I., Metzger, J., & Saypol, E. (2005). Choosing psychotherapy as a career: Why did we cross that road? *Journal of Clinical Psychology: In Session, 61*, 1009-31.

Foster, R. (2010). *Ballet Pedagogy.* Gainesville: University Press of Florida.

Frank, J. D. & Frank, J. B. (1993). *Persuasion and Healing.* Baltimore, MD: Johns Hopkins University Press.

Frankl, V. (1988). *The Will to Meaning: Foundations and Applications of Logotherapy.* New York: New American Library.

Frederickson, J. (2013). *Co-Creating Change: Effective Dynamic Therapy Techniques.* Kansas City, MO: Seven Leaves Press.

Freud, S. (1958). The future prospects of psychoanalytic psychotherapy. In J. Strachey (Ed. & Trans.), *The Standard Edition of the Complete Psychological Works of Sigmund Freud* (Vol. 11, pp. 141-51). London: Hogarth Press (original work published 1910).

Friedlander, M. L., Sutherland, O., Sandler, S., Kortz, L., Bernardi, S., Lee, H.-H., & Drozd, A. (2011). Exploring corrective experiences in a successful case of short-term dynamic psychotherapy. *Psychotherapy, 49*(3), 349-63. doi: 10.1037/a0023447

Fulton, P. R. (2013). Mindfulness as clinical training. In C. K. Germer, R. D. Siegel, & P. R. Fulton (Eds), *Mindfulness and Psychotherapy.* New York: Guilford Press.

Gallway, W. T. (1997). *The Inner Game of Tennis.* New York: Random House.

Gawande, A. (2011). Personal best. *New Yorker*, retrieved from http://goo.gl/zthIyW

Gelso, C. J. & Hayes, J. A. (2007). *Countertransference and the Therapist's Inner Experience: Perils and Possibilities.* Mahwah, NJ: Erlbaum.

Germer, C. K. (2013). Mindfulness. In C. K. Germer, R. D. Siegel, & P. R. Fulton (Eds), *Mindfulness and Psychotherapy.* New York: Guilford Press.

Germer, C. K., Siegel, R. D. & Fulton, P. R. (2013). *Mindfulness and Psychotherapy* (2nd Ed.). New York: Guilford Press.

Gladwell, M. (2008). *Outliers.* New York: Little, Brown and Company.

Goldberg, S., Rousmaniere, T. G., Miller, S. D., Whipple, J., Nielsen, S. L., Hoyt, W., & Wampold, B. E. (2016). Do psychotherapists improve with time and experience? A longitudinal analysis of real world outcome data. *Journal of Counseling Psychology, 63*, 1-11.

Goodyear, R. (2015). Using accountability mechanisms more intentionally: A framework and its implications for training professional psychologists. *American Psychologist, 70*(8), 736-43. doi: http://dx.doi.org/10.1037/a0039828

Goodyear, R. & Rousmaniere, T. G. (in press). Helping therapists to each day become a little better than they were the day before: The expertise-development model of supervision and consultation. In Rousmaniere, T. G., Goodyear, R., Miller, S. D., & Wampold, B. (Eds), *The Cycle of Excellence: Using Deliberate Practice to Improve Supervision and Training.* London: Wiley.

Greason, P. B. & Cashwell, C. S. (2009). Mindfulness and counseling self-efficacy: The mediating role of attention and empathy. *Counselor Education and Supervision, 49*, 2–19. doi: 10.1002/j.1556-6978.2009.tb00083.x

Greenberg, L. S. (2010). *Emotion-Focused Therapy*. Washington, DC: American Psychology Association Press.

Greenwald, A. G. (1980). The totalitarian ego: Fabrication and revision of personal history. *American Psychologist, 35*(7), 603–18. http://psycnet.apa.org/?&fa=main. doiLanding&doi=10.1037/0003-066X.35.7.603

Grepmair, L., Mitterlehner, F., Loew, T., Bachler, E., Rother, W., & Nickel, M. (2007). Promoting mindfulness in psychotherapists in training influences the treatment results of their patients: A randomized, double-blind, controlled study. *Psychotherapy and Psychosomatics, 76*(6), 332–8. http://doi.org/10.1159/000107560

Hackney, H. L. & Bernard, J. M. (in press). *Professional Counseling: A Process Guide to Helping*. New York: Merrill.

Haggerty, G. & Hilsenroth, M. J. (2011). The use of video in psychotherapy supervision. *British Journal of Psychotherapy, 27*(2), 193–210.

Hambrick, D. Z., Oswald, F. L., Altmann, E. M., Meinz, E. J., Gobet, F., & Campitelli, G. (2014). Deliberate practice: Is that all it takes to become an expert? *Intelligence, 45*, 34–45. doi: 10.1016/j.intell.2013.04.001

Hannan, C., Lambert, M. J., Harmon, C., Nielsen, S. L., Smart, D. W., Shimokawa, K., & Sutton, S. W. (2005). A lab test and algorithms for identifying clients at risk for treatment failure. *Journal of Clinical Psychology: In Session, 61*, 155–63.

Hashimoto, D. A., Sirimanna, P., Gomez, E. D., Beyer-Berjot, L., Ericsson, K. A., Williams, N. N., Darzi, A., & Aggarwal, R. (2014). Deliberate practice enhances quality of laparoscopic surgical performance in a randomized controlled trial: From arrested development to expert performance. *Surgical Endoscopy*. doi: 10.1007/s00464-014-4042-4

Hatcher, R. L. (2015). Interpersonal competencies: Responsiveness, technique, and training in psychotherapy. *American Psychologist, 70*(8), 747–57. doi: 10.1037/a0039803

Hatfield, D., McCullough, L., Frantz, S. H., & Krieger, K. (2010). Do we know when our clients get worse? An investigation of therapists' ability to detect negative client change. *Clinical Psychology & Psychotherapy, 17*, 25–32.

Hattie, J. A., Sharpley, C. F., & Rogers, H. J. (1984). Comparative effectiveness of professional and paraprofessional helpers. *Psychological Bulletin, 95*, 534–41. http://dx.doi.org/10.1037/0033-2909.95.3.534

Hayes, S. C., Bissett, R., Roget, N., Padilla, M., Kohlenberg, B. S., Fisher, G., Masuda, A., ... Niccolls, R. (2004). The impact of acceptance and commitment training and multicultural training on the stigmatizing attitudes and professional burnout of substance abuse counselors. *Behavior Therapy, 35*, 821–35.

Hayes, S. C., Follette, V. M., & Linehan, M. M. (Eds). (2004). *Mindfulness and Acceptance: Expanding the Cognitive Behavioral Tradition*. New York: Guilford Press.

Hembree, E. A., Rauch, S. A. M., & Foa, E. B. (2003). Beyond the manual: The insider's guide to prolonged exposure therapy for PTSD. *Cognitive and Behavioral Practice, 10*(1), 22–30.

Hendlin, S. J. (2014). Finding expertise in the process. *Psychotherapy Bulletin, 49*, 9–11.

Hick, S. F. & Bien, T. (2008). *Mindfulness and the Therapeutic Relationship*. New York: Guilford Press.

Hill, C. E. & Knox, S. (2013). Training and supervision in psychotherapy: Evidence for effective practice. In M. J. Lambert (Ed.), *Handbook of Psychotherapy and Behavior Change* (6th ed., pp. 775–811). New York: Wiley.

Hill, C. E. & Lent, R. W. (2006). A narrative and meta-analytic review of helping skills training: Time to revive a dormant area of inquiry. *Psychotherapy: Theory, Research, Practice, Training, 43*(2), 154–72.

Hill, C. E., Chui, H., & Baumann, E. (2013). Revisiting and re-envisioning the outcome problem in psychotherapy: An argument to include individualized and qualitative measurement. *Psychotherapy, 50,* 68–76.

Hill, C. E., Lystrup, A., Kline, K., Gebru, N. M., Birchler, J., Palmer, G., Robinson, J., Um, M., Griffin S., Lipsky, E., Knox, S., & Pinto-Coelho, K. (2013). Aspiring to become a therapist: Personal strengths and challenges, influences, motivations, and expectations of future psychotherapists. *Counselling Psychology Quarterly, 26*(3/4), 267–93. doi: 10.1080/09515070.2013.825763

Hill, C. E., Baumann, E., Shafran, N., Gupta, S., Morrison, A., Rojas, A. E. P., Spangler, P. T., Griffin, S., Pappa, L., & Gelso, C. J. (2015). Is training effective? A study of counseling psychology doctoral trainees in a psychodynamic/interpersonal training clinic. *Journal of Counseling Psychology, 62,* 184–201.

Hill, N. M. & Schneider, W. (2006). Brain changes in the development of expertise: Neuroanatomical and neurophysiological evidence about skill-based adaptation. In K. A. Ericsson, N. Charness, P. J. Feltovich, & R. R. Hoffman (Eds), *The Cambridge Handbook of Expertise and Expert Performance* (pp. 653–82). Cambridge: Cambridge University Press.

Hilsenroth, M. J. & Diener, M. J. (in press). Some effective strategies for the supervision of psychodynamic psychotherapy. In Rousmaniere, T. G., Goodyear, R., Miller, S. D., & Wampold, B. (Eds), *The Cycle of Excellence: Using Deliberate Practice to Improve Supervision and Training.* London: Wiley.

Hilsenroth, M. J., Kivlighan, D. M., & Slavin-Mulford, J. (2015). Structured supervision of graduate clinicians in psychodynamic psychotherapy: Alliance and technique. *Journal of Counseling Psychology.* http://dx.doi.org/10.1037/cou0000058

Horvath, A. O., Del Re, A. C., Flückiger, C., & Symonds, D. (2011). Alliance in individual psychotherapy. *Psychotherapy, 48*(1), 9–16. doi: 10.1037/a0022186

Hubble, M. A., Duncan, B. L., & Miller, S. D. (1999). *The Heart and Soul of Change: What Works in Therapy.* Washington, DC: American Psychological Association.

Imel, Z. E., Laska, K., Jakupcak, M., & Simpson, T. L. (2013). Meta-analysis of dropout in treatments for posttraumatic stress disorder. *Journal of Consulting and Clinical Psychology, 81*(3), 394–404. doi: 10.1037/a0031474

James, W. (1907). The energies of men. *Science, 25,* 321–32.

Johnson, M. B., Tenenbaum, G., & Edmonds, W. A. (2006). Adaptation to physically and emotionally demanding conditions: The role of deliberate practice. *High Ability Studies, 17*(1), 117–36. doi: 10.1080/13598130600947184

Johnson, S. M. (2002). *Emotionally Focused Couple Therapy with Trauma Survivors: Strengthening Attachment Bonds.* New York: Guilford Press.

Kabat-Zinn, J. (1994). *Wherever You Go, There You Are.* New York: Hyperion.

Kagan, H. K. & Kagan, N. I. (1997). Interpersonal process recall: Influencing human interaction. In C. E. Watkins, Jr. (Ed.), *Handbook of Psychotherapy Supervision* (pp. 296–309). New York: Wiley.

Kageyama, N. (2016). *Hi! I'm Noa Kageyama.* Retrieved on February 14, 2016 from www.bulletproofmusician.com/about/

Kantrowitz, J. T. & Citrome, L. (2011). Schizoaffective disorder: A review of current research themes and pharmacological management. *CNS Drugs, 25*, 317-31. doi: 10.2165/11587630-000000000-00000

Kazdin, A. E. (2009). Understanding how and why psychotherapy leads to change. *Psychotherapy Research, 19*(4-5), 418-28. doi: 10.1080/10503300802448899

Kenny, D. T. (2014). *From Id to Intersubjectivity*. New York: Karnac.

Klein, G. A. (2008). Naturalistic decision making. *Human Factors, 50*(3), 456-60. doi: 10.1518/001872008X288385

Klein, G. A., Calderwood, R., & Clinton-Cirocco, A. (2010). Rapid decision making on the fireground: The original study plus a postscript. *Journal of Cognitive Engineering and Decision Making, 4*, 186-209. doi: 10.1518/155534310X12844000801203

Kohut, H. (1977). *The Restoration of the Self*. New York: International Universities Press.

Kraus, D. R., Castonguay, L., Boswell, J. F., Nordberg, S. S., & Hayes, J. A. (2011). Therapist effectiveness: Implications for accountability and patient care. *Psychotherapy Research, 21*(3), 267-76. doi: 10.1080/10503307.2011.563249

Krause, M. S. & Lutz, W. (2009). Process transforms inputs to determine outcomes: Therapists are responsible for managing process. *Clinical Psychology: Science and Practice, 16*, 73-81.

Ladany, N. & Inman, A. G. (2012). Training and supervision. In E. M. Altmaier & J. C. Hansen (Eds), *The Oxford Handbook of Counseling Psychology* (pp. 179-207). New York: Oxford University Press.

Ladany, N., Hill, C. E., Corbett, M. M., Nutt, E. A. (1996). Nature, extent, and importance of what psychotherapy trainees do not disclose to their supervisors. *Journal of Counseling Psychology, 43*(1), 10-24.

Ladany, N., Friedlander, M., & Nelson, M. (2016). *Critical Events in Psychotherapy Supervision*. Washington, DC: American Psychological Association.

Laing, R. (1971). *The Politics of the Family and Other Essays*. New York: Routledge.

Lambert, M. J. (2013). The efficacy and effectiveness of psychotherapy. In. M. J. Lambert (Ed.), *Bergin & Garfield's Handbook of Psychotherapy and Behavior Change* (6th ed., pp. 169-218). Hoboken, NJ: Wiley.

Lamm C., Batson, C. D., & Decety, J. (2007). The neural substrate of human empathy: Effects of perspective-taking and cognitive appraisal. *Journal of Cognitive Neuroscience, 19*(1), 42-58. doi: 10.1162/jocn.2007.19.1.42. PMID 17214562

Lampropoulos, G. K. (2011). Failure in psychotherapy: An introduction. *Journal of Clinical Psychology, 67*(11), 1093-5. doi: 10.1002/jclp.20858

Laska, K. M., Smith, T. L., Wislocki, A. P., & Wampold, B. E. (2013). Uniformity of evidence-based treatments in practice? Therapist effects in the delivery of cognitive processing therapy for PTSD. *Journal of Counseling Psychology, 60*, 31-41. doi: 10.1037/a0031294

Lehmann, A. C. & Ericsson, K. A. (1998). The historical development of domains of expertise: Performance standards and innovations in music. In A. Steptoe (Ed.), *Genius and the Mind* (pp. 67-94). Oxford: Oxford University Press.

Levitt, H. M. (2015). Qualitative psychotherapy research: The journey so far and future directions. *Psychotherapy, 52*, 31-7.

Lichtenberg, J. W. & Goodyear, R. K. (2012). Informal learning, incidental learning, and deliberate continuing education: Preparing psychologists to be effective lifelong learners. In G. J. Neimeyer & J. M. Taylor (Eds), *Continuing Professional Development and Lifelong Learning: Issues, Impacts and Outcomes* (pp. 71-80). Hauppauge, NY: Nova Science.

Locke, E. A. & Latham, G. P. (2002). Building a practically useful theory of goal setting and task motivation: A 35-year odyssey. *American Psychologist, 57*, 705–17.

Loftus, G. R. & Loftus, E. F. (1976). *Human Memory: The Processing of Information.* Hillsdale, NJ: Erlbaum Associates.

Macnamara, B. N., Hambrick, D. Z., & Oswald, F. L. (2014). Deliberate practice and performance in music, games, sports, education, and professions: A meta-analysis. *Psychological Science.* doi: 10.1177/0956797614535810

Martin, R. (2013). *Reminder: Our Memories Are Less Reliable than We Think.* Book review. retrieved on November 19, 2015 from http://goo.gl/irC2k

McCullough, L., Bhatia, M., Ulvenes, P., Berggraf, L., & Osborn, K. (2011). Learning how to rate video-recorded therapy sessions: A practical guide for trainees and advanced clinicians. *Psychotherapy, 48*(2), 127–37. doi: 10.1037/a0023131

McGaghie, W. C. (in press). Advances in medical education from mastery learning and deliberate practice. In T. G. Rousmaniere, R. Goodyear, D. D. Miller, & B. E. Wampold (Eds), *The Cycle of Excellence: Using Deliberate Practice to Improve Supervision and Training.* London: Wiley Publishers.

McGaghie, W. C. & Fisichella, P. M. (2014). The science of learning and medical education. *Medical Education, 48*(2), 106–8. http://doi.org/10.1111/medu.12396

McGaghie, W. C. & Kristopaitis, T. (2015). Deliberate practice and mastery learning: Origins of expert medical performance. In J. Cleland & S. J. Durning (Eds), *Researching Medical Education.* Chichester: John Wiley & Sons. doi: 10.1002/9781118838983.ch19

McGaghie, W. C., Issenberg, S. B., Barsuk, J. H., & Wayne, D. B. (2014). A critical review of simulation-based mastery learning with translational outcomes. *Medical Education, 48*(4), 375–85. http://doi.org/10.1111/medu.12391

McLeod, J. (2010). *Case Study Research in Counselling and Psychotherapy.* London: Sage.

McLeod, J. (2013). Qualitative research: Methods and contributions. In M. J. Lambert (Ed.), *Bergin and Garfield's Handbook of Psychotherapy and Behavior Change* (5th ed., pp. 49–84). New York: Wiley.

McLeod, J. (2016). *Using Research in Counselling and Psychotherapy.* London: Sage.

McLeod, J. (in press). Qualitative methods for routine outcome measurement. In T. G. Rousmaniere, R. Goodyear, D. D. Miller, & B. E. Wampold (Eds), *The Cycle of Excellence: Using Deliberate Practice to Improve Supervision and Training.* London: Wiley.

McWilliams, N. (1999). *Psychoanalytic Case Formulation.* New York: Guilford Press.

Mehr, K. E., Ladany, N., & Caskie, G. I. L. (2010). Trainee nondisclosure in supervision: What are they not telling you? *Counselling and Psychotherapy Research, 10*(2), 103–13. doi: 10.1080/14733141003712301

Miller, S. D., Duncan, B. L., Brown, J., Sparks, J. A., & Claud, D. A. (2003). The outcome rating scale: A preliminary study of the reliability, validity, and feasibility of a brief visual analog measure. *Journal of Brief Therapy, 2*, 91–100.

Miller, S. D., Hubble, M. A., and Duncan, B. L. (2007). Supershrinks: Learning from the field's most effective practitioners. *Psychotherapy Networker, 31*, 26–35, 56.

Miller, S. D., Hubble, M. A, Chow, D. L., & Seidel, J. A. (2013). The outcome of psychotherapy: Yesterday, today, and tomorrow. *Psychotherapy, 50*(1): 88–97. doi: 10.1037/a0031097

Miller, S. D., Hubble, M. A., Chow, D., & Seidel, J. (2015). Beyond measures and monitoring: Realizing the potential of feedback-informed treatment. *Psychotherapy, 52*(4), 449–57. http://doi.org/10.1037/pst0000031

Miller, S. D., Hubble, M. A., & Chow, D. (in press). Professional development: From oxymoron to reality. In Rousmaniere, T. G., Goodyear, R., Miller, S. D., & Wampold,

B. (Eds), *The Cycle of Excellence: Using Deliberate Practice to Improve Supervision and Training*. London: Wiley.

Miller, S. D., Prescott, D., & Maeschalck, S. (in press). *Reaching for Excellence: Feedback-Informed Treatment in Practice*. Washington, DC: APA Books.

Miller, W. R. & Rollnick, S. (2012). *Motivational Interviewing* (3rd ed.). New York: Guilford Press.

Minami, T., Wampold, B. E., Serlin, R. C., Hamilton, E., Brown, G. S., & Kircher, J. (2008). Benchmarking the effectiveness of psychotherapy treatment for adult depression in a managed care environment: A preliminary study. *Journal of Consulting and Clinical Psychology, 76*, 116-24. doi: 10.1037/0022-006X.76.1.116

Minami, T., Brown, G., McCulloch, J., & Bolstrom, B. J. (2012). Benchmarking therapists: Furthering the benchmarking method in its application to clinical practice. *Quality & Quantity, 46*(6), 1699-708. doi: 10.1007/s11135-011-9548-4

Mohr, D. C. (1995). Negative outcome in psychotherapy: A critical review. *Clinical Psychology: Science and Practice, 2*(1), 1-27. http://doi.org/10.1111/j.1468-2850.1995.tb00022.x

Moreno, J. L. (1932). *First Book on Group Therapy*. New York: Beacon House.

Myers, D. G. (2015). *Exploring Social Psychology* (7th ed.). New York: McGraw Hill Education.

Neimeyer, G. J. & Taylor, J. M. (2010). Continuing education in psychology. In J. C. Norcross, G. R. VandenBos, & D. K. Freedheim (Eds), *History of Psychotherapy: continuity and change* (pp. 663-71). Washington, DC: American Psychological Association.

Newman, J. W. (1996). *Disciplines of Attention*. New York: Peter Lang Publishing.

Nissen-Lie, H. A., Monsen, J. T., & Rønnestad, M. H. (2010). Therapist predictors of early patient-rated working alliance: A multilevel approach. *Psychotherapy Research: Journal of the Society for Psychotherapy Research, 20*(6), 627-46. doi: 10.1080/10503307.2010.497633

Nissen-Lie, H. A., Rønnestad, M. H., Høglend, P. A., Havik, O. E., Solbakken, O. A., Stiles, T. C., & Monsen, J. T. (2015). Love yourself as a person, doubt yourself as a therapist? *Clinical Psychology & Psychotherapy*. http://doi.org/10.1002/cpp.1977

Norcross, J. C. (2011). *Psychotherapy Relationships that Work: Evidence-Based Responsiveness* (2nd ed.). Oxford: Oxford University Press.

Norem, J. K. & Cantor, N. (1986). Anticipatory and post hoc cushioning strategies: Optimism and defensive pessimism in "risky" situations. *Cognitive Therapy and Research, 10*(3), 347-62.

Okiishi, J., Lambert, M. J., Nielsen, S. L., & Ogles, B. M. (2003). Waiting for supershrink: An empirical analysis of therapist effects. *Clinical Psychology & Psychotherapy, 10*(6), 361-73. doi: 10.1002/cpp.383

Okiishi, J. C., Lambert, M. J., Eggett, D., Nielsen, L., Dayton, D. D., & Vermeersch, D. A. (2006). An analysis of therapist treatment effects: Toward providing feedback to individual therapists on their clients' psychotherapy outcome. *Journal of Clinical Psychology, 62*, 1157-72. http://dx.doi.org/10.1002/jclp.20272

Orlinsky, D. E. & Ronnestad, M. H. (2005). *How Psychotherapists Develop*. Washington, DC: American Psychological Association.

Osborn, K. & Bhatia, M. (2015). Online supervision in affect phobia therapy. In T. G. Rousmaniere & E. Renfro-Michele (Eds), *Using Technology for Clinical Supervision: A Practical Handbook* (pp. 203-22). Alexandria, VA: American Counseling Association Press.

Osler, W. (1932). *Aeuquanimitas* (3rd ed.). Philadelphia, PA: P. Blakiston's Son & Co.

Öst, L. G. (2008). Efficacy of the third wave of behavioral therapies: A systematic review and meta-analysis. *Behaviour Research and Therapy, 46*(3), 296-321. doi: 10.1016/j.brat.2007.12.005

Owen, J. & Hilsenroth, M. J. (2014). Treatment adherence: The importance of therapist flexibility in relation to therapy outcomes. *Journal of Counseling Psychology, 61*, 280-8. doi: 10.1037/a0035753

Owen, J., Adelson, J., Budge, S., Wampold, B., Kopta, M., Minami, T., & Miller, S. (2015). Trajectories of change in psychotherapy. *Journal of Clinical Psychology, 71*(9), doi: 10.1002/jclp.22191

Owen, J., Wampold, B. E., Rousmaniere, T. G., Kopta, M., & Miller., S. (2016). As good as it gets? Therapy outcomes of trainees over time. *Journal of Counseling Psychology, 63*, 12-19.

Perls, F. (1973). *The Gestalt Approach and Eye Witness to Therapy*. New York: Science and Behavior Books.

Preston, S. D. & de Waal, F. B. M. (2002). Empathy: Its ultimate and proximate bases. *Behavioral and Brain Sciences, 25*, 1-72. doi: 10.1017/s0140525x02000018

Rast, K., Herman, J., Rousmaniere, T. G., Swift, J., & Whipple, J. (in review). Supervisor effects on client outcomes: The perspectives of practicing supervisors and supervisees.

Reese, R. J., Usher, E. L., Bowman, D. C., Norsworthy, L. A., Halstead, J. L., Rowlands, S. R., & Chisholm, R. R. (2009). Using client feedback in psychotherapy training: An analysis of its influence on supervision and counselor self-efficacy. *Training and Education in Professional Psychology, 3*, 157-68. doi: 10.1037/a0015673

Riksrevisionen (2015). Rehabgarantin fungerar inte: Tänk om eller lägg ner [The rehabilitation system does not work: Rethink or terminate the project]. Report from Riksrevisionen to the Swedish Government (RIR 2015: 19). Stockholm: Riksdagens Interntryckeri. Retrieved on August 20, 2016 from https://goo.gl/yjOC9B

Rogers, C. (1961). *On Becoming a Person*. London: Constable.

Rosenzweig, S. (1936). Some implicit common factors in diverse methods of psychotherapy. *American Journal of Orthopsychiatry, 6*(3), 412-15.

Ross, G. K., Shafer, J. L., & Klein, G. (2006). Professional judgments and "naturalistic decision making." In K. A. Ericsson, N. Charness, P. J. Feltovich, & R. R. Hoffman (Eds), *The Cambridge Handbook of Expertise and Expert Performance* (pp. 683-703). Cambridge: Cambridge University Press.

Roth, A. D. (2016). A new scale for the assessment of competencies in cognitive and behavioural therapy. *Behavioural and Cognitive Psychotherapy*, 1-5. doi: 10.1017/S1352465816000011

Rothaupt, J. W. & Morgan, M. M. (2007). Counselors' and counselor educators' practice of mindfulness: A qualitative inquiry. *Counseling & Values, 52*, 40-54.

Rousmaniere, T. G. & Ellis, M. V. (2013). Developing the construct and measure of collaborative clinical supervision: The supervisee's perspective. *Training and Education in Professional Psychology, 7*, 300-8. doi: 10.1037/a0033796

Rousmaniere, T. G. & Frederickson, J. (2013). Internet-based one-way-mirror supervision for advanced psychotherapy training. *Clinical Supervisor, 32*, 40-55. doi: 10.1080/07325223.2013.778683

Rousmaniere, T. G. & Frederickson, J. (2015). Remote live supervision: Videoconference for one-way-mirror supervision. In T. G. Rousmaniere & E. Renfro-Michele (Eds), *Using Technology for Clinical Supervision: A Practical Handbook* (pp. 157-74). Alexandria, VA: American Counseling Association Press.

Rousmaniere, T. G. & Kuhn, N. (2015). Internet security for clinical supervisors. In T. G. Rousmaniere & E. Renfro-Michele (Eds), *Using Technology for Clinical Supervision: A Practical Handbook* (pp. 103–16). Alexandria, VA: American Counseling Association Press.

Rousmaniere, T. G., Swift, J. K., Babins-Wagner, R., Whipple, J. L., & Berzins, S. (2014). Supervisor effects on client outcome in routine practice. *Psychotherapy Research*, 1–10.

Rousmaniere, T. G., Goodyear, R., Miller, S. D., & Wampold, B. (Eds) (in press). *The Cycle of Excellence: Using Deliberate Practice to Improve Supervision and Training*. London: Wiley.

Rowe, C. E. & Isaac, D. S. M. (2000). *Empathic Attunement: The "Technique" of Psychoanalytic Self Psychology*. New York: Jason Aronson.

Russell, T. A., Green, M. J., Simpson, I., & Coltheart, M. (2008). Remediation of facial emotion perception in schizophrenia: Concomitant changes in visual attention. *Schizophrenia Research, 103*, 248–56.

Safran, J. D., Muran, J. C., & Eubanks-Carter, C. (2011). Repairing alliance ruptures. *Psychotherapy, 48*(1), 80–7. doi: 10.1037/a0022140

Scherr, S. R., Herbert, J. D., & Forman, E. M. (2015). The role of therapist experiential avoidance in predicting therapist preference for exposure treatment for OCD. *Journal of Contextual Behavioral Science, 4*(1), 21–9. http://doi.org/10.1016/j.jcbs.2014.12.002

Schöttke, H., Flückiger, C., Goldberg, S. B., Eversmann, J., & Lange, J. (2016). Predicting psychotherapy outcome based on therapist interpersonal skills: A five-year longitudinal study of a therapist assessment protocol. *Psychotherapy Research, 33*(7), 1–11. doi: 10.1080/10503307.2015.1125546

Schure, M. B., Christopher, J., & Christopher, S. (2008). Mind-body medicine and the art of self care: Teaching mindfulness to counseling students through yoga, meditation and qigong. *Journal of Counseling and Development, 86*, 47–56.

Schwartz, D. L., Chase, C. C., & Bransford, J. D. (2012). Resisting overzealous transfer: Coordinating previously successful routines with needs for new learning. *Educational Psychologist, 47*, 204–14. doi: 10.1080/00461520.2012.696317

Segal, Z. V., Williams, J. M. G., & Teasdale, J. D. (2002). *Mindfulness-Based Cognitive Therapy for Depression: A New Approach to Preventing Relapse*. New York: Guilford Press.

Seligman, E. P. (2012). *Flourish: A Visionary New Understanding of Happiness and Well-being*. New York: Free Press.

Shapiro, S. L. & Carlson, L. E. (2009). *The Art and Science of Mindfulness: Integrating Mindfulness into Psychology and the Helping Professions*. Washington, DC: American Psychological Association.

Shapiro, S. L., Brown, K. W., & Biegel, G. M. (2007). Teaching self-care to caregivers: Effects of mindfulness-based stress reduction on the mental health of therapists in training. *Training and Education in Professional Psychology, 1*, 105–15. doi: 10.1037/1931-3918.1.2.105

Sherman, J. J. & Cramer, A. (2005). Measurement of changes in empathy during dental school. *Journal of Dental Education, 69*(3), 338–45. https://www.ncbi.nlm.nih.gov/pubmed/15749944

Siegel, D. J. (2007). *The Mindful Brain: Reflection and Attunement in the Cultivation of Well-being*. New York: Norton.

Spengler, P. M., White, M. J., Ægisdóttir, S., Maugherman, A. S., Anderson, L. A., Cook, R. S., Nichols, C., Lampropoulos, G., Walker, B., Cohen G., & Rush, J. D. (2009).

The meta-analysis of clinical judgment project: Effects of experience on judgment accuracy. *Counseling Psychologist, 37,* 350–99. http://dx.doi.org/10.1177/0011000006295149

Stein, D. M. & Lambert, M. J. (1984). On the relationship between therapist experience and psychotherapy outcome. *Clinical Psychology Review, 4,* 127–42. http://dx.doi.org/10.1016/0272-7358(84)90025-4

Stein, D. M. & Lambert, M. J. (1995). Graduate training in psychotherapy: Are therapy outcomes enhanced? *Journal of Consulting and Clinical Psychology, 63,* 182–96. http://dx.doi.org/10.1037/0022-006X.63.2.182

Stephen, S., Elliott, R., & Macleod, R. (2011). Person-centred therapy with a client experiencing social anxiety difficulties: A hermeneutic single case efficacy design. *Counselling and Psychotherapy Research, 11,* 55–66.

Stiles, W. B. (2009). Responsiveness as an obstacle for psychotherapy outcome research: It's worse than you think. *Clinical Psychology: Science and Practice, 16*(1), 86–91. doi: 10.1111/j.1468-2850.2009.01148.x

Stiles, W. B., Honos-Webb, L., & Surko, M. (1998). Responsiveness in psychotherapy. *Clinical Psychology Science and Practice, 39*(4), 490–8. doi: 10.1111/j.1468-2850.1998.tb00166.x

Strupp, H. H. & Hadley, S. W. (1979). Specific vs nonspecific factors in psychotherapy: A controlled study of outcome. *Archives of General Psychiatry, 36,* 1125–36. doi:10.1001/archpsyc.1979.01780100095009. http://jamanetwork.com/journals/jamapsychiatry/article-abstract/492193

Sudnow, D. (2001). *Ways of the Hand.* Cambridge, MA: MIT Press.

Suzuki, S. (1970). *Zen Mind, Beginner's Mind.* New York: Weatherhill.

Swift, J. K. & Greenberg, R. O. (2014). *Premature Termination in Psychotherapy: Strategies for Engaging Clients and Improving Outcomes.* Washington, DC: American Psychological Association.

Swift, J. K., Rousmaniere, T. G., Babins-Wagner, R., Berzins, S., & Whipple, J. L. (in review). Predicting client dropout based on outcome and alliance changes in the sessions preceding the event.

Tallman, K. & Bohart, A. C. (1999). The client as a common factor: Clients as self-healers. In M. A. Hubble, B. L. Duncan, & S. D. Miller (Eds), *The Heart and Soul of Change.* Washington, DC: American Psychological Association.

Tatkin, S. (2012). *Wired for Love.* Berkeley, CA: New Harbinger Publications.

Taylor, J. M. & Neimeyer, G. J. (2015). The assessment of lifelong learning in psychologists. *Professional Psychology: Research and Practice,* July 20. http://dx.doi.org/10.1037/pro0000027

Taylor, J. M. & Neimeyer, G. J. (in press). Lifelong professional improvement: The evolution of continuing education. In Rousmaniere, T. G., Goodyear, R., Miller, S. D., & Wampold, B. (Eds), *The Cycle of Excellence: Using Deliberate Practice to Improve Supervision and Training.* London: Wiley.

Tracey, T. J. G., Wampold, B. E., Lichtenberg, J. W., & Goodyear, R. K. (2014). Expertise in psychotherapy: An elusive goal? *American Psychologist, 69,* 218–29.

Tracey, T. J. G., Wampold, B. E., Goodyear, R. K., & Lichtenberg, J. W. (2015). Improving expertise in psychotherapy. *Psychotherapy Bulletin, 50*(1), 7–13.

Underhill, E. (2002). *Mysticism: A Study in the Nature and Development of Spiritual Consciousness.* New York: Dover Publications.

Vallerand, R. J., Blanchard, C. M., Mageau, G. A., Koestner, R., Ratelle, C., Léonard, M., Gagné, M., & Marsolais, J. (2003). Les passions de l'âme: On obsessive and harmonious passion. *Journal of Personality and Social Psychology, 85,* 756–67.

Vallerand, R. J., Mageau, G. A., Elliot, A. J., Dumais, A., Demers, M.-A., & Rousseau, F. (2008). Passion and performance attainment in sport. *Psychology of Sport and Exercise, 9*, 373–92. http://dx.doi.org/10.1016/j.psychsport.2007.05.003

Vallerand, R. J., Houlfort, N., & Forest, J. (2014). Passion for work: Determinants and outcomes. In M. Gagne (Ed.), *Oxford Handbook of Work Engagement, Motivation, and Self-Determination Theory* (pp. 85–105). New York: Oxford University Press.

Vygotsky, L. S. (1978). *Mind in Society: The Development of Higher Psychological Processes.* Cambridge, MA: Harvard University Press.

Waelde, L. C., Uddo, M., Marquett, R., Ropelato, M., Freightman, S., Pardo, A., & Salazar, J. (2008). A pilot study of meditation for mental health workers following hurricane Katrina. *Journal of Traumatic Stress, 21*, 497–500. doi: 10.1002/jts.20365

Walfish, S., McAlister, B., O'Donnell, P., & Lambert, M. J. (2012). An investigation of self-assessment bias in mental health providers. *Psychological Reports, 110*(2), 639–44. doi: 10.2466/02.07.17.PR0.110.2.2

Walsh, R. & Shapiro, S. L. (2006). The meeting of meditative disciplines and Western psychology: A mutually enriching dialogue. *American Psychologist, 61*, 227–39. doi: 10.1037/0003-066X.61.3.227

Wampold, B. (in press). What should we practice? A contextual model for how psychotherapy works. In Rousmaniere, T. G., Goodyear, R., Miller, S. D., & Wampold, B. (Eds), *The Cycle of Excellence: Using Deliberate Practice to Improve Supervision and Training.* London: Wiley.

Wampold, B. E. & Brown, G. S. (2005). Estimating variability in outcomes attributable to therapists: A naturalistic study of outcomes in managed care. *Journal of Consulting and Clinical Psychology, 73*, 914–23. http://dx.doi.org/10.1037/0022-006X.73.5.914

Wampold, B. E. & Holloway, E. L. (1997). Methodology, design, and evaluation in psychotherapy supervision research. In C. E. Watkins (Ed.), *Handbook of Psychotherapy Supervision* (pp. 11–27). New York: Wiley.

Wampold, B. E. & Imel, Z. (2015). *The Great Psychotherapy Debate: The Evidence for What Makes Psychotherapy Work* (2nd ed.). New York: Routledge.

Watkins, C. E. (2011). Does psychotherapy supervision contribute to patient outcomes? Considering thirty years of research. *Clinical Supervisor, 30*, 235–56. doi: 10.1080/07325223.2011.619417

Watson, J. B. (1930). *Behaviorism.* New York: W. W. Norton.

Webb, C. A., DeRubeis, R. J., & Barber, J. P. (2010). Therapist adherence/competence and treatment outcome: A meta-analytic review. *Journal of Consulting and Clinical Psychology, 78*(2), 200–11. doi: 10.1037/a0018912

Webster, T. G. (1971). National priorities for the continuing education of psychologists. *American Psychologist, 26*, 1016–19. http://dx.doi.org/10.1037/h0032256

Weisberg, R. (2006). Modes of expertise in creative thinking: Evidence from case studies. In K. A. Ericsson, N. Charness, P. J. Feltovich, & R. R. Hoffman (Eds), *The Cambridge Handbook of Expertise and Expert Performance* (pp. 761–87). Cambridge: Cambridge University Press. http://doi.org/10.1017/CBO9780511606915.003

Weiss, J. (1993). *How Psychotherapy Works: Process and Technique.* New York: Guilford Press.

Werbart, A., von Below, C., Brun, J., & Gunnarsdottir, H. (2014). "Spinning one's wheels": Nonimproved patients view their psychotherapy. *Psychotherapy Research.* doi: 10.1080/10503307.2014.989291

Williams, E. N., Hayes, J. A., & Fauth, J. (2007). Therapist self-awareness: Interdisciplinary connections and future directions. In S. D. Brown & R. W. Lent (Eds), *Handbook of Counseling Psychology* (4th ed.). New York: Wiley.

Wilson, K. G. & Dufrene, T. (2008). *Mindfulness for Two: An Acceptance and Commitment Therapy Approach to Mindfulness in Psychotherapy.* Oakland, CA: New Harbinger Publications.

Winner, R. (1996). The rage to master: The decisive role of talent in the visual arts. In K. A. Ericsson (Ed.), *The Road to Excellence: The Acquisition of Expert Performance in the Arts and Sciences, Sports and Games* (pp. 271-301). Hillsdale, NJ: Erlbaum.

Wise, E. H., Sturm, C. A., Nutt, R. L., Rodolfa, E., Schaffer, J. B., & Webb, C. (2010). Life-long learning for psychologists: Current status and a vision for the future. *Professional Psychology: Research and Practice, 41*(4), 288-97. http://doi.org/10.1037/a0020424

Yalom, I. D. (1980). *Existential Psychotherapy.* New York: Basic Books.

Zimmerman, B. J. (2006). Development and adaptation of expertise: The role of self-regulatory processes and beliefs. In K. A. Ericsson, N. Charness, P. J. Feltovich, & R. R. Hoffman (Eds), *The Cambridge Handbook of Expertise and Expert Performance* (pp. 683-703). Cambridge: Cambridge University Press.

INDEX

Page numbers in *italics* denote references to Figures and Tables.

Abbass, Allan 24, 26, 27
accessibility of deliberate practice 186–7
Ackerman, S. J. 102, 187
active learning 174–5, 177, 182–3
adaptation 28, 51–2, 140
adherence to psychotherapy model 147–8
Aldrich, B. J. 58
ambition 57
American Psychological Association (APA) 9, 21
anger 50, 116, 143–4
anxiety: accepting 98; caused by guilt 143–4; client 37, 100, 101; nausea as sign of 37; nonverbal signaling 39–40; simplistic approach to 103–5; therapist 81
anxiety-regulation techniques 97
appropriate responsiveness 145–6
assessment 123–4; *see also* performance assessment
Association of Counselor Education and Supervision 9
attunement: to client's body language 130–3, 138, 141; to client's verbal language 133–5, 138, 141; experiential

reflection 135; microexpressions 131; to therapists' experience 135–7, 138, 141; through videotape review 46
authenticity 73–4, 134
automaticity 134
autonomous internalization of activity 162–3
awareness 147
Axline, Virginia 98

Bandura, Albert 159
basic therapy-related interpersonal skills 125–6
behavioral self-regulation 159
Beutler, L. E. 8
biased data 8–10
biased memory 9, 17, 47, 83, 94
Blanchard, Matt 93
blind spots 182
Bloom, Benjamin 158, 186
body language 38
Bohart, A. C. 11
boundaries 178
Bruce, Noah 109
Buddhism 107
bulletproofmusician.com 77

California Board of Psychology 66
Callahan, Jennifer 8
The Cambridge Handbook of Expertise and Expert Performance (Ericsson) 59
Campitelli, G. 188
career-long repetition *115*, 117
CBT therapy models 101, 103, 151–2
Chow, Daryl 30, 53
Clement, Paul 87
client distress, handling 103–5
client outcome: adherence to model and 177; disconnect between clinical training and 12; performance assessment through 121, 123, 152–4, 177, 183–4; supervision's impact on 7–8, 11–12, 25; training to improve 63–4, 108; variability between therapists 15
client resistance 89
client-centered psychotherapy 151
clients, bonding with 4–5
clinical experience, prolonged 60
clinical judgment 120
clinical mastery, path to 26–7
clinical mindfulness 109–10, 126–30
clinical portfolio 66
clinical rationalizations 101
clinical role play 116
clinical supervision: biased data in 9–10; challenges of 11; client outcome from 7–8, 11–12; collaborative 34; defined 6, 173; goals of 6–7, 167–8; harmful 34–5; inadequate 34–5; incorporating deliberate practice in 173; limited benefit of 10; reading assignments in 41; in real time 81; resistance to 79–80; transcript excerpt *82*; *see also* coaches/coaching
clinical training: active learning 174–5; for basic psychotherapy skills 12; behavioral skill rehearsal 116; continuing education 170; deliberate practice for 29–30; disconnect from client outcomes and 12; effective

pedagogy 35; effectiveness of 12–13; for experiential avoidance 103; group process 35; homework 41–2, 176; integrating deliberate practice in 65; medical education and 61; passive learning 174–5; post-graduate 170; skill-focused 64, 174; stimulation-based 62; traditional 116, 174, 177; venue for 170–2; *see also* clinical supervision; lifelong learning
clinical videos 18
clinical wisdom 88, 89, 92
coaches/coaching: consultation groups 171; effectiveness of 167; individual consultation 171; long-term relationship with 183; morale from 167; peer consultation 171; selection of 168–70; *see also* clinical supervision; clinical training
coach/therapist judgment 120
coasting 119
Coker, Jerry 78
Colgan, Philip 80
collaboration: with clients 81, 130; in jazz 130; with supervisor 100–1, 175; with trainee 175
collaborative supervision 34
collateral information 121
common-factor variables of therapy outcomes 47
communication 47
competency 166–7
compliance 69–70, 166, 175
congruence 130
consultation groups 171
continuing education 180, 181
control, assessment of 147
Coughlan, E. K. 51
Coughlin, Patricia 23–4, 27, 30–1
countertransference 9
couples therapy, case example 143–5
creative genius 39
culture, professional 71–2
curiosity 57

Darwin, Charles 157
Davis, Daphne 109
decision skills training 93
deep domain-specific expertise 39
defensive pessimism 182
deliberate practice: challenges to 186-9; core challenge of 51; defined 28; described 27-30; in graduate school 165-7; *see also* solitary deliberate practice
deliberate practice exercises: attunement with client 130-7; building endurance 139-42; clinical mindfulness 126-30; couples therapy 143-5; drama therapy 137; learning goals 153-4; microexpressions 131; psychotherapist activity/model assessment 146-8; psychotherapy warm-ups 137-9; videotape study 149-50
deliberate practice journal 53, 123
deliberate practice model: developing 59; implementation 59
deliberate practice routine: career-long repetition 115; effectiveness of 119; identifying cases for 120; learning principles 115; processes of 114-15; role play 118-19; sample schedule 123; selecting exercises for 122
deteriorating clients 5-7, 16, 36-7, 94, 181-2
deteriorating in therapy 93
deterioration, focus on 5-6, 19, 124, 144
deterioration rates 14, 19, 25, 43
Disciplines of Attention (Newman) 106
disidentification 106; *see also* mindfulness
disillusionment, in psychotherapy models 13-14
dodo bird verdict 21
domain-specific expertise 39
drama therapy 137
dropouts, therapy 6, 8, 25n1, 94
dualistic model of passion 162
Duckworth, Angela 160-1
Duncan, Barry 21, 85

duration, for deliberate practice routine 122
dynamic therapy 13, 17, 22-4, 71

Ellis, Michael 7, 34
emotional endurance 51-3
emotional resiliency 105
emotional self-awareness 49-50, 102
emotional training block 101
emotion-focused therapy 151, 152-3
empathy 130, 135
empirically supported training methods 189
environmental self-regulation 159
Ericsson, K. Anders: defining deliberate practice 31n1; on deliberate practice learning 166, 174, 176; discovery of deliberate practice 27-8; on extensive experience vs. expertise 86-7, 180; on long-term follow-up 124; on mental representations 39; on overloading 52; on pathfinders 191-2; on performance improvement 52; on purposeful practice 189; redefining deliberate practice 189; simulation-based training benefits 40-1; videotape use for deliberate practice 36, 50-1
Eskreis-Winkler, Lauren 161
experience vs. expertise 86-8, 180
experiential avoidance: anxiety and 81-2; case example 97, 99; cognitive justification for 101; described 98; as impediment to training 177-8; lifelong learning and 184; rationalization for 101; recognizing one's own 42, 127, 129-30; of therapist 102-3
experiential exercises 116
experiential reflection 135
experiential self-awareness 126-7
expert performance 29, 187-8
expertise model of learning 76, 86-8, 187

facilitative interpersonal skills 119, 125-6
failing successfully 84-5
failure, productive use of 84-5

Fairbanks, Alaska 58
Falender, Carol 7
Farber, Barry 93
feedback 93–4, 120, 153
Fernyhough, Charles 9
flow ("being in the zone") 42, 43n1, 51
follow-through 161
follow-up 124, 184
Forest, J. 162–3
four-step model for decision skills training 93
Frank, J. B. 48
Frank, J. D. 48
Frederickson, Jon 24, 32–3, 37–8, 72, 76, 79–80
Freud, Sigmund 59
further education *see* continuing education

gatekeeping 103
Gawande, Atul 184
Gladwell, Malcolm 45
Gobet, F. 188
Goldberg, Simon 20, 87, 193
Goodyear, Rodney 94, 180
graduate school 165–7
grit 160–2
Guatama, Siddhärtha 107

Hagerty, G. 94–5
Hambrick, D. Z. 187, 188
Handbook of Expertise and Expert Performance (Ericsson) 105
harmonious passion 162–3, 179
harsh supervision 35
Hatcher, R. L. 145–6
Hayes, Jeffrey 109
The Heart and Soul of Change (Hubble) 21, 27
Hendlin, Steven 87–8
Herget, Mary 17, 34
Hilsenroth, M. J. 94–5, 102
Holloway, E. L. 12
Holmes, Oliver Wendell, Jr. 60
homeostasis 52
homework 41–2, 176, 183

Houlfort, N. 162–3
"How being bad can make you better" (article) 85
Howard, M. 8
Hoyt, Bill 20
Hubble, Mark 21, 85

immersion-experience model 75
improvisation, rule-governed paths for 78
individual consultation 171
Inman, A. G. 8
inner game: coach support for 167, 178–9; defined 157–8; grit 160–2; harmonious passion 162–3, 179; lifelong learning 184; self-regulation 159–60
intensive short-term dynamic psychotherapy (ISTDP) 23–4, 142; *see also* deliberate practice exercises
interpersonal functioning 26–7
interpersonal process recall 127
inter-rater reliability 66
intrapsychic functioning 26–7
isolation 57

James, William 107–8, 157
jazz 78–9

Kageyama, Noa 77, 85
Kazdin, Alan 14, 146
knowledge acquisition 182–3

Ladany, Nicholas 7, 8
Lambert, M. J. 15, 19
learning goals 153–4
Lichtenberg, James 94, 180
lifelong learning: defined 180; format for 180–1; improving 181–4; passive learning 181; training formats *181*
listening, careful value of 134
location, for deliberate practice routine 122
long-term dynamic model of therapy 71

Macnamara, B. N. 188
mastery learning 79–81

McGaghie, William 61, 62–3, 79
medical education: deliberate practice in 61–2; natural method of 60–2; reform of 61
medically unexplained disorders 24
meditation 106
memory/memories: biased 9; described 9; limits of 94–5
mental health 59, 189
mental models 92
mental representations 39
metacognition 92
metacompetency 146
metaknowledge 146
microexpressions 131
Miller, Scott 21, 27, 28, 39, 85
mindfulness 106–9; *see also* clinical mindfulness
mindfulness training 108–9
mirror neurons 135
model and style of therapy 66–70
modern medical education 61
Moltke, Helmuth 49
mood disorder 74
morale 167
Moreno, Jacob 116
motivation 157–8; *see also* inner game
motivational interviewing 151
multisystemic stressors 5
Muran, John 108–9
musical training: deliberate practice in 33; jazz 78–9; model of learning 76; performance enhancement 77; solitary deliberate practice routines 77–8

narrative therapy 17, 22
natural decision making 90–2
natural method of learning 74–5
nausea 37
Neimeyer, Greg 180–1
Newman, John 106
Nielsen, S. L. 15
Nissen-Lie, H. A. 105, 163
nonresponders 6

nonverbal microexpressions 47
nonverbal signaling 38, 39–40
Norcross, John 47

obsessive passion 163
Ogles, B. M. 15
Okiishi, J. 15
optimal learning zone 37–8, 175
Orlinsky, David 19
Osler, William 60
Oswald, F. L. 188
outcome data: analysis of 16, 20; assessing performance 153; self-assessment of 27; tracking of 15; use of 72n1
Outliers (Gladwell) 45
overloading 52
overzealous transfer 148

passive compliance 175
passive learning 117, 174–5, 181, 183
passivity 37–8
pathfinders 191–2
patterns, awareness of 47–8
peer consultation 171
perceptual skills 92
performance assessment 177, 183–4
performance data 14–15
performance enhancement 77
performance feedback 72, 93, 167, 184
personal introspection 103
personal self-regulation 159
pioneering practitioners 191–2
play therapy 100
Pool, R. 31n1, 166, 174, 189
positive psychology 160–1, 162–3
practice, defined 188–9
procedural memory 42
professional culture 71–2
professional external feedback 94
professional obsolescence 183
professional self-doubt 182
prolonged clinical experience 60
psychodynamic psychotherapy 151
psychodynamic therapy 4, 13, 18, 22

psychotherapy: adherence to model 147–8; compared to jazz 78; compared to other professions 105; difficult situation factors 90; dropout rates 8; effectiveness of 10–12, 148; failure in 125; fit of 148; homework for 41–2; integrating deliberate practice in 65; learning from master clinicians 17–18; mechanical approach to 41; mindfulness for 107–8; model and style of therapy 66–70; negative reactions to 93–4; performance data 14–15; therapeutic timing in 81–3; treatment models 151–4; variability between therapists 15–17, 88–90; variation among clients' rates of improvement 15–17; *see also* therapists
psychotherapy endurance 51–2
psychotherapy model: community-and-feeling methods 14; faith-based idealism in 13–14; fit of 48–9; scientific evidence and 14–15; selection factors 14; strict adherence to 89
psychotherapy theories, described 48–9
psychotherapy tourism 172
psychotherapy training *see* clinical training
psychotherapy training programs 170–2
psychotherapy.net 27
purposeful practice 31n1, 189

qualitative data 121

rapid response 5
Recognition of Psychotherapy Effectiveness (APA) 21
Recognition-Primed Decision Model (RPD) 91–2
redirecting clients 99–100
relational skills 126
repetition 57, *115*, 117, 176, 177
repetitive behavioral rehearsal 153, 154
repetitive clinical role play 40
rock climbing 113
role play 27, 39–40, 80, 116–19, 134, 152–4, 183

Ronnestad, Michael 19
Rosenzweig, S. 21
Ross, G. K. 92
routine outcome monitoring 121

Safran, Jeremy 108–9
Salathé Wall 113
schedule, for deliberate practice routine 122
schizoaffective disorder 74
self-assessment 27
self-awareness: emotional 49–50, 102; experiential 126–7
self-doubt 182
self-efficacy 159
self-esteem 163
self-identity 187
self-monitoring 92
self-regulation 159–60, 179
self-restraint 174
sequential progression 76
Session Rating Scale (SRS) 69, 120
Shafranske, Edward 7
short outcome 121
short-term dynamic model of therapy 71, 153–4
simulation-based behavioral rehearsal 117
simulation-based mastery learning 40–1, 104
simulation-based training 117–19
skill acquisition 182, 184
skill deficits 83–4
skill development 167
skill-focused clinical exercises 39–40
skill-focused homework 176
skill-focused training 64, 174
slow responders to therapy 5
small-group training 172
smart compliance 166
solitary deliberate practice: benefits of 46, 117, 176; deeper attunement 47; difficulties of 50–1; emotional endurance 51–3; emotional self-awareness 49–50; motivation for 57;

pattern awareness 47–8; plan 44–6; psychotherapy model examination 48–9; schedule 45; videotape supervision vs. 50

solitary deliberate practice journal 53

solitary repetition 42

somatization 24

spiritual practices 106

sporadic learning 181

stalled clients 7, 36, 93, 120, 151, 182

standardized role play 119; see also role play

stimulation-based training 62

sudden gains 5

Sudnow, David 78

supervision see clinical supervision

supervision resistant 79–80

Suzuki, Shinichi 77

Swedish National Audit Office 64

symptom change 121

Tallman, K. 11

Taylor, Jennifer 180–1

10-year rule 45

10,000-hour rule 45

theoretical learning 117

therapeutic alliance measure 121

therapeutic authenticity 134

therapeutic relationship: as basis for psychodynamic work 4–5; couples therapy 145; important elements of 130; psychotherapy training and 12; ROM data 121; therapists' personal attributes effecting 102

therapeutic timing 81–3

therapeutic working alliance 73–4

therapist countertransference 89

therapist development 19

therapist variability 15–17

therapists: authenticity of 73–4; characteristics of 102; developing mindfulness skills 127; effectiveness of 18–20; emotional self-awareness 102; mindfulness training for 108–9;

outcome data self-assessment 27; self-appraisal 19–20

therapy see psychotherapy

therapy outcomes, common-factor variables of 47

threshold of tolerance 36–7

timing, for deliberate practice routine 122

Tracey, Terrence 94

traditional medical education 60

traditional supervision 177

translational education 65

translational science 63–5

utility estimate 90–1

Vallerand, Robert 162–3

videotaped sessions: client's view of 83–4; for deliberate practice 36, 118; explained to clients 95; observing own work 153–4; as path to clinical mastery 26; as standard of practice 95; studying expert 149–50; in supervision sessions 35–8, 116; therapists avoidance to 83–4

Vygotsky, Lev 36

Wampold, B. E. 12

Wampold, Bruce 20, 94

Watkins, Ed 8

Watson, John 157

Watson, Thomas 85

Weisberg, R. 39

Werbart, A. 13

Whipple, Jason 18–19

willpower 57, 163

Winner, R. 166

Yalom, Victor 27, 134

Zazen practice 107

Zen meditation 108

zone of optimal learning 37–8

zone of proximal development (theory) 36–7